ACCOUNTING SKILLS

Margaret Nicholson

MACMILLAN

First published 1989

Published by
MACMILLAN EDUCATION LTD
Houndmills, Basingstoke, Hampshire RG21 2XS
and London
Companies and representatives
throughout the world

Printed in Hong Kong

British Library Cataloguing in Publication Data
Nicholson, Margaret
Accounting skills.
I. Title
657
ISBN 0–333–49156–4

Contents

Acknowledgements

The author and publishers wish to thank the following for use of examination questions in the book:

Royal Society of Arts Examinations Board;
Joint Matriculation Board;
Pitman Examinations Institute;
The London Chamber of Commerce and Industry Examinations Board.

They also wish to thank Barclays Bank Plc for use of the specimen cheque and paying-in slip in Module 9.

The author would also like to express her appreciation to Elaine Mellor and to Tony Ripley of Wildings.

Introduction

This book is designed to be used as a main text and aims to cover the requirements of the Royal Society of Arts Examination Board Book-keeping Stage I; Pitman Examinations Institute Book-keeping and Accounts Elementary Stage; London Chamber of Commerce and Industry Book-keeping Elementary Stage. In addition most of the requirements of the various Boards for the new General Certificate of Secondary Education are covered, and should prove invaluable in most foundation courses where certain aspects of accounting are required.

It is the writer's intention to combine straightforward explanations with sufficient interesting practice to enable the student, from the beginning, to carry out the actual 'mechanical operation' of book-keeping and the preparation of accounts. Each new module is clearly and precisely defined and contains a fully worked example to illustrate each new principle together with easy-to-follow instructions on how to enter and record the business transactions.

The progressive modular approach is intended to enable students to gain confidence quickly through understanding and practice, and the modules are linked to provide continuous revision of the topics covered. The methods and procedure are based upon definite principles which are logical and consistent throughout. A summary of the essential points covered in each module is included and should prove most helpful to students.

In the later modules, dealing with the type of questions frequently encountered in examinations, there are specific, step by step instructions for the student to follow, dealing with layout, presentation and 'what the examiner will look for'. Many of the exercises given at the end of each module are from very recent past examination papers, giving students invaluable experience practice.

Book-keeping can only be mastered by practice and, therefore, it must be emphasised that the carefully chosen exercises should always be regarded as an integral part of each module. It would be inadvisable for the student to progress to the next module before mastering the exercises in the current one.

This book will provide students with a sound understanding of both the theory and the practice requirements of basic accounting. It is especially suitable for students working towards the Royal Society of Arts Book-keeping Stage I Examinations. It would be advisable, therefore, for students to determine the syllabus requirements relating to a particular Examination Board and to compare these with the topics listed in the contents to ascertain which modules are necessary for their individual course of study.

At the present time, the provision for bad debts, calculating depreciation for fixed assets and the double entry system for depreciation are not required to be covered by candidates taking the Royal Society of Arts, Book-keeping Stage I Examination.

It may also be of interest to candidates taking The Royal Society of Arts Examinations that these are now marked on three criteria: concepts, accuracy and presentation, each criterion being marked separately and candidates having to achieve a satisfactory mark in all three before being awarded a pass. The examination now consists of five questions, *all compulsory*. Question 5, which is always a final accounts type of question, is only used to discriminate between a Pass and a Pass with Credit.

1 An Introduction to Assets, Liabilities and Capital

OBJECTIVES   To distinguish and classify assets, liabilities, capital, debtors, creditors and to understand the accounting equation and a simple balance sheet.

All businesses, however small, require some form of accounting. The most straightforward example of a firm or business would be a sole trader – a man or woman in business, buying and selling goods with the intention of making a profit. The transactions which are the business dealings of the firm are kept completely separate from those of the owner of the business.

The whole of financial accounting is based on the accounting equation, and the accounting equation is expressed in a document called a balance sheet. A balance sheet has two sides, a right-hand side and a left-hand side.

Assets

These are the resources possessed by the firm, consisting of: property of all kinds, such as buildings and premises, plant and machinery, stocks of goods, motor vehicles, the amount of money in cash and in the bank account, debts owing by customers to the firm. A person who owes the firm money for goods or services is known as a *debtor*. Some of these assets may have been supplied by the owner of the business. The total amount supplied by the owner of the business is known as *capital*.

Liabilities

Liabilities consist of money owing for goods purchased. (Example: if a firm buys some goods and agrees to pay for them in a month's time, the firm receives the goods immediately, and the liability is created; the firm has become liable to pay for the goods received.) A person to whom money is owed for goods or services is known as a *creditor*. Money owing for expenses such as gas, electricity, rates, rent, telephone and loans made to the firm are also liabilities.

The formula is:

$$\text{capital} + \text{liabilities} = \text{assets}$$

The actual assets, capital and liabilities will constantly change, as illustrated in the following examples, but the formula will always hold true, no matter how many transactions are entered into. A balance sheet is always drawn up at a specific date. For this example, a sole trader commenced business on 1 January 19–7 with £20,000. The balance sheet would appear as follows:

Balance Sheet as at 1 January 19–7

Assets		Capital and Liabilities	
Cash at Bank	20,000	Capital	20,000
	£20,000		£20,000

On 7 January 19–7, the sole trader decides to buy a motor vehicle for £4,000 and he pays for this out of his business bank account. The balance sheet would now appear as follows:

Balance Sheet as at 7 January 19–7

Assets		Capital and Liabilities	
Motor Vehicles	4,000	Capital	20,000
Cash at Bank	16,000		
	£20,000		£20,000

The sole trader's capital remains £20,000 but instead of it only being in the form of cash at the bank it is now made up of cash at bank and a motor vehicle.

On 12 January, 19–7, the trader buys some premises for £5,000 and pays by cheque – this transaction will reduce his cash at bank, but will increase his assets. His balance sheet will now appear as follows:

Balance Sheet as at 12 January 19–7

Assets		Capital and Liabilities	
Premises	5,000	Capital	20,000
Motor Vehicle	4,000		
Cash at Bank	11,000		
	£20,000		£20,000

At this point, the trader decides to buy a stock of goods, which he eventually hopes to re-sell. On 18 January 19–7, he buys some goods for £600 from Munro & Son and agrees to pay for them in one month's time. This transaction will again affect the balance sheet, and the liability of a creditor will have been created. (The name *creditor* is given in accounting language to a person to whom the firm owes money, for goods or services.) The balance sheet will now appear as follows:

Balance Sheet as at 18 January 19–7

Assets		Capital and Liabilities	
Premises	5,000	Capital	20,000
Motor Vehicle	4,000	Creditor	600
Stock of Goods	600		
Cash at Bank	11,000		
	£20,600		£20,600

On 25 January 19–7, goods which had cost £300 were sold to D. Davey, who agreed to pay for the goods in one month's time. (The name *debtor* is given, in accounting language, to a person who owes the firm money.) This transaction will again affect the balance sheet – by decreasing the asset of the stock of goods, and by the creation of another asset, a debtor. The balance sheet would now appear as follows:

Balance Sheet as at 25 January 19–7

Assets		Capital and Liabilities	
Premises	5,000	Capital	20,000
Motor Vehicle	4,000	Creditor	600
Stock of Goods	300		
Debtor	300		
Cash at Bank	11,000		
	£20,600		£20,600

On 28 January 19–7, the trader decides to buy some office equipment costing £1,000, paying by cheque, and further goods on credit, costing £2,000. Also an associate of the trader, A. Goodson lends the firm £3,000. This is placed in the business bank account. The effect of these transactions on the balance sheet will be as follows:

Balance Sheet as at 28 January 19–7

Assets		Capital and Liabilities	
Premises	5,000	Capital	20,000
Motor Vehicle	4,000	Creditors	2,600
Stock of Goods	2,300	Loan – A. Goodson	3,000
Debtor	300		
Office Equipment	1,000		
Cash at Bank	13,000		
	£25,600		£25,600

The student should now gain essential practice by completing the following assignment exercises.

Assignment Exercises

1.1
Classify the following items into assets and liabilities:
Premises
Creditor
Debtor
Motor Vehicle
Office Equipment
Capital
Cash at Bank

1.2
Classify the following items into assets and liabilities:
Stock of Goods
Premises
Owing to Bank
Machinery
Loan from D. James
Motor Vehicles
Creditors

1.3

Classify the following items into assets and liabilities and draw up a balance sheet dated 31 December 19–7.

	£
Cash at Bank	1,500
Capital	22,250
Debtors	5,525
Creditors	2,450
Office Equipment	8,425
Stock of Goods	9,250

1.4

Classify the following items into assets and liabilities and draw up a balance sheet dated 31 July 19–7

	£
Machinery	2,275
Capital	15,000
Fixtures	10,000
Creditors	1,800
Stock of Goods	1,750
Debtors	825
Cash at Bank	4,950
Loan from D. Davies	3,000

1.5

Classify the following items and draw up a balance sheet dated 30 April 19–7.

	£
Fixtures and Fittings	4,200
Creditors	2,600
Motor Vehicle	4,000
Capital	19,800
Stock of Goods	5,750
Cash at Bank	6,250
Loan from C. Green	2,000
Debtors	3,880
Cash in Hand	320

1.6

Classify the following items and draw up a Balance Sheet dated 31 May 19–8.
Debtors £6,750, Creditors £3,425, Fixtures and Fittings £6,900, Plant and Machinery £8,880, Capital £35,205, Stock of Goods £4,550, Loan from G. Grove £5,000, Cash at Bank £5,450, Cash in Hand £600, Motor Vehicles £10,500.

1.7

In the following question you are required to calculate the amount of the capital.

	Assets	Liabilities	Capital
(a)	42,000	17,300	?
(b)	87,500	26,500	?
(c)	59,750	19,950	?
(d)	71,450	22,750	?
(e)	64,500	25,000	?

1.8

In the following question you are required to calculate the amount of the capital.

	Assets	Liabilities	Capital
(a)	51,500	19,700	?
(b)	92,200	27,500	?
(c)	57,750	18,950	?
(d)	63,330	14,500	?
(e)	81,000	17,850	?

1.9

In the following question you are required to calculate the missing figure.

	Assets	Liabilities	Capital
(a)	65,000	?	32,250
(b)	?	16,750	27,900
(c)	78,350	?	59,450
(d)	?	12,750	18,350
(e)	45,000	?	20,200

1.10

In the following question you are required to calculate the missing figure.

	Assets	Liabilities	Capital
(a)	?	18,250	28,950
(b)	51,500	?	16,450
(c)	?	27,800	28,900
(d)	31,150	17,250	?
(e)	48,750	?	26,650

1.11

W. Dyson sets up a new business. He has the following assets and liabilities:
Premises £7,000, Stock of Goods £3,250, Motor Vehicle £5,750, Creditors £2,200, Debtors £3,950, Loan from D. James £5,000, Office Equipment £1,750, Machinery £2,700, Cash at Bank £5,860.
You are required to calculate the amount of his capital and draw up his balance sheet as at 31 December 19–8.

2 Opening the Double Entry Accounts in the Ledger

OBJECTIVES   To enable students to understand and practise the basic principles of the double entry system of book-keeping.

The transactions of the business are the day-to-day dealings of the business. Every transaction will affect *two items*, and it is this 'dual aspect' which is the basis of the double entry system. The double entry system has an account for every asset, every liability and for capital.

For example, if a business buys a motor vehicle for cash the business will receive the motor vehicle and will pay out the cash; the two items concerned are the motor vehicle and the cash. This transaction must be recorded in the books of the business; this is done in a ledger. An example of ledger paper is set out below:

	DEBIT SIDE					CREDIT SIDE			
Date	Details	Folio	£	p	Date	Details	Folio	£	p

The student should purchase a supply of ledger paper. The page is divided into two halves; think of it as having a wall down the centre. The left-hand side of the page is called the *debit side*. The right-hand side of the page is called the *credit side*. The name of the account is written across the top of the page, in the centre. Each account would be shown on a separate page in the ledger.

In a business each account has a separate page in the Ledger and two accounts would *NEVER* appear on the same page in the Ledger. However, for student practice, it would be a great waste of paper to show every account on a separate page, and it is, therefore, customary in student practice for several accounts to be shown on the same page, leaving a few lines of space between each account.

In all business dealings there are two separate and distinct aspects – one of which is regarded as the *receiving* aspects, the other as the *giving* or *paying* aspect. Two separate accounts are involved in every transaction, one account recording the 'debit'

7

entry' (receiving aspect) the other account recording the 'credit entry' (giving or paying aspect).

The account which receives value or benefit is *debited*. The account which gives or pays benefit is *credited*. The double entry is:

debit the receiver
credit the giver

Example transaction. The firm buys a motor vehicle costing £5,000 for cash. The entries for this transaction would be as follows:

Motor Vehicle Account

Jan 1 Cash	5,000	

Cash Account

	Jan 1 Motor Vehicle	5,000

The firm would receive the motor vehicle, therefore the debit side entry is recorded in the account which 'receives'. The firm would pay out the cash, therefore a credit side entry is recorded in the account which pays.

POINTS TO REMEMBER
The most important basic principle in book-keeping is that every debit side entry must have a corresponding credit side entry; this is the meaning of 'double entry system'. For every transaction *two entries must be made*, at the debit side of one account and at the credit side of the other.

The date of the transaction will be the same in both accounts, as will be the amount of money. The details column is completed by cross-reference, and will identify and describe the account in which the corresponding entry is made.

Further worked examples are now considered. On 3 January the firm bought office equipment costing £350 paying by cheque. The firm would *receive* the office equipment, therefore, a debit entry is recorded in the office equipment account, as follows:

Office Equipment Account

Jan 3 Bank	350	

The firm would pay (give) out a cheque, therefore the credit side entry would be in the bank account, as follows:

Bank Account

	Jan	3	Office Equipment	350

Finally, consider the following. On 5 January the firm bought a second-hand machine costing £150 paying in cash. The firm would *receive* the machine, therefore a debit entry is recorded in the machinery account, as follows:

Machinery Account

Jan	5	Cash	150	

The firm would pay (give) out the cash, therefore, the credit side entry would be in the cash account, as follows:

Cash Account

	Jan	5	Machinery	150

The proprietor is the owner of the business. If he puts money into the business this will increase the capital, as shown in the following example, when the proprietor started a business with £2,000 in cash. The double entry would be as follows: the cash account would *receive*, therefore a debit entry is recorded in the cash account:

Cash Account

Date	Capital	2,000	

The account which is 'giving' or paying in the example is the capital account (the proprietor has given £2,000 to the business), therefore a credit entry is made in the capital account, as follows:

Capital Account

	Date	Cash	2,000

Assignment Exercises

Before actually beginning to use the ledger and opening the double entry accounts, it is advisable to work through the first two exercises.

2.1

Complete the blank spaces by inserting the name of the account to be debited and the name of the account to be credited. The first transaction is completed for you as an example.

(a) Bought a motor car, paying in cash.

    Debit   (Motor Car)   Account   Credit   (Cash)   Account

(b) Bought Machinery paying by cheque.

    Debit _____ Account   Credit _____ Account

(c) A debtor, M. Dyson pays the firm in cash.

    Debit _____ Account   Credit _____ Account

(d) Paid a creditor, J. Smith by cheque.

    Debit _____ Account   Credit _____ Account

(e) Sold some machinery and received cash.

    Debit _____ Account   Credit _____ Account

(f) M. Field lends the firm money, giving it to us by cheque.

    Debit _____ Account   Credit _____ Account

(g) Proprietor puts further money into the business by cheque.

    Debit _____ Account   Credit _____ Account

(h) P. Dexter, a debtor, pays the firm in cash.

    Debit _____ Account   Credit _____ Account

2.2

Complete the blank spaces by inserting the name of the account to be debited and the name of the account to be credited.

(a) Repaid part of loan from M. Fieldhouse by cheque.

    Debit _____ Account   Credit _____ Account

(b) Sold a motor car for cash.

    Debit _____ Account   Credit _____ Account

(c) A debtor, B. Dixon pays us by cheque.

    Debit _____ Account   Credit _____ Account

(d) Paid S. Smith, a creditor, in cash.

    Debit _____ Account   Credit _____ Account

(e) Bought machinery on credit from C. Cliff.

    Debit _____ Account   Credit _____ Account

(f) Proprietor puts a further amount of cash into the firm.

Debit _____ Account   Credit _____ Account

(g) A loan is received from P. Bellamy, by cheque.

Debit _____ Account   Credit _____ Account

(h) Returned some Machinery to C. Cliff.

Debit _____ Account   Credit _____ Account

2.3

This is a worked example exercise, showing the transaction, the account to be debited and the account to be credited.

Feb 1 Proprietor started business with £3,000, putting the money into a business bank account.
     Debit Bank Account   Credit Capital Account

Feb 3 Bought a motor van costing £2,000 on credit from Nichols Garages.
     Debit Motor Van Account Credit Nichols Garages Account

Feb 5 Bought some office furniture costing £750, paying by cheque.
     Debit Office Furniture A/c Credit Bank Account

Feb 17 Withdrew £200 from the bank and placed it in the cash box.
     Debit Cash Account   Credit Bank Account

Feb 22 Sold some office furniture (£50) to T. Groves on credit.
     Debit T. Groves Account   Credit Office Furniture A/c

Feb 24 A loan of £1,000 is received from W. Old by cheque.
     Debit Bank Account   Credit W. Old (Loan) Account

The completed double entry accounts for the above transactions would appear as follows:

Bank Account

Feb	1	Capital	3,000	Feb	5 Office furniture	750
Feb	24	W. Old (Loan)	1,000	Feb	17 Cash	200

Capital Account

	Feb	1 Bank	3,000

Motor Van Account

Feb	3 Nichols Garages	2,000	

Nichols Garages Account

				Feb	3 Motor Van		2,000

Office Furniture Account

Feb	5 Bank		750	Feb	22 T. Groves		50

Cash Account

Feb	17 Bank		200		

T. Groves Account

Feb	22 Office Furniture		50		

W. Old (Loan) Account

			Feb	24 Bank		1,000

2.4

In the ledger, write up the double entry accounts required to record the following transactions.

Mar 1 Started business with £2,000 in cash.

  2 Bought a motor van on credit from J. Jackson, costing £750.

12 Bought office fixtures, £100, paying in cash.

15 Received a loan of £1,000 by cheque from D. Pickles. The money was placed in a bank account for the business.

24 Paid J. Jackson £750 in cash.

29 Bought a second-hand machine costing £250, paying in cash.

30 Bought display equipment costing £300, paying by cheque.

2.5

In the ledger, write up the double entry accounts required to record the following transactions.

Apr 1 Started a new business with £3,000 in a business bank account.

  2 Bought some machinery costing £800 on credit from Lupton Ltd.

  4 Bought a motor van costing £500, paying by cheque.

  5 Withdrew £100 from the bank and put it in the cash box.

  8 Bought office furniture costing £650 on credit from Systems Ltd.

12 Sold some surplus machinery (£200) on credit to B. Smith.

15 Paid Lupton Ltd. £800 by cheque.

18 Received a loan of £1,000 by cheque from J. Clubman.

25 Received £200 in cash from B. Smith.

2.6

In the ledger, write up the double entry accounts needed to record the following transactions.

May 1 Started business with £15,000 in cash.
     3 Bought some machinery costing £800, paying in cash.
     5 Bought office equipment (£750) on credit from Ellis Supplies.
     7 Paid £14,000 of the cash into a business bank account.
     9 Bought shop fittings costing £1,600, paying by cheque.
   12 Withdrew £500 from the bank and put it in the cash box.
   14 Returned faulty office equipment (£150) to Ellis Supplies.
   16 Bought motor van (£3,000) on credit from Wallace Garages.
   20 Sold some surplus shop fittings (£350) on credit to J. Dunn.
   25 Paid Ellis Supplies the amount owing, £600, by cheque.
   31 Received £350 in cash from J. Dunn.

2.7

In the ledger, write up the double entry accounts needed to record the following transactions.

Jun 1 Started a new business with £8,000 in a business bank account.
     3 Bought shop fittings costing £900 on credit from Nyson Ltd.
     5 Withdrew £500 from the bank and placed it in the cash box.
     9 Bought office furniture costing £550, paying by cheque.
   12 Returned some faulty shop fittings (£250) to Nyson Ltd.
   15 Bought a motor van costing £3,000 on credit from White & Son.
   17 Bought machinery costing £150, paying in cash.
   19 Received a loan of £1,000 by cheque from L. Myers.
   21 Bought further office furniture costing £750 on credit from Parkinsons Ltd.
   24 Paid Nyson Ltd. £650 by cheque.
   28 Bought further machinery costing £250, paying in cash.
   29 Repaid part of loan to L. Myers (£250) by cheque.
   30 Paid White & Son £3,000 by cheque.

2.8

In the ledger, write up the double entry accounts needed to record the following transactions.

Aug 1 Started business with £15,000 in cash.
     2 Paid £14,000 of the cash into a business bank account.
     5 Bought display equipment (£1,500) on credit from Chanings Ltd.
     7 Bought motor van (£2,000) paying by cheque.
   10 Bought office furniture costing £650, paying in cash.
   12 Withdrew £500 cash from the bank.
   13 Bought machinery costing £950 on credit from Grovehall Ltd.
   15 Received a loan of £5,000 by cheque from T. Mason.
   18 Sold surplus office furniture (£150) on credit to M. Wilkinson.
   19 Returned faulty display equipment (£300) to Chanings Ltd.
   20 Paid Grovehall Ltd. £950 by cheque.

26 Bought shop fittings (£150), paying in cash.

28 Received a cheque of £150 from M. Wilkinson.

29 Repaid part of loan (£500) to T. Mason by cheque.

30 Bought further display equipment costing £750 on credit from Chanings Ltd.

2.9

You are required to open the double entry accounts necessary to record the following transactions.

Oct 1 Started a new business with £10,000 in a business bank account.

3 Bought office equipment costing £750 on credit from Modern Offices Ltd.

5 Withdrew £500 from the business bank account and placed it in the cash box.

7 Bought shop fittings costing £450, paying in cash.

10 Bought motor vehicle costing £4,000 on credit from Swansons Garages Ltd.

15 Received a loan of £1,000 in cash from A. Moss.

16 Bought machinery costing £750, paying in cash.

18 Bought further office equipment costing £250 on credit from Modern Offices Ltd.

20 Sold some machinery costing £200, surplus to requirements to J. Green on credit.

27 Paid Swansons Garages £4,000 by cheque.

30 Received a cheque of £200 from J. Green.

31 Paid a cheque of £500 to Modern Offices Ltd.

3 The Double Entry System for Sales and Purchases

OBJECTIVES To enable students to understand and practise the double entry system for the sale of goods on credit and for cash, and the purchase of goods on credit and for cash.

So far we have seen the double entry accounts which are required for the assets, liabilities and the capital of the business. In the same way all other transactions of the business must be recorded. Usually, in business the main objective is to buy and sell goods in order to make a profit, and it is essential that the purchases of the business and the sales of the business are kept completely separate and are not confused.

Business transactions may be carried out either for cash or on credit – in credit transactions the goods are received immediately but payment is made at a later date. Credit transactions require the opening of *personal accounts*. A personal account is an account opened in the name of a person or company.

Purchase of Goods on Credit

When a firm buys goods with the intention of resale, these are called purchases. Study the following example: on 1 March goods costing £250 are bought on credit from M. Dyson. Consider the two-fold effect. The firm will receive the goods, therefore the debit entry will be in the purchases account, where a record of all the purchases of goods is kept.

The credit entry (giving aspect) is recorded in the account of the person who has supplied the goods, in this example M. Dyson. The double-entry accounts for this example would appear as follows:

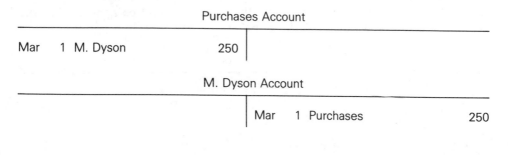

	Purchases Account	
Mar 1 M. Dyson	250	

	M. Dyson Account	
	Mar 1 Purchases	250

Cash Purchases

With regard to cash purchases, and these are so called whether payment is made in cash or by cheque, the goods purchased would be received, therefore a debit entry is made in the purchases account; and because payment is made immediately the goods are bought (either in cash or by cheque) this would reduce the amount of cash, so the credit entry (paying aspect) would be in the cash account or the bank account, as shown in the following example. On 4 March goods costing £65 are bought, cash being paid immediately. The double-entry accounts for this example would appear as follows:

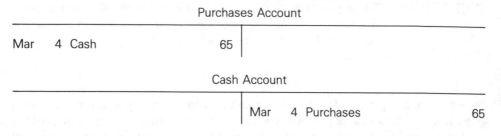

Purchases Account

Mar 4 Cash	65	

Cash Account

	Mar 4 Purchases	65

Consider another example: on 10 March goods costing £95 are bought, a cheque being paid immediately. The double entry accounts for this example would appear as follows:

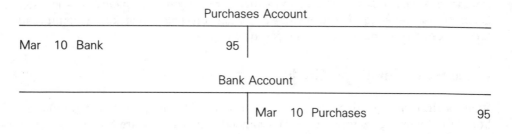

Purchases Account

Mar 10 Bank	95	

Bank Account

	Mar 10 Purchases	95

Sales of Goods on Credit

When a firm sells goods in which the firm normally deals, these are sales. Again consider the two-fold effect in order that the book-keeping entries can be made. Study the following example: on 1 March goods are sold on credit for £350 to W. Benn. W. Benn will receive the goods, therefore the debit entry will be in the personal account of W. Benn, as shown below:

W. Benn Account

Mar 1 Sales	350	

The credit entry will be in the sales account, where a record of all the sales of goods is kept, as shown below:

Sales Account

	Mar 1 W. Benn	350

Cash Sales

With regard to cash sales, and these are so called whether payment is received in cash or by cheque, payment is received immediately, therefore the debit entry (receiving aspect) would be in the cash account if cash is received, or in the bank account if payment is received by cheque. The credit entry (giving aspect) would be recorded in the sales account. Consider the following example: on 6 March goods are sold for £50, cash being received immediately. The double entry accounts would appear as follows:

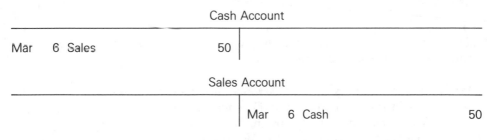

Cash Account

Mar 6 Sales 50	

Sales Account

	Mar 6 Cash 50

Again, consider the following example: on 14 March goods are sold for £75, a cheque being received immediately. The double entry accounts would appear as follows:

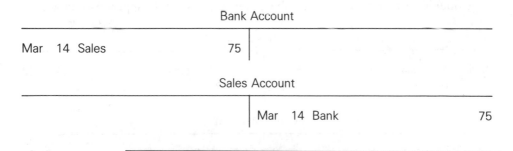

Bank Account

Mar 14 Sales 75	

Sales Account

	Mar 14 Bank 75

POINTS TO REMEMBER In accounting terms *purchases* are goods bought with the intention of selling. An example of this could be an electrical business, with the firm buying television sets. If a firm buys something else, for instance office equipment, this would not be regarded as purchases, as the office equipment was bought for use within the business, and would be an *asset*, and not for resale.

17

Sales in accounting terms applies to the goods in which the firm normally deals, as in the example, with an electrical business buying and selling television sets – goods were bought with the intention of selling.

When entering the transactions in the double entry accounts, never write 'goods'. If goods are bought, these are *purchases*, and the word 'purchases' should be written in the personal account, for purchases on credit; the word 'purchases' should appear in the cash account or the bank account in the case of 'cash purchases'.

Similarly, when goods are sold, these are *sales*, and the word 'sales' should be written in the personal account, for sales on credit; the word 'sales' should appear in the cash account or the bank account in the case of 'cash sales'.

Assignment Exercises

3.1
This is a worked example exercise, showing the transactions and then the completed double entry accounts.

Mar 1 Started a business with £5,000 in a business bank account.
   4 Bought goods on credit from D. James (£550).
   8 Bought machinery (£350) paying by cheque.
  15 Sold goods on credit (£200) to W. Preston.
  20 Bought goods (£45) paying by cheque.
  26 Sold goods (£150), a cheque being received immediately.

The double entry accounts for the above transactions would appear as follows:

Bank Account

Mar	1	Capital	5,000	Mar	8 Machinery	350
	26	Sales	150		20 Purchases	45

Capital Account

	Mar	1 Bank	5,000

PURCHASES ACCOUNT

Mar	4	D. James	550
	20	Bank	45

18

D. James Account

	Mar 4 Purchases	550

Machinery Account

Mar 8 Bank	350	

Sales Account

	Mar 15 W. Preston	200
	26 Bank	150

W. Preston Account

Mar 15 Sales	200	

3.2

Complete the blank spaces by inserting the name of the account to be debited
and the name of the account to be credited.

(a) Bought goods on credit from R. Rice.

 Debit _____ Account   Credit _____ Account

(b) Sold goods for cash.

 Debit _____ Account   Credit _____ Account

(c) Sold machinery and received a cheque.

 Debit _____ Account   Credit _____ Account

(d) Bought goods paying in cash.

 Debit _____ Account   Credit _____ Account

(e) Sold goods on credit to B. Drake.

 Debit _____ Account   Credit _____ Account

(f) Sold goods, a cheque was received immediately.

 Debit _____ Account   Credit _____ Account

3.3

Complete the blank spaces by inserting the name of the account to be debited
and the name of the account to be credited.

(a) Bought goods, paying by cheque.

 Debit _____ Account   Credit _____ Account

(b) Bought office furniture, paying in cash.

Debit _____ Account   Credit _____ Account

(c) Sold goods on credit to J. Jackson.

Debit _____ Account   Credit _____ Account

(d) Bought goods for cash.

Debit _____ Account   Credit _____ Account

(e) Sold surplus office furniture and received a cheque.

Debit _____ Account   Credit _____ Account

(f) Sold goods for cash.

Debit _____ Account   Credit _____ Account

3.4

Complete the blank spaces by inserting the name of the account to be debited and the name of the account to be credited.

(a) Bought goods on credit from E. Smith.

Debit _____ Account   Credit _____ Account

(b) Bought motor van, paying by cheque.

Debit _____ Account   Credit _____ Account

(c) Goods sold on credit to T. Dean.

Debit _____ Account   Credit _____ Account

(d) Sold goods and received payment by cheque.

Debit _____ Account   Credit _____ Account

(e) Paid a creditor, D. Sadler, in cash.

Debit _____ Account   Credit _____ Account

(f) A Debtor, M. Moore, pays us by cheque.

Debit _____ Account   Credit _____ Account

3.5

Complete the blank spaces, showing which accounts should be debited and which are to be credited.

(a) Sold goods on credit to J. Morgan.

Debit _____ Account   Credit _____ Account

(b) Goods bought for cash.

Debit _____ Account   Credit _____ Account

(c) M. Myers paid his account by cheque.

Debit _____ Account   Credit _____ Account

(d) Sold goods, a cheque being received immediately.

Debit _____ Account   Credit _____ Account

(e) Bought goods on credit from W. James.

Debit _____ Account   Credit _____ Account

(f) Paid a creditor, P. Ellis, by cheque.

Debit _____ Account   Credit _____ Account

3.6
You are required to enter the following transactions in the double entry accounts.
May 1 Started business with £8,000 in cash.
       3 Paid £7,000 of the cash into a business bank account.
       5 Bought goods on credit from G. Moore (£350).
       9 Bought office furniture (£700), paying by cheque.
      14 Sold goods on credit to F. Green (£450).
      17 Bought motor van (£5,000) on credit from Newtown Motors.
      20 Sold goods (£50) for cash.
      25 Paid G. Moore a cheque for £350.
      30 Bought goods (£75), paying in cash.

3.7
You are required to enter the following transactions in the double entry accounts.
Jun 1 Started business with £5,000 in a business bank account.
       3 Bought goods (£150) on credit from C. Clifton.
       5 Sold goods (£250), receiving payment by cheque.
       7 Sold goods for cash (£150).
       9 Bought goods (£50), paying in cash.
      11 Bought goods on credit from K. Ingram (£660).
      14 Sold goods on credit (£500) to E. Mason.
      15 Bought motor vehicle (£2,000), paying by cheque.
      20 W. Wilson lends the firm £1,000, paying the money by cheque.
      22 Paid a creditor, C. Clifton, £150 by cheque.
      26 Bought goods (£70), paying by cheque.
      30 Sold goods on credit (£90) to G. Spink.

3.8
You are to enter the following transactions in the double entry accounts.
Aug 1 Started business with £10,000 in cash.
       2 Paid £8,500 of the opening cash into a bank account.

3 Bought goods (£150), paying in cash.
5 Sold goods (£100) on credit to F. Fieldhouse.
7 Bought office equipment (£250) on credit from Nelsons Ltd.
12 Bought goods on credit (£650) from J. Black Ltd.
15 Sold goods (£200) for cash.
20 Sold goods on credit to J. Smith (£150) and W. Wiseman (£120).
24 Bought motor van (£4,000) on credit from Bright Motors Ltd.
26 Cash purchases £450.
27 Paid Nelsons Ltd. £250 in cash.
28 F. Fieldhouse paid £100 by cheque.
29 Bought display equipment (£350), paying by cheque.
30 Paid J. Black £650 by cheque.
31 Sold goods (£220), receiving payment by cheque.

3.9

Enter the following transactions in the double entry accounts.
Nov 1 Started business with £5,000 in a business bank account.
2 Bought goods on credit (£490) from W. Rycroft.
3 Withdrew £250 cash from the bank and placed it in the cash box.
4 Bought goods (£175), paying in cash.
5 Sold goods on credit (£325) to J. Buckley.
6 Bought display equipment (£550) on credit from Thompson Ltd.
7 Cash sales £225.
9 Bought goods on credit from G. Stewart (£595); W. Rycroft (£355).
10 Sold surplus display equipment (£150) on credit to E. Somes.
12 Sold goods on credit to F. Armitage (£220); J. Buckley (£295).
14 Proprietor puts a further £500 cash into the business.
16 Bought motor van (£1,500) paying by cheque.
18 Cash purchases £420.
19 Bought some shop fittings (£150), paying in cash.
20 Received a cheque (£150) from E. Somes.
21 Bought goods on credit from G. Stewart (£225).
24 Sold goods for £190 cash.
25 Paid W. Rycroft £490 by cheque.
26 Credit sales to B. Armstrong (£125); F. King (£90).
27 J. Buckley paid £325 in cash.
28 Goods bought on credit (£395) from G. Stewart.
29 Bought further shop fittings (£220), paying by cheque.
30 F. Armitage paid £220 by cheque.

4   The Double Entry System for Returns

OBJECTIVES   To enable students to understand and practise the double entry system for the returns inwards and returns outwards of goods.

In the normal course of business, every day goods are bought, goods are sold and goods are returned. The two accounts concerned regarding the return of goods are the returns inwards account and the returns outwards account.

The reasons why the goods are returned are of no concern with regard to the book-keeping entries; it may be the goods supplied were of the wrong colour, wrong size and so on. It is the entries that are required in the double entry accounts which we must consider.

Goods are returned in two ways. Goods returned *to the firm* by its customers are *returns inwards*. Goods returned *by the firm* to its suppliers are *returns outwards*.

Returns Inwards

Returns inwards are goods returned to the firm by its customers. Consider the following example: on 1 May, goods which had been previously sold to K. Sadler for £50 are now returned by him. Again consider what has happened, in order that the book-keeping entries can be made. The goods are received by the firm, therefore the debit entry will be in the returns inwards account. The credit entry (giving aspect) is recorded in the account of the person who has returned the goods, in this example K. Sadler. The double entry accounts for this example would appear as follows:

Returns Inwards Account

May 1 K. Sadler	50	

K. Sadler Account

	May 1 Returns Inwards	50

Returns Outwards

Returns outwards are goods returned by the firm to its suppliers. Consider the following example: on May 9, goods previously purchased for £75 are now returned to the supplier, R. Linton. The goods are received by R. Linton, therefore, the debit entry will be in the personal account of R. Linton. The credit entry (giving aspect) will be in the returns outwards account. The double entry accounts for this example would appear as follows:

R. Linton Account

May 9 Returns Outwards 75	

Returns Outwards Account

	May 9 R. Linton 75

POINTS TO REMEMBER   Another name for the returns inwards account is the *sales returns account* – derived from the fact that these are sales which have been returned.

Another name for the returns outwards account is the *purchases returns account* – derived from the fact that these were purchases which have been returned to the supplier.

As with sales and purchases, avoid the use of the word 'goods' in the double entry accounts. The transaction itself will usually refer to the items as 'goods' but when recording the transaction in the double entry accounts write 'returns inwards' or 'returns outwards', as the case may be.

In the following worked example, consider each transaction carefully and proceed to find the entries in the double entry accounts.

Feb 1 Bought goods on credit (£150) from S. Singer.
     4 Sold goods for cash (£75).
     6 Bought goods on credit (£450) from V. Hood.
    10 Returned goods to S. Singer (£20).
    12 Sold goods on credit (£125) to A. Towers.
    15 Bought goods (£50), paying in cash.
    20 A. Towers returned £25 goods to us.
    22 Bought goods on credit (£600) from D. Davine.
    25 Sold goods on credit (£250) to A. Towers.
    28 Returned goods (£150) to D. Davine.

The double entry accounts would appear as follows:

Purchases Account

Feb	1	S. Singer	150
	6	V. Hood	450
	15	Cash	50
	22	D. Davine	600

S. Singer Account

Feb	10	Returns Outwards	20	Feb	1	Purchases	150

Cash Account

Feb	4	Sales	75	Feb	15	Purchases	50

Sales Account

				Feb	4	Cash	75
					12	A. Towers	125
					25	A. Towers	250

V. Hood Account

				Feb	6	Purchases	450

Returns Outwards Account

				Feb	10	S. Singer	20
					28	D. Davine	150

A. Towers Account

Feb	12	Sales	125	Feb	20	Returns Inwards	25
	25	Sales	250				

Returns Inwards Account

Feb	20	A. Towers	25				

D. Davine Account

Feb	28	Returns Outwards	150	Feb	22	Purchases	600

Assignment Exercises

4.1
Complete the blank spaces by inserting the name of the account to be debited and the name of the account to be credited.

(a) Bought goods for cash.

Debit _____ Account   Credit _____ Account

(b) Returned goods to D. Davine.

Debit _____ Account   Credit _____ Account

(c) Sold goods on credit to P. Packman.

Debit _____ Account   Credit _____ Account

(d) Goods bought on credit from C. Overton.

Debit _____ Account   Credit _____ Account

(e) Goods returned to us by J. Kind.

Debit _____ Account   Credit _____ Account

(f) Bought motor van, paying by cheque.

Debit _____ Account   Credit _____ Account

4.2
Complete the blank spaces by inserting the name of the account to be debited and the name of the account to be credited.

(a) Goods sold on credit to L. Young.

Debit _____ Account   Credit _____ Account

(b) Bought goods, paying in cash.

Debit _____ Account   Credit _____ Account

(c) We returned goods to E. Smythe.

Debit _____ Account   Credit _____ Account

(d) Bought office furniture on credit from N. Newton.

Debit _____ Account   Credit _____ Account

(e) L. Young returns goods to us.

Debit _____ Account   Credit _____ Account

(f) Machinery returned to T. Tomkinson.

Debit _____ Account   Credit _____ Account

4.3

Complete the blank spaces by inserting the name of the account to be debited and the name of the account to be credited.

(a) Goods bought on credit from J. Mackey.

Debit _____ Account   Credit _____ Account

(b) Goods returned to us by G. Grimes.

Debit _____ Account   Credit _____ Account

(c) We paid a creditor, B. Bright by cheque.

Debit _____ Account   Credit _____ Account

(d) Sold goods for cash.

Debit _____ Account   Credit _____ Account

(e) We returned goods to W. Preston.

Debit _____ Account   Credit _____ Account

(f) A debtor, B. Dixon, pays us by cheque.

Debit _____ Account   Credit _____ Account

4.4

Complete the blank spaces by inserting the name of the account to be debited and the name of the account to be credited.

(a) Sold goods on credit to D. Marsh.

Debit _____ Account   Credit _____ Account

(b) We returned goods to R. Chalker.

Debit _____ Account   Credit _____ Account

(c) Bought motor van on credit from Appleyard Garages.

Debit _____ Account   Credit _____ Account

(d) D. Marsh returns goods to the firm.

Debit _____ Account   Credit _____ Account

(e) Sold goods, a cheque being received immediately.

Debit _____ Account   Credit _____ Account

(f) Goods returned to D. Davine.

Debit _____ Account   Credit _____ Account

4.5

Enter the following transactions in the double entry accounts.

May 1 Started business with £7,000 in cash.
2 Paid £6,500 of the opening cash into a bank account for the business.
3 Bought goods on credit (£500) from M. Trenholme.
5 Bought motor van (£3,000) on credit from Linton Garages.
6 Returned goods (£60) to M. Trenholme.
8 Sold goods on credit (£250) to D. Davey.
9 Bought office furniture (£300), paying by cheque.
10 Sold goods for cash (£50).
12 D. Davey returned goods to us (£40).
15 Bought goods on credit (£750) from R. Marples.
18 Bought goods (£145), paying in cash.
20 Sold goods (£75), a cheque being received immediately.
22 Returned goods (£80) to R. Marples.
24 Credit sales to R. Sinclair (£145); K. Bray (£221).
26 Paid a cheque for £440 to M. Trenholme.
27 Goods returned by K. Bray £21.
28 Bought goods on credit (£350) from R. Marples.
29 Paid £250 by cheque to Linton Garages.
30 Goods returned to R. Marples (£25).
31 Received a cheque (£210) from D. Davey.

4.6

The following transactions are to be entered in the double entry accounts of T. Fountain, for the month of June 19–8.

Jun 1 Started business with £10,000 in the Bank.
2 Bought goods on credit from M. Webb (£900) and T. Rose (£500).
4 Bought display equipment (£250) on credit from Carr & Co.
5 Returned goods (£125) to M. Webb.
7 Sold goods for £300 cash.
9 Sold goods on credit (£425) to V. Reed.
11 Returned goods (£50) to T. Rose.
12 Goods bought on credit (£600) from G. Appleby.
14 V. Reed returned goods (£75).
16 Sold goods on credit (£350) to F. Redman.
17 Bought goods (£150), paying in cash.
20 Withdrew £500 cash from the bank.
22 F. Redman returned goods (£25).
24 Bought machinery (£190), paying by cheque.
25 Paid M. Webb the amount owing to him, by cheque.
26 Credit sales to F. Redman (£230); M. Dyson (£195).
28 Received a cheque (£350) from V. Reed.
29 Cash purchases (£225).
30 Paid Carr & Co. £250 in cash.

4.7

Enter the following transactions in the double entry accounts.

Aug 1 Started business with £5,000 in cash.
      3 Bought goods on credit (£875) from T. Mann.
      5 Paid £4,500 of the opening cash into a business bank account.
      7 Returned goods (£75) to T. Mann.
      8 Bought office furniture (£295), paying by cheque.
      9 Sold goods on credit to James Seymore (£580) and E. Yates (£65).
    10 Bought goods (£420), paying by cheque.
    12 Bought motor van (£4,500) on credit from Greens Garages.
    13 James Seymore returned goods £40.
    14 Credit Sales to T. Williams (£165); B. Groves (£330).
    15 Sold goods (£124) cash.
    18 Bought goods on credit (£300) from T. Mann.
    19 T. Williams returns goods (£36).
    20 J. Kelly lends the firm £3,000, paying the money by cheque.
    22 Returned goods (£30) to T. Mann.
    25 Received a cheque (£65) from E. Yates.
    27 Paid instalment to Greens Garages (£200) by cheque.
    28 Sold goods on credit to James Seymore (£175).
    29 Paid money owing to T. Mann by cheque.
    30 Cash purchases (£320).
    31 T. Williams paid the amount owing (£129) in cash.

5 The Double Entry System for Expenses

OBJECTIVES To enable students to understand and practise the double entry system for the expenses incurred in the day to day running of a business, with an examination of the proprietor's drawings account and the revenue receivable accounts.

Expenses

We have already seen that for each business transaction *two* things happen: some form of value is received in exchange for another form of value given.

In the day-to-day running of a business there will be many expenses incurred, including such items as rent, salaries, wages, telephone, gas, electricity, rates, motor expenses and so on. If the business kept only one account, called 'expenses account', this would only give the overall total of all the expenses. However, the business will need to know exactly how much is spent on each individual expense and, therefore, to meet this requirement an expense account is opened for each type of expense. The double entry for expense accounts is as follows:

Expense account   (receiving)   debit entry
The payment – bank or cash account   (paying)   credit entry

To illustrate the two-fold effect, consider the following transaction: on 1 March, paid wages of £50 in cash. The double entry accounts would appear as follows:

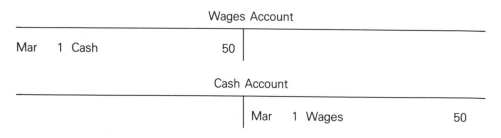

Wages Account

Mar	1	Cash	50		

Cash Account

			Mar	1 Wages	50

Another example of an expense account could be motor expenses; these are petrol, oil, servicing and repairs. Consider the following: on 2 March, paid motor expenses of £75 by cheque. The double entry accounts would appear as follows:

Motor Expenses Account

Mar 2 Bank	75	

Bank Account

	Mar 2 Motor Expenses	75

The Proprietor's Drawings Account

From time to time, the proprietor, who is the owner of the business, may require to take money or goods out of the business for his private use. Whether he takes cash or goods, these withdrawals are known in book-keeping as *drawings*. We have already seen that the proprietor's original investment in the business is recorded in the capital account. This is a very important account, and in order to prevent numerous entries being made in it, any withdrawals from the business by the proprietor are recorded in a drawings account. At the end of the financial year the total of the drawings account will be transferred to the capital account. The double entry accounts required to record the drawings are illustrated in the following examples.

On 8 March, the proprietor takes £100 cash out of the business for his personal use. The double entry accounts would appear as follows:

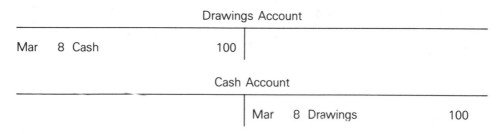

Drawings Account

Mar 8 Cash	100	

Cash Account

	Mar 8 Drawings	100

On 15 March, the proprietor takes £60 goods out of the business for his own use. The double entry accounts would appear as follows:

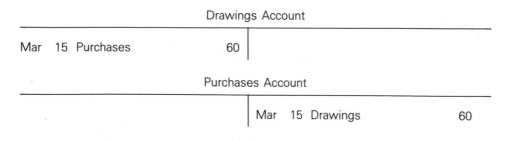

Drawings Account

Mar 15 Purchases	60	

Purchases Account

	Mar 15 Drawings	60

Revenue Receivable Accounts

Special attention is required with regard to revenue receivable accounts – this is revenue (income) which is received by the business. An example of this could be if a business occupied a large building with three floors and decided to sub-let part of the building, one complete floor; the business would receive the rent for this part of the building. This would be rent receivable, and is illustrated in the following example.

On 15 March, received rent of £45 by cheque from sub-tenant. Consider the two-fold effect: the money would be received, therefore a debit entry is made in the bank account. The credit entry would be in the rent receivable account. This is a completely separate account from the rent account, which is an expense. The double entry accounts would appear as follows:

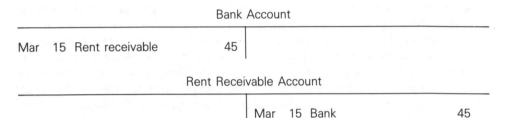

Bank Account

Mar 15 Rent receivable	45	

Rent Receivable Account

	Mar 15 Bank	45

Another example of revenue received could be commission received. Consider the following transaction: on 20 March, received sales commission of £75 in cash. The cash would be received, therefore a debit entry is made in the cash account. The credit entry would be in the commissions receivable account. The double entry accounts would appear as follows:

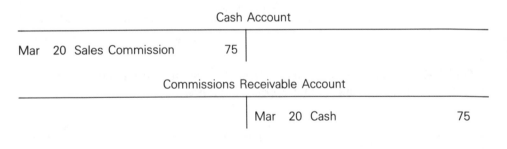

Cash Account

Mar 20 Sales Commission	75	

Commissions Receivable Account

	Mar 20 Cash	75

POINTS TO REMEMBER

The expenses of the business are kept in separate accounts. This is necessary to enable the business to see exactly how much is spent on each individual expense.

Drawings are withdrawals from the business by the owner of the business, and are called drawings whether he takes cash or goods. The accounts which are required with regard to revenue receivable transactions require careful consideration, and are particularly popular with examiners, as they are an excellent test of a students knowledge of the double entry system.

Assignment Exercises

5.1
Complete the blank spaces by inserting the name of the account to be debited and the name of the account to be credited.

(a) Paid motor expenses in cash.

Debit _____ Account   Credit _____ Account

(b) Paid rent by cheque.

Debit _____ Account   Credit _____ Account

(c) Proprietor took cash out of the business for his own use.

Debit _____ Account   Credit _____ Account

(d) Paid rates by cheque.

Debit _____ Account   Credit _____ Account

(e) Received commission in cash.

Debit _____ Account   Credit _____ Account

(f) Paid insurance by cheque.

Debit _____ Account   Credit _____ Account

5.2
Complete the blank spaces by inserting the name of the account to be debited and the name of the account to be credited.

(a) Bought goods, paying in cash.

Debit _____ Account   Credit _____ Account

(b) Received rent by cheque.

Debit _____ Account   Credit _____ Account

(c) Paid motor expenses by cheque.

Debit _____ Account   Credit _____ Account

(d) Sold goods on credit to J. Kendall.

Debit _____ Account   Credit _____ Account

(e) Bought motor van on credit from Leaders Garages.

Debit _____ Account   Credit _____ Account

(f) Paid wages in cash.

Debit _____ Account   Credit _____ Account

5.3

Complete the blank spaces by inserting the name of the account to be debited and the name of the account to be credited.

(a) Paid electricity bill by cheque.

Debit _____ Account   Credit _____ Account

(b) Sold goods for cash.

Debit _____ Account   Credit _____ Account

(c) Received commission by cheque.

Debit _____ Account   Credit _____ Account

(d) Bought office furniture, paying by cheque.

Debit _____ Account   Credit _____ Account

(e) Goods returned to the firm by J. Kilburn.

Debit _____ Account   Credit _____ Account

(f) Proprietor took cash out of the business for private use.

Debit _____ Account   Credit _____ Account

5.4

Complete the blank spaces by inserting the name of the account to be debited and the name of the account to be credited.

(a) We returned goods to R. Bright.

Debit _____ Account   Credit _____ Account

(b) Paid rates by cheque.

Debit _____ Account   Credit _____ Account

(c) Sold goods on credit to K. Williams.

Debit _____ Account   Credit _____ Account

(d) Proprietor took goods for his own use.

Debit _____ Account   Credit _____ Account

(e) Goods returned to the firm by K. Williams.

Debit _____ Account   Credit _____ Account

(f) Received a refund of rates in cash.

Debit _____ Account   Credit _____ Account

5.5

You are to enter the following transactions for the month of May 19–7 in the double entry accounts.

May 1 Started business with £5,000 in a business bank account.
      2 Bought goods on credit (£750) from J. Richardson.
      4 Withdrew £500 cash from the bank.
      6 Returned £40 goods to J. Richardson.
      7 Proprietor took £100 cash for personal use.
      9 Sold goods (£250), receiving a cheque immediately.
   11 Sold goods on credit to K. Stead (£150); M. Day (£229).
   12 Paid rent (£75) by cheque.
   14 K. Stead returned goods to the firm (£24).
   15 Paid motor expenses in cash (£58).
   16 Received rent for premises sub-let (£30) by cheque.
   19 Bought goods on credit (£950) from S. Ramsden.
   22 Paid wages (£150) in cash.
   24 Received £126 by cheque from K. Stead.
   25 Cash sales (£88).
   26 Credit sales, T. Barnett (£122); M. Day (£159).
   27 Returned goods (£68) to S. Ramsden.
   28 Bought office furniture (£200), paying in cash.
   29 The proprietor took £50 by cheque for his own use.
   30 Paid J. Richardson the amount owing (£710) by cheque.
   31 Paid rent (£75) in cash.

5.6

Enter the following transactions in the double entry accounts in the books of K. Wilson for the month of June 19–7.

Jun 1 Started business with £10,000 in cash.
      2 Bought goods (£500), paying in cash.
      3 Paid rent by cash (£100).
      6 Paid £9,000 of the cash into a business bank account.
      8 Sold goods on credit (£250) to J. Stevens.
      9 Received sales commission of £50 in cash.
   10 Credit purchases, A. Dawson (£329); C. Page (£172).
   12 The proprietor, K. Wilson, took £75 cash for his own use.
   14 J. Stevens returned goods (£25).
   15 Bought motor van (£4,000) on credit from Northtown Garages.
   16 Returned goods (£22) to C. Page.
   18 Paid rates by cheque (£150).
   20 Bought goods (£750), paying by cheque immediately.
   22 Bought stationery (£18), paying in cash.
   23 Sold goods on credit (£495) to G. Blackman.
   24 K. Wilson took £120 by cheque for personal use.
   26 Cash sales (£265).
   27 Received sales commission (£28) by cheque.
   28 J. Stevens paid his account (£225) by cheque.

29 G. Blackman returned goods to the firm (£58).

30 Paid motor expenses (£55) in cash.

5.7

You are required to open the double entry accounts in the books of D. Shelley for the month of August 19–7.

Aug 1 Started business with £5,000 in the bank.

2 Purchased goods on credit (£359) from Smith & Weston Ltd.

4 Bought office furniture on credit (£460) from Newstylax.

5 Bought goods (£675), paying by cheque.

7 Returned goods (£29) to Smith & Weston Ltd.

9 Sold goods on credit (£450) to H. Gibson.

10 Withdrew £300 cash from the bank.

12 D. Shelley took £50 cash for his personal use.

14 Paid rent (£200) in cash.

15 Sold goods (£150), receiving a cheque immediately.

16 Paid insurance (£30) by cheque.

18 Received a loan of £2,000 from R. Cawood by cheque.

19 H. Gibson returned goods (£40).

20 Paid Smith & Weston a cheque (£330).

21 Received part of amount owing from H. Gibson (£200) in cash.

22 Paid wages in cash (£175).

23 Paid electricity bill (£68) by cheque.

24 Credit sales to J. Youngman (£278); H. Dale (£181).

26 Paid Newstylax a cheque (£460).

27 Goods returned by J. Youngman (£58).

28 Received rent (£50) in cash for part of premises sub-let.

29 Cash purchases (£45).

30 The insurance was overpaid. A refund of £5 is received by cheque.

31 H. Dale paid us by cheque (£181).

5.8

You are to enter the following transactions in the double entry accounts in the books of T. Garside for the month of October 19–8.

Oct 1 Started business with £7,000 in the business bank account and £500 in cash.

2 Bought goods on credit from T. Richie (£750); R. Kemp (£375); P. Douglas (£480).

3 Paid rates (£75) by cheque.

4 Bought motor van on credit (£2,000) from Abbot Garages.

5 Sold goods on credit to D. Jenkins (£295); A. Andrews (£190).

6 Returned goods (£45) to R. Kemp.

7 Paid insurance (£150) in cash.

8 Cash sales (£65).

9 Received commission by cheque (£75).

10 Bought goods on credit from R. Kemp (£267); W. Wallace (£290).

11 A. Andrews returned goods (£38).

12 Paid motor expenses (£35) in cash.
13 Sold goods for cash (£150).
14 Received refund of £20 by cheque; rates overpaid.
15 Paid wages (£250) in cash.
16 Received a loan of £4,000 by cheque from A. Goldman.
17 Bought office fixtures (£195) on credit from Burton Supplies.
18 A. Andrews paid the firm by cheque £152.
19 Bought goods on credit from R. Kemp (£360).
20 Cash purchases (£150).
21 Paid T. Richie by cheque £750.
22 Returned goods to R. Kemp (£55).
23 Sold goods on credit to D. Jenkins (£130); R. Smythe (£276).
24 Commission received in cash (£95).
24 Paid wages (£200) in cash.
25 Paid R. Kemp the amount owing, a cheque for £902.
26 Received a cheque from D. Jenkins (£425).
27 Paid motor expenses (£22) in cash.
28 T. Garside took £150 for his personal use, by cheque.
29 R. Smythe returned goods (£26).
30 Paid instalment of £150 by cheque to Abbot Garages.
31 Sold goods for cash (£96).

5.9

You are required to open the double entry accounts in the books of F. Perry for the month of November 19–8.

Nov 1 Started business with £4,000 in the bank and £350 in cash.
2 Bought goods on credit from J. Dean (£650); R. Reagan (£467); M. Nichols (£265).
3 Sold goods for cash (£150).
4 A loan is received of £2,500 by cheque from J. Franks.
5 Paid rates by cheque (£212).
6 Bought motor van on credit (£1,500) from Websters Garages.
7 Sold goods on credit to E. Barker (£221); J. Armitage (£357); S. Grey (£128).
8 Paid motor expenses (£35) in cash.
9 The proprietor, F. Perry, took £80 cash for his own use.
10 Paid insurance (£55) by cheque.
11 Bought goods on credit from R. Reagan (£330); J. Dean (£125).
12 Sold goods for cash (£245).
13 A refund of rates (£25) is received by cheque.
14 Paid wages in cash (£130).
15 Returned goods (£45) to R. Reagan.
16 Sold goods on credit to E. Barker (£325); S. Grey (£250).
17 Paid electricity bill (£124) by cheque.
18 Received rent (£55) in cash from sub-tenant.
19 Bought goods on credit from M. Nichols (£356); B. Harris (£95).
20 Bought stationery (£47), paying by cheque.

21 Returned goods to M. Nichols (£38).
22 F. Perry took £150 by cheque for private use.
23 Paid J. Dean the amount outstanding (£775) by cheque.
24 Received £378 from S. Grey by cheque.
25 Cash sales (£200).
25 Bought office fixtures (£150), paying in cash.
26 Received a cheque (£357) from J. Armitage.
27 Paid wages in cash (£75).
28 Paid Websters Garages £1,500 by cheque.
29 Bought goods on credit from B. Harris (£450).
30 Returned goods (£65) to B. Harris.

6   Balancing Accounts

OBJECTIVES   To enable students to ascertain the 'balance' on an account.

The term 'balance' is the accounting word for the amount of the difference between the two sides of an account. To 'balance off' an account the procedure is as follows:

1. Add up the side of the account which is the greatest in value.
2. Add up the other side of the account.
3. Deduct the smaller total; the difference between the two sides is the 'balance'.
4. The 'balance' is first entered on the side which is smallest in value.
5. The two totals are then entered at both sides of the account, the writer making sure that the two totals are written parallel with each other.
6. The 'balance' is then brought down, to the correct side of the account.

Consider the following cash account:

Cash Account

Mar	1 Sales		350	Mar	2 Motor expenses	35
					4 Rent	50
					9 Stationery	15
					15 Wages	70

The cash received is recorded at the debit side of the account, the cash paid out is recorded at the credit side. The debit side total is £350. The credit side totals £170; the difference between these two figures is 'the balancing figure' of £180, and represents the amount of cash which remains. The cash account when balanced off will appear as follows:

Cash Account

Mar	1 Sales		350	Mar	2 Motor expenses	35
					4 Rent	50
					9 Stationery	15
					15 Wages	70
					31 Balance c/d	180
			350			350
Apr	1 Balance b/d		180			

In most firms the accounts are balanced at the end of each month. The balance carried down, abbreviated as (c/d), is written in the account on the last day of the current month. The balance is brought down (b/d) on the first day of the next month. These two balancing entries are a 'double entry'. If the balance brought down is at the debit side of an account, it is referred to as a 'debit balance'. If the balance brought down is at the credit side of an account, it is referred to as a 'credit balance'.

Consider the following personal account, before balancing.

B. Senior Account

Apr	3	Sales	235	Apr	10 Returns Inwards	46
	15	Sales	350		28 Bank	189
	25	Sales	145			

To balance this account, the same principle will apply: total the side which is greatest in value, in this example the debit side, which is £730; total the credit side, £235; the difference between the two sides is the balance. After balancing the account will appear as follows:

B. Senior Account

Apr	3	Sales	235	Apr	10 Returns Inwards	46
	15	Sales	350		28 Bank	189
	25	Sales	145		30 Balance c/d	495
			730			730
May	1	Balance b/d	495			

Further examples, before balancing:

F. Reedman Account

Apr	12	Returns Outwards	25	Apr	7 Purchases	725
	29	Bank	700		17 Purchases	300

After balancing, F. Reedman's account would appear as follows:

F. Reedman Account

Apr	12	Returns Outwards	25	Apr	7 Purchases	725
	29	Bank	700		17 Purchases	300
	30	Balance c/d	300			
			1,025			1,025
				May	1 Balance b/d	300

40

If an account contains only one entry on each side which are equal to each other, totals are not required. A double line is ruled under each side, as shown in this example:

T. Gordon Account

Apr	4 Sales	250	Apr	28 Bank	250

If accounts contain only one entry, as shown in the following:

Motor Van Account

Apr	2 Lintons Garages	3,000

the balance should be written in, a double line ruled under each side, and the balance brought down, as follows:

Motor Van Account

Apr	2 Lintons Garages	3,000	Apr	30 Balance c/d	3,000
May	1 Balance b/d	3,000			

Personal Accounts

Every *personal account* has the name of a 'person' with whom the business deals. These may be sole traders, such as R. Moore, or partnerships, such as Black & Green, or limited companies, such as R. Smith & Co. Ltd. Whichever kind of 'person' they are, their account will keep a record of the firms dealings with them.

The capital account is a very special case among personal accounts. The value of the proprietor's investment in the business is recorded in this account.

Real Accounts

Every *real account* has the name of an asset. These assets are real things, such as office furniture, a motor vehicle, machinery, premises, cash. All asset accounts are real accounts.

Nominal Accounts

The word 'nominal' means in name only. Every *nominal account* has the name of a loss or profit of the business. Examples might include electricity account, gas account, rent account, wages account, rent receivable account. The business keeps a record of these losses and profits during the year, and at the end of the year uses them to calculate the profit and loss account of the business.

A good illustration of a nominal account is the wages account. There may be £500 debited in the wages account, but the money is there in name only – it has been paid in wages to the employees.

Assignment Exercises

6.1
Complete the blank spaces by inserting the correct classification of the following accounts; the first one is completed as an example:

(a) D. Wilson   Personal Account

(b) Display equipment   _____ Account

(c) Telephone   _____ Account

(d) Motor van   _____ Account

(e) Smith & Pearson Ltd.   _____ Account

(f) Cash   _____ Account

6.2
Complete the blank spaces by inserting the correct classification of the following accounts.

(a) Works machinery   _____ Account

(b) Rent received   _____ Account

(c) T. Greenwood   _____ Account

(d) Office furniture   _____ Account

(e) Electricity   _____ Account

(f) Stylax Ltd.   _____ Account

6.3
Enter the following items in the personal accounts only; do not write up the other accounts. Balance each personal account at the end of the month and bring down the balance.

Jan 1 Bought goods on credit from D. Hall (£348); L. Walker (£576); B. Hagston (£850).

4 Purchases on credit from L. Walker (£125); B. Dickson (£367).
9 Returned goods to B. Hagston (£50); L. Walker (£55).
16 Bought goods on credit from B. Dickson (£146); J. Dunn (£85).
18 Returned goods to B. Dickson (£67).
26 Paid D. Hall £348 by cheque.
30 Paid B. Dickson £300 in cash.

6.4

Enter the following transactions in the personal accounts only; do not write up the other accounts. Balance each personal account at the end of the month and bring down the balance.

Feb 1 Sold goods on credit to M. Harding (£360); J. Johnstone (£98); E. Briggs (£450); T. Myers (£212).
3 Sales on credit to R. Godfrey (£330); P. Ellis (£421).
6 Goods returned by J. Johnstone (£24); E. Briggs (£50).
9 Sold goods on credit to T. Myers (£152); R. Godfrey (£135).
12 Returns inwards from M. Harding (£60).
15 Received £300 in cash from M. Harding.
18 Sales on credit to E. Briggs (£220); T. Myers (£240).
19 P. Ellis paid £421 by cheque.
20 Goods returned by T. Myers (£52).
25 Received a cheque (£400) from E. Briggs.
27 Sales on credit to R. Kemp (£350); E. Briggs (£90).
28 Received £74 in cash from J. Johnstone.

6.5

Enter the following transactions in the personal accounts only; do not write up the other accounts. Balance each personal account at the end of the month and bring the balance down.

Mar 1 Purchases on credit from J. Radcliffe (£525); P. Coates (£450); W. James (£695); P. Williams (£155).
4 Sold goods on credit to J. Burns (£158); S. Daniel (£350); D. Hall (£212); P. Harper (£90).
6 Returned goods to P. Coates (£55); P. Williams (£25).
8 Purchases on credit from W. James (£152); P. Coates (£295); J. Allen (£355).
12 Credit sales to S. Daniel (£395); D. Hall (£422); J. Nixon (£125).
15 Paid J. Radcliffe £525 by cheque.
18 Goods returned to the firm by J. Nixon (£20); S. Daniel (£45).
21 Received £158 in cash from J. Burns.
25 Sold goods on credit to P. Harper (£155); J. Nixon (£120).
27 Purchased goods on credit from P. Williams (£240); J. Allen (£170).
29 Returned goods to J. Allen (£28).
30 Paid cheques to P. Coates (£395); P. Williams (£130).
31 Received £212 by cheque from D. Hall.

6.6

Enter the following transactions in the personal accounts only; do not write up the other accounts. Balance each personal account at the end of the month and bring down the balance.

Apr 1 Bought goods on credit from R. Pearson (£459); S. Dean (£360); L. Gregg (£126); N. Banks (£280).

    3 Credit sales to P. Lodge (£240); D. Simons (£120).

    5 Goods returned to S. Dean (£30); L. Gregg (£26).

    7 Sold goods on credit to J. Watson (£195); P. Lodge (£150); R. Sutcliffe (£95); T. Barnsdale (£360).

  10 Credit purchases: L. Gregg (£326); R. Pearson (£231).

  11 Credit sales to D. Simons (£97); J. Watson (£219).

  12 Bought goods on credit from N. Banks (£350); S. Dean (£195).

  15 Sold goods on credit to J. Watson (£175); R. Sutcliffe (£150); F. McKay (£220); T. Barnsdale (£155).

  18 Returned goods to S. Dean (£45); N. Banks (£50).

  21 Goods returned to the firm by F. McKay (£20); J. Watson (£25).

  23 Paid R. Pearson £459 by cheque.

  25 Received £200 in cash from F. McKay.

  26 Sold goods on credit to R. Sutcliffe (£235); D. Simons (£190).

  27 Bought goods on credit from K. Stocks (£490); S. Dean (£280); N. Banks (£125); J. Carlton (£175).

  28 Received £360 by cheque from T. Barnsdale.

  29 Returned goods to K. Stocks (£35); J. Carlton (£25).

  30 Paid L. Gregg £426 and N. Banks £230 by cheque.

6.7

Enter the following transactions in the double entry accounts; write up all the accounts. Balance the accounts at the end of the month and bring the balances down.

May 1 Started business with £2,500 in a business bank account.

    3 Bought goods on credit from M. Seal (£240); J. Green (£195); S. Sutcliffe (£280).

    5 Sold goods on credit to E. Phillips (£125); W. Lodge (£178).

    6 Withdrew £500 cash from the bank.

    7 Returned goods to J. Green (£35); S. Sutcliffe (£20).

    8 Paid rent in cash (£75).

    9 The proprietor took £50 cash for his private use.

  12 Received a loan of £1,000 by cheque from G. Normanton.

  14 Cash sales (£120).

  15 Bought office stationery (£45), paying by cheque.

  18 Received a cheque (£125) from E. Phillips.

  20 Paid insurance (£95) in cash.

  22 Bought goods on credit from J. Green (£450); M. Seal (£335).

  24 Cash purchases (£250).

  25 Proprietor took £50 cash for own use.

  27 Paid rent by cheque (£75).

28 Paid by cheque S. Sutcliffe (£260); M. Seal (£240).
30 Sold goods on credit to W. Lodge (£258); E. Phillips (£160).

6.8

Enter the following transactions in the double entry accounts; write up all the accounts. Balance the accounts at the end of the month and bring the balances down.

Jun
1 Started business with £6,000 in a bank account and £250 in cash.
2 Bought goods on credit from B. Lewis (£619); E. Daley (£197).
3 Bought stationery (£24), paying in cash.
4 Returned faulty goods to E. Daley (£29).
5 Paid rent by cheque (£125).
6 Credit sales to D. Mills (£136); J. Kendall (£333); W. Barry (£85).
7 Machinery bought on credit (£316) from Groves & Bean Ltd.
8 Paid wages (£65) in cash.
9 Goods returned to the firm by J. Kendall (£23).
10 Bought motor vehicle (£950) on credit from Lockwood Motors.
11 Sold some surplus machinery (£125) on credit to B. Freeman.
12 Proprietor took £50 cash for personal use.
13 Credit purchases D. Trent (£367); E. Daley (£522); B. Todd (£168).
14 Paid motor expenses in cash (£48).
15 Received rent from sub-tenant (£25) by cheque.
16 Cash sales (£155).
17 Returned goods to D. Trent (£47); B. Todd (£18).
18 Paid wages in cash (£75).
19 Cash purchases (£76).
20 Bought another motor van (£800), paying by cheque.
21 Sold goods on credit to W. Barry (£96); D. Mills (£134).
22 Proprietor took £50 by cheque for own use.
23 B. Freeman paid £125 in cash.
24 Credit purchases from B. Lewis (£447); E. Daley (£292).
25 Received by cheque £181 from W. Barry.
26 Goods returned by D. Mills (£22).
27 Paid D. Trent £320 by cheque.
28 Goods bought on credit from B. Todd (£275); B. Lewis (£196).
29 Received £310 in cash from J. Kendall.
30 Paid Lockwood Motors £950 by cheque.

7 The Trial Balance

OBJECTIVES   To enable students to understand the function and purpose of a trial balance, and to recognise that the trial balance is only a proof of the arithmetical accuracy of the books.

The principle of the double entry system states that every debit entry should have a corresponding credit entry. Two separate accounts are involved in every transaction, one account recording the debit entry, the other account recording the credit entry. At the end of each month, it is normal procedure for the accounts to be totalled and the 'balance' remaining on each account to be ascertained. All items recorded in the accounts on the debit side should equal in total all the items recorded on the credit side of the books; this principle is the basis for the structure and preparation of a trial balance.

The trial balance is prepared by making a complete list of all the balances remaining in the ledger. The 'balances' are placed in two separate columns, side by side, with the headings 'Debit' and 'Credit'. When there is a debit balance on the account, the amount of the balance is entered in the column for debit balances; when there is a credit balance on the account, the amount of the balance is placed in the column for credit balances. Accounts which equal each other on debit and credit sides should never be included; only the accounts which have a 'balance' are used.

A trial balance, therefore, consists of a list of the 'balances' only, arranged according to whether they are debit balances or credit balances on the accounts. When all the 'balances' are entered, the two columns are totalled. The two columns should agree. When they do so, they are said to 'strike a balance', and this is usually considered to be a good indication that the book-keeping has been methodically carried out.

A trial balance is usually drawn up periodically for the purpose of testing the arithmetical accuracy of the book-keeping. The 'balance' or agreement of the trial balance does not positively prove that no errors have been made: it has certain limitations, which are considered later in Module 27.

A trial balance is always taken out at a specific date, and this date should be clearly written as part of the heading. A trial balance is *not* an account, and should not be placed in a ledger; it is a summary of all the balances remaining on the ledger accounts at a specific date. The headings of the two columns are usually abbreviated to Dr. and Cr.

The ruling on journal paper, having two columns on the right-hand side, is very suitable for the construction of a trial balance. The following is an example of a trial balance:

Trial Balance as at 31 May 19–7

	Dr. £	Cr. £
Capital		2,500
Bank	2,505	
Purchases	1,750	
Sales		841
Cash	100	
M. Seal		335
J. Green		610
E. Phillips	160	
W. Lodge	436	
Returns Outwards		55
Rent	150	
Drawings	100	
G. Normanton (Loan)		1,000
Office Stationery	45	
Insurance	95	
	5,341	5,341

POINTS TO REMEMBER

If the trial balance totals do not agree, the following procedure will very often reveal the errors:

1. Re-check the addition of the totals, to make sure the error is not a simple matter of addition.
2. Check the balances – have debit balances in the ledger been incorrectly entered in the credit column of the trial balance, and vice versa? Check that no balances have been missed completely.
3. Check for transposition of figures, for example a balance of £890 written in the trial balance as £980.
4. Re-calculate the balances on the accounts to ensure that these are correct.

Errors can occur which are not revealed by the trial balance. These limitations are covered in Modules 27, which considers errors not affecting trial balance agreement.

What the Examiner Will Look For

Ensure that the transactions are correctly recorded in the double entry accounts. The accounts should be neatly written and crossing out should be avoided. Marks can be lost for careless and untidy work.

In questions where a trial balance is required, the accounts must be 'balanced off' and the balances brought down. Balancing the accounts uses more lines on the paper, therefore the accounts should be positioned several lines apart to avoid a 'jumbled' appearance.

A trial balance is taken out at a specific date; this date should be clearly written as part of the heading. Clear and concise headings are a mandatory examination requirement.

Frequently in examination questions the student is initially given a list of 'balances'; these could be in the form of a trial balance or a balance sheet. These 'balances' should be entered in the appropriate accounts before the recording of any further transactions is begun.

Assignment Exercises

7.1

Record the following transactions of James Carrington for the month of July 19–8 in the double entry accounts. Balance off all the accounts and extract a trial balance as at 31 July 19–8.

Jul 1 Started business with £5,500 in cash.
  2 Bought goods for cash (£200).
  3 Put £5,000 of the cash into a business bank account.
  4 Bought goods on credit from M. Morgan (£300); R. Draper (£480); S. Sykes (£186); D. Hammond (£340).
  5 Bought motor van (£1,500) on credit from Silver Garages.
  6 Paid Rent by cheque (£65).
  8 Sold goods on credit to B. Hedges (£180); V. McKay (£195); S. Draper (£150); J. Nixon (£210).
  10 Paid insurance in cash (£78).
  11 Bought office furniture (£196), paying by cheque.
  12 Paid wages (£150) in cash.
  14 Returned goods to R. Draper (£40); S. Sykes (£10).
  16 Cash sales (£130).
  17 Credit purchases: S. Sykes (£126); M. Morgan (£260).
  18 Goods returned to us by V. McKay (£25); S. Draper (£40).
  19 Received a cheque (£12); a refund of insurance overpaid.
  20 Sold goods on credit to J. Nixon (£150); B. Hedges (£115); J. Peters (£90).
  22 V. McKay paid £170 in cash.
  24 Paid M. Morgan £560 by cheque.
  25 Paid wages (£75) in cash.
  26 Goods returned to the firm by J. Nixon (£20).
  27 J. Carrington took £50 cash for his own use.
  28 Bought stationery (£45), paying by cheque.

29 J. Peters paid £90 by cheque.
30 Received £180 in cash from B. Hedges.
31 Paid Rent (£65) in cash.

7.2
You are required to open the necessary double entry ledger accounts and enter
the following transactions for the month of March, in the books of Brian Stones.
At the end of the month balance off the accounts and extract a trial balance as at
31 March 19–8.

Mar 1 Commenced business with £6,000 in a business bank account.
    2 Bought office fixtures (£400), paying by cheque.
    3 Bought goods on credit (£840) from Thompson Ltd.
    5 Paid rent (£420) by cheque.
    6 Cash sales (£400).
    8 Paid insurance (£74) by cheque.
    9 Paid wages in cash (£45).
  10 Cash purchases (£200).
  11 Bought goods on credit (£600) from Thompson Ltd.
  14 Cash sales (£210).
  16 Returned goods (£45) to Thompson Ltd.
  18 Paid Thompson Ltd. the balance on their account by cheque.
  20 Sold goods (£440) on credit to S. Lawson.
  26 Paid wages in cash (£45).
  27 S. Lawson returned goods (£40).
  28 Withdrew £60 in cash for private use.
  31 S. Lawson settled his account by cheque.

7.3
Ron Stewart is a wholesaler. On 1 January 19–7 he had the following balances in
his ledger.

	Dr. £	Cr. £
Capital		6,800
A. Frazer		880
Motor vehicle	3,800	
A. Hodges	1,100	
J. Jennings	740	
Bank	2,040	

During the month of January 19–7 his trading transactions were as follows:

Jan 2 Received £740 from J. Jennings by cheque.
    3 Bought goods on credit (£1,070) from A. Frazer.
    4 Bought office equipment (£560), paying by cheque.
    5 Sold goods on credit to A. Hodges (£930).

8 Paid A. Frazer £880 by cheque.
11 A. Hodges returned goods (£37).
14 Sold goods on credit to J. Jennings (£590).
17 Drawings (£500) by cheque.
20 Purchased goods on credit (£760) from A. Frazer.
22 Received £1,100 by cheque from A. Hodges.
26 Sold goods on credit to A. Hodges (£710).
28 Returned goods to A. Frazer (£98).
31 Paid salaries by cheque (£480).

Write up Ron Stewart's ledger for the month of January 19–7, and extract a trial balance as at 31 January 19–7.

7.4
The following information refers to a small engineering business owned by Douglas Whitby.

Balance Sheet as at 31 October 19–8

Premises	6,250	Capital	9,000
Debtors: P. Cave	1,580	Loan: G. Franks	2,000
R. Webster	1,640	Creditors: T. Cummings	1,250
V. Bruce	870	G. Fenland	730
Balance at Bank	2,640		
	£12,980		£12,980

During the month of November 19–8 his transactions were as follows:

Sales on Credit
8 Nov	V. Bruce	130
10 Nov	P. Cave	810
24 Nov	H. Crossley	480

Purchase Returns
6 Nov	T. Cummings	115

Cheques received from:
26 Nov	P. Cave	1,580
29 Nov	V. Bruce	870

Purchases on Credit
2 Nov	T. Cummings	855
12 Nov	G. Fenland	330
13 Nov	T. Cummings	914
18 Nov	I. Shaw	295

Paid the following-
by cheque
4 Nov	Purchase of Van	2,000
7 Nov	T. Cummings	1,250
15 Nov	Rates	600
25 Nov	Repairs to Van	90
30 Nov	Drawings	250

You are required to write up Douglas Whitby's ledger for the month of November 19–8 and extract a trial balance as at 30 November 19–8.

50

7.5

The trial balance of Ken Stevens on 30 April 19–4 was as follows:

Trial Balance as at 30 April 19–4

	Dr. £	Cr. £
Sales		20,750
Purchases	13,170	
General Expenses	4,972	
Fixtures	2,500	
K. Gibson	1,130	
T. Lowe		700
Bank	1,720	
Drawings	2,800	
Capital		7,228
Stock	2,386	
	28,678	28,678

During the month of May the following transactions took place:

May 1 Bought goods on credit from T. Lowe (£85).
May 2 Sold goods on credit to K. Gibson (£105).
May 18 Banked cash sales (£400).
May 20 K. Gibson paid £680 by cheque in part settlement of his account.
May 26 Paid general expenses by cheque (£97). Sent a cheque value £300 to T. Lowe in part settlement of his account.
May 28 Paid general expenses by cheque (£275).
May 30 Withdrew £300 from the bank for own use.

You are required to:
(a) Open the accounts at 1 May 19–4.
(b) Record the transactions directly in the accounts by means of double entries.
(c) Extract a trial balance at 31 May 19–4.

(Royal Society of Arts)

7.6

J. Fisher runs a small mail order business. A bank account is kept in which all amounts received and paid are entered. Amounts paid for packing materials and postage are entered into the general expenses account. On 30 September 19–6 the following balances remain in the books.

	£	£
G. Rogers	675	
N. Fuller	120	
A. Lewis		75
Bank	360	
Capital		1,080
	1,155	1,155

You are required to:
(1) Open ledger accounts for the above items and enter the balances as at 1 October 19–6
(2) Post the transactions indicated direct to the appropriate ledger accounts and open any other accounts which may be required.
(3) Balance the accounts where necessary and extract a trial balance on 31 October.

Purchases on Credit			Sales on Credit		
October		£	October		£
6	A. Lewis	80	15	G. Rogers	50
13	A. Lewis	40	24	N. Fuller	80
			28	G. Rogers	20

Payments Received			Payments Made		
October		£	October		£
2	G. Rogers	675	1	Packing materials	15
30	N. Fuller	200	15	Postage	25
			21	A. Lewis	75

(Royal Society of Arts)

8 Separating the Accounts into Four Main Ledgers

OBJECTIVES   To enable the student to divide and separate the accounts into four main ledgers and a cash book and to understand the necessity for this division.

Even in a relatively small business it would be very difficult to keep all the accounts in one main ledger, and this would mean only one person would be able to use the ledger at any given time. Therefore it is necessary to divide the ledger into four separate ledgers, and to classify the accounts.

Private Ledger

This ledger will contain the capital account and the drawings account of the proprietor. It may also contain details of loan accounts. Loans made to the business, and loans made by the business. These accounts are of a confidential nature.

Purchases Ledger or Bought Ledger

This ledger will contain all the suppliers' personal accounts.

Sales Ledger

This ledger will contain all the customers' personal accounts.

General Ledger or Nominal Ledger

This ledger will contain all the remaining real and nominal accounts including the sales account, purchases account, returns inwards account and the returns outwards account.

Cash Book

This is the book of original entry concerned only with the receiving and paying out of money, both in cash and by cheque. It is the bank account and the cash account taken out of the ledger and placed together in a separate book.

The private ledger contains the accounts which are of a private
and confidential nature.

The personal accounts of the suppliers contain the essential
information relating to the purchase of goods on credit, these
are grouped together, for convenience in a separate ledger, this
is known as the purchase ledger or the bought ledger.

The personal accounts of the customers contain important
information relating to the sales of goods on credit, these are
grouped together, for convenience in a separate ledger, this is
known as the sales ledger and is sometimes referred to as the
debtors ledger.

The cash book contains the cash account and the bank
account. All the remaining accounts are in the general ledger,
this is also known as the nominal ledger.

Assignment Exercises

8.1
Complete the blank spaces by inserting the name of the ledger in which the
following accounts would appear.

(a) Purchases account   _____ Ledger

(b) S. Smith – suppliers' personal account   _____ Ledger

(c) Returns inwards account   _____ Ledger

(d) J. Jones – customers' personal account   _____ Ledger

(e) Sales account   _____ Ledger

(f) Fixtures account   _____ Ledger

8.2
Complete the blank spaces by inserting the name of the ledger in which the
following accounts would appear.

(a) Returns outwards account   _____ Ledger

(b) Brown & Co. Ltd. – customers' personal account   _____ Ledger

(c) Motor vehicle account   _____ Ledger

(d) Wages account   _____ Ledger

(e) Capital account   _____ Ledger

(f) Walsh & Pine Ltd. – suppliers' personal account   _____ Ledger

8.3

Complete the blank spaces by inserting the name of the ledger in which the following accounts would appear.

(a) Rent account   _____ Ledger

(b) Drawings account   _____ Ledger

(c) Office equipment account   _____ Ledger

(d) D. Lawrence – customers' personal account   _____ Ledger

(e) Stylax Ltd. – supplier of display equipment   _____ Ledger

(f) J. Norbury – suppliers' personal account   _____ Ledger

9   Banking

OBJECTIVES   To gain an understanding of the banking system and to consider Current Accounts, Deposit Accounts, and the detailed completion of paying-in-slips and cheques.

Banks operate two main types of account, a current account and a deposit or savings account.

Deposit Accounts

This type of account is normally concerned with saving, and interest is given on the balance held in the account. Money placed in a deposit account cannot be drawn upon by cheque and, in some cases, notice may be required before money can be withdrawn.

Current Accounts

The main function and use of current accounts is the paying in and withdrawing of money. With this type of account the bank will issue a cheque book to enable the customer to make payments by cheque. The customer will also be given a paying-in book to enable him to pay cash and cheques into the account. Interest is not usually given on current accounts.

A great number of private individuals and practically all businesses have Current Accounts.

Bank Charges

Many banks will make a charge for their services and also charge interest on any money borrowed by customers. Special arrangements can be made for customers to 'overdraw' their current accounts. When banks pay out more money than has been deposited, this is referred to as a 'bank overdraft'. When a bank account has been overdrawn this is usually indicated by the placing of the abbreviation DR or O/D after the balance on the bank statement.

Standing Orders

These are special instructions given by the customer to his bank to pay a stated sum of money to a named party at certain stated dates until further orders. This is a service offered by banks to their customers in return for a small charge for each payment, and is much used for paying fixed amounts which fall due on known dates, such as insurance premiums, rents, subscriptions and so on.

Direct Debit

This is another way of making payments. A customer arranges for his bank to pay money to certain organizations when they present their bills direct to the bank, and to debit the amounts to his account.

Credit Transfers

This is another method of payment which makes it possible for any person to pay money into a clearing bank for the credit of the account of any customer of the banks operating the system. In 1967 the name of the credit transfer was changed to Bank Giro, with which was also merged the direct debiting system.

Refer to Drawer

This is a note or answer written or stamped by the drawer's bank on a cheque that the bank will not honour. This is usually because: there is not a sufficient credit balance in the drawer's account; because the cheque has been stopped by the drawer; because the amount in words and in figures on the cheque do not agree; or because the drawer has been made bankrupt. The words mean that the payee should ask the drawer to pay or to explain why the cheque is not being honoured. The abbreviation, is R/D.

At regular intervals, usually once a month, the bank will provide the customer with a copy of their account. This is known as a statement of account or a bank statement, and will give full details of all the transactions during the period, and also details of any bank charges.

Cheques

The following is an example of a completed cheque:

The person writing the cheque and using it for payment is called the *drawer* – in this example, J. M. England. The person to whom the cheque is to be paid is called the *payee* – in this example E. Wilding. The cheque is dated in the top right-hand corner; the date should also be written on the counterfoil along with the remainder of the details as a record. The amount of the cheque is written in figures in the appropriate box, and the same amount then stated in words. Most banks personalise their cheques by printing the name of the account holder. The cheque must be signed beneath the printed name.

Cheques are identified by the numbers which are positioned along the bottom. In this example, the first set of numbers – 239547 – is the number of the cheque. The second set of numbers – 20–99–93 – is the number of the particular branch of the bank, in this example, High Street, Caxton, London N99 4XX, and is often referred to as the 'Code Number'. The third set of numbers – 10324965 – is the individual account number of J. M. England.

The cheque illustrated is a crossed cheque; it has two parallel lines printed vertically across the front. A crossed cheque cannot be 'cashed on demand' – it must be paid into a bank account. A cheque can be further safeguarded by use of a special 'crossing'. These are in the form of a specific instruction to the bank. An excellent example of a special crossing is: 'Account Payee only'. When this is written between the two parallel lines, the cheque can only be paid into the account of the payee.

Paying-in Slips

When paying money into a current account a paying-in slip must be completed, stating the total amount to be paid in and the form it takes, whether in cash, notes or cheques. Any cheques or money orders should be listed separately and totalled on the reverse side of the paying-in slip, and the total amount of any cheques and/or money orders then inserted in the appropriate box, on the front of the paying-in slip, under the amount of 'total cash'. This is an illustration of the front and the reverse side of a paying-in slip.

The following is a worked example of a paying-in slip. You are employed as a cashier by Reed & Co. They keep a current account at the Bond Street branch of Barclays Bank. The account number is 87655678. On 15 July 19–8 you are required to bank the following on their behalf:

3	£50 notes
4	£20 notes
7	£10 notes
125	£1 coins
35	50p coins
26	20p coins
15	10p coins
50	2p coins

Cheques made payable to Reed & Co. from:

T. Green	£161.17
G. Moore	£245.15
B. Bingley	£ 78.84
H. Fellows	£159.95

BARCLAYS BANK PLC — CREDIT

54 LOMBARD STREET BRANCH

DATE

ACCOUNT

Paid in by

ACCOUNT NUMBER

	£
Notes: £50	
Notes: £20	
Notes: £10	
Notes: £5	
Notes/Coin: £1	
50p	
20p	
Silver	
Bronze	
TOTAL CASH	
Cheques,PO's,etc (Listed overleaf)	
TOTAL CREDIT £	

Customers are advised that the Bank reserves the right at its discretion to postpone payment of cheques drawn against uncleared effects which may have been credited to the account.

PLEASE DO NOT WRITE OR MARK BELOW THIS LINE

CS2E 3/82

||"20"0000|: 60

Counterfoil

Date

Credit the account of

Account Number

	£
Notes: £50	
Notes: £20	
Notes: £10	
Notes: £5	
Notes/Coin: £1	
50p	
20p	
Silver	
Bronze	
TOTAL CASH	
Cheques,PO's,etc (Listed overleaf)	
TOTAL CREDIT £	

Cheques etc.

TOTAL CARRIED OVERLEAF £

The completed paying-in slip is as follows:

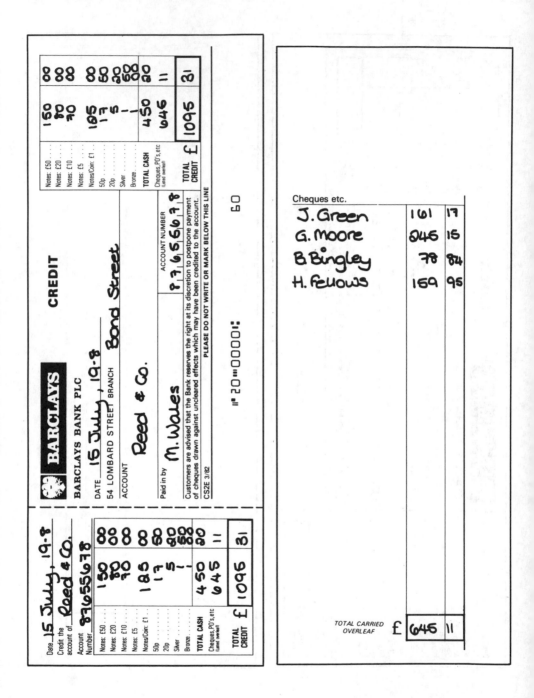

Date 15 July, 19-8
Credit the account of Reed & Co.
Account Number 87655678

	£	
Notes: £50	150	00
Notes: £20	80	00
Notes: £10	70	00
Notes: £5	185	00
Notes/Coin: £1	17	00
50p	5	50
20p	—	—
Silver	—	—
Bronze	450	00
TOTAL CASH	645	00
Cheques, PO's, etc (Land overleaf)		
TOTAL CREDIT £	1096	31

BARCLAYS BANK PLC   CREDIT

DATE 16 July, 19-8
54 LOMBARD STREET BRANCH   Bond Street
ACCOUNT   Reed & Co.
Paid in by   M. Wales

ACCOUNT NUMBER
87655678

Customers are advised that the Bank reserves the right at its discretion to postpone payment of cheques drawn against uncleared effects which may have been credited to the account.

PLEASE DO NOT WRITE OR MARK BELOW THIS LINE

CS2E 3/82

II⁗ 20 ⁗0000I: 60

	£	
Notes: £50	150	00
Notes: £20	80	00
Notes: £10	70	00
Notes: £5	185	00
Notes/Coin: £1	17	00
50p	5	50
20p	—	—
Silver	—	—
Bronze	450	00
TOTAL CASH	645	00
Cheques, PO's, etc (Land overleaf)		
TOTAL CREDIT £	1096	31

Cheques etc.

J. Green	161	17
G. Moore	245	15
B Bingley	78	84
H. Fellows	159	95
TOTAL CARRIED OVERLEAF £	**645**	**11**

POINTS TO **REMEMBER**	A business bank account offers many advantages and services to a firm, and practically all businesses have a current account. This enables them to make payments by cheque and receive payments through the normal banking system.

Most banks personalise their cheques by printing the name of the account holder; the cheque *must* always be signed beneath the printed name. A crossed cheque cannot be cashed on demand, it must be paid into a bank account.

The cash and cheques received by the business are paid into the bank by completing a paying-in slip. The details of notes and coins are listed on the front; the cheque/and money orders are listed on the reverse side, this total is then carried forward to the front of the slip and added to the total cash. The counterfoil is stamped by the cashier at the bank as a proof of the deposit.

All the following exercises are taken from past examination papers, to enable the student to gain practice in the preparation of cheques/counterfoils, paying-in slips and banking.

Assignment Exercises

9.1
Your employers, Adam and Eve, keep a current account at the High Street branch of Barclays Bank. The account number is 2345678. You are to bank the following on their behalf:

3 notes of £20 each
358 notes of £1 each
12 bags of £5 each in silver
18 bags of 50p each in bronze
Cheques for £194.67; £218.54; £18.50 and a money order for £37.50.

Write up the paying-in slip set out below.

(The Royal Society of Arts)

9.2
On 7 June 19–3 you received an account from Modern Office Equipment Ltd. for the supply of two new electric typewriters. The amount due for payment is £1,890 and is subject to a small discount of $2\frac{1}{2}$ per cent if paid within 28 days. You settle the account on 21 June 19–3. The balance at bank prior to this transaction was £3,113.18. Required:
(a) Complete the cheque below settling the account.

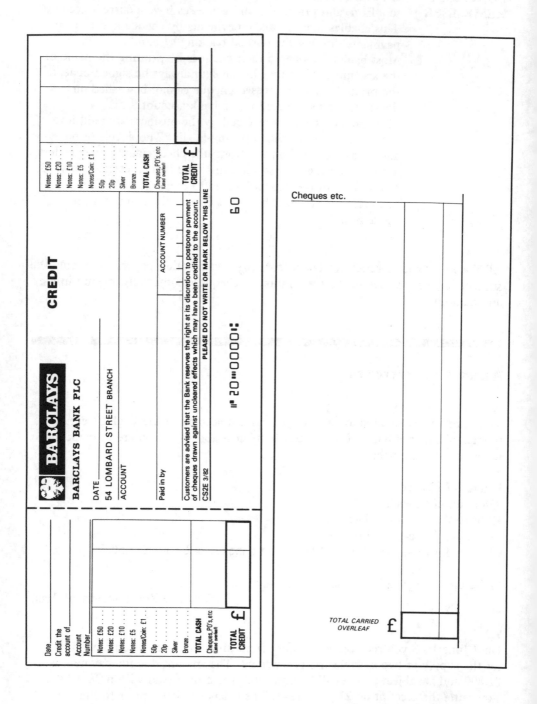

(b) Fill in the counterfoil showing clearly the new balance to be carried forward.

(The Royal Society of Arts)

9.3

You are employed by White & Co as a cashier at their Westminster Branch. Their bank current account, number 76543211, is maintained at the Lombard Street Branch of Barclays Bank. On 15 May 19–7 you pay the following items into the local branch of Barclays Bank.

5	£50 notes
2	£20 notes
8	£10 notes
130	£1 coins
55	50p coins
24	20p coins
20	10p coins
100	2p coins

Cheques made payable to White & Co from:

R. S. Adams	£169.95
T. Bromley	£261.14
A. Kent	£ 61.24

You are required to complete all parts of the paying-in slip set out below:

(The Royal Society of Arts)

9.4

(a) On 5 June 19–5 your cheque book counterfoil shows you have £238.37 in your account at the bank. On the same day you receive an account from R. S. Andrews for goods received, value £80.50. Using today's date, which is 20 June 19–5, complete and sign the cheque and counterfoil to settle Andrews' account after deducting 2 per cent cash discount.
N.B. Your counterfoil should show the balance at bank after completion of this transaction.

BARCLAYS

BARCLAYS BANK PLC

CREDIT

DATE

54 LOMBARD STREET BRANCH

ACCOUNT

Paid in by

ACCOUNT NUMBER

Customers are advised that the Bank reserves the right at its discretion to postpone payment
of cheques drawn against uncleared effects which may have been credited to the account.

PLEASE DO NOT WRITE OR MARK BELOW THIS LINE

CS2E 3/82

1" 20 "0000 : 60

Notes: £50		
Notes: £20		
Notes: £10		
Notes: £5		
Notes/Coin: £1		
50p		
20p		
Silver		
Bronze		
TOTAL CASH		
Cheques, PO's, etc (Listed overleaf)		
TOTAL CREDIT	£	

Date

Credit the account of

Account Number

Notes: £50		
Notes: £20		
Notes: £10		
Notes: £5		
Notes/Coin: £1		
50p		
20p		
Silver		
Bronze		
TOTAL CASH		
Cheques, PO's, etc (Listed overleaf)		
TOTAL CREDIT	£	

Cheques etc.

TOTAL CARRIED OVERLEAF   £

(b) Give one advantage to the supplier of accepting cheques in payment and give one advantage to the customer of using cheques for payment.

(The Royal Society of Arts)

9.5

Diane Glover

in account with

NORTHERN JOINT BANK PLC

Date	Description	Debit	Credit	Balance
19–6		£	£	£
May 1	Balance			125 O/D (a)
2	000344 (b)	220 (c)		345 O/D
3	Sundries		200	145 O/D
4	Standing Order (d)	10		155 O/D
5	Credit Transfer		195	40
6	D. Allday (R/D) (e)	85		? (f)

(a) Would Diane Glover have shown the balance as a current asset or a current liability on her balance sheet as at 30 April 19–6?

. . . .

(b) To what do the numbers 000344 refer? . . . .

(c) Was the item (c) paid in or withdrawn? . . . .

(d) Briefly explain the meaning of the term 'standing order' . . . .

. . . .

(e) What does the abbreviation R/D stand for? . . . .

Give a reason why a cheque may be marked R/D . . . .

. . . .

(f) What is the new balance on 6 May? . . . .

(Joint Matriculation Board)

10 Two-Column Cash Books

OBJECTIVES   To enable students to understand and practise the use of the cash book.

The cash book is the book of original entry for all payments and receipts, whether in cash or by cheque. Previously these have been shown as two separate ledger accounts, but, because of the considerable number of daily entries required in the bank account and the cash account, these two accounts are removed from the ledger and are brought together in the cash book.

In the cash book, the cash account and the bank account still remain *separate* accounts, but are set out side by side. The ruling is known as two-column. The student should obtain an exercise cash book. The first, single, side is not used. The cash book has the entire left-hand page for the debit side and the entire right-hand page for the credit side. The cash book is ruled so that the debit column of the cash account is placed alongside the debit column of the bank account, and similarly the credit column of the cash account is placed alongside the credit column of the bank account.

The bank column at the debit side will record the details of payments into the bank, the credit side will record withdrawals from the bank. The following is an example showing the cash account and the bank account as they would have appeared previously, as two separate accounts, followed by an illustration of the same two accounts as they appear when brought together in a two-column cash book.

Cash Account

19–8			£	19–8			£
May	1	Balance b/d	270	May	4	Insurance	58
	7	M. Fellows	105		11	D. Riley	86
	10	E. Ashby	94		16	Rates	116
	18	D. Douglas	62		19	Motor Expenses	42
	29	H. Sinclair	75		25	Wages	55
					27	Drawings	25
					31	Balance c/d	224
			606				606
Jun	1	Balance b/d	224				

66

Bank Account

19–8		£	19–8		£
May	1 Balance b/d	859	May	2 Rent	175
	6 J. Wiseman	255		13 T. Norbury	187
	12 D. Glover	392		17 A. Longdon	422
	24 B. McCann	576		30 J. Lyons	385
				31 Balance c/d	913
		2,082			2,082
Jun	1 Balance b/d	913			

The cash account and the bank account now brought together in a two-column cash book:

Cash Book

19–8		Cash £	Bank £	19–8		Cash £	Bank £
May	1 Balances b/d	270	859	May	2 Rent		175
	6 J. Wiseman		255		4 Insurance	58	
	7 M. Fellows	105			11 D. Riley	86	
	10 E. Ashby	94			13 T. Norbury		187
	12 D. Glober		392		16 Rates	116	
	18 D. Douglas	62			17 A. Longdon		422
	24 B. McCann		576		19 Motor Expenses	42	
	29 H. Sinclair	75			25 Wages	55	
					27 Drawings	25	
					30 J. Lyons		385
					31 Balances c/d	224	913
		606	2,082			606	2,082
Jun	1 Balances b/d	224	913				

The cash column and the bank column are totalled and balanced separately, in the usual way.

Bank Overdraft

The amount of the difference between the debit side bank column and the credit side bank column is the bank balance or bank overdraft. A bank overdraft only occurs when the total of the bank column at the credit side exceeds the total of the bank column at the debit side.

The person appointed to keep the cash book would be a responsible person and is usually called the cashier.

Contra Entries

Contra entries are a very important part of the cash book. They can only occur because there are two accounts set out side by side. The word 'contra' is the Latin word for 'opposite'. Contra entries appear on both sides of the cash book because the bank account and the cash account are affected in opposite ways. This is the only place in the accounts where both halves of a double entry are visible on the same page, because it is the only place where two ledger accounts appear side by side. The letter 'C' is placed in the folio column against each 'Contra Entry'; this denotes that double entry has taken place within the cash book.

Contra entries are transfers of money, used when cash is paid into the bank and when cash is withdrawn from the bank for business use. Consider the following example: on 1 June £200 is taken from the office cash and paid into the bank. The entries in the two-column cash book would appear as follows:

Cash Book

			Cash	Bank					Cash	Bank
Jun	1 Cash	C		200	Jun	1 Bank	C	200	

Against the credit side payment of £200 is shown the word 'bank', to indicate that the other half of the double entry is in the bank account. Against the debit side entry of £200 is shown the word 'cash', to indicate that the other half of the double entry is in the cash account, and the letter 'C' in the folio column indicates that these items do not require posting, as the double entry has taken place in the cash book.

Similarly there are occasions when a firm will require cash for business use, and will have insufficient cash in hand. Consider a further example of a contra entry, when cash is withdrawn from the bank for use in the business. On 9 June £350 cash is withdrawn from the bank for business use. The entries for this transaction would appear in the two-column cash book, as follows:

Cash Book

			Cash	Bank					Cash	Bank
Jun	9 Bank	C	350		Jun	9 Cash	C		350

The following is a fully worked example, showing the cash and bank transactions for the month of March 19–8.

19–8

			£
Mar	1	Balances brought forward from last month:	
		Cash	147
		Bank	850
	2	Cash sales	152
	3	Received cheque from F. Lewis	355
	4	Paid rent in cash	60
	6	Bank £100 of the office cash	100
	8	Cash purchases	75
	10	Paid M. Robson by cheque	216
	12	Cash sales paid direct into bank	78
	15	Paid wages in cash	50
	17	Received a cheque from C. Miles	498
	20	Cash sales	143
	22	Withdrew cash from bank for business use	150
	25	Paid insurance by cheque	48
	27	Cash purchases	69
	31	Paid S. Dwyer in cash	140

The following is an illustration of the above transactions as they would appear in a two-column cash book. Take each item separately, in date order, and trace the item to where it appears in the following two-column cash book:

Cash Book

				Cash £	Bank £					Cash £	Bank £
Mar	1	Balances b/d		147	850	May	4	Rent		60	
	2	Sales		152			6	Bank	C	100	
	3	F. Lewis			355		8	Purchases		75	
	6	Cash	C		100		10	M. Robson			216
	12	Sales			78		15	Wages		50	
	17	C. Miles			498		22	Cash	C		150
	20	Sales		143			25	Insurance			48
	22	Bank	C	150			27	Purchases		69	
							31	S. Dwyer		140	
							31	Balances c/d		98	1,467
				592	1,881					592	1,881
Apr	1	Balances b/d		98	1,467						

Both the cash account and the bank account are ledger accounts. For convenience they are set out, side by side, in the two-column cash book to enable the cashier to keep the accounts entered up to date and the cash and so that bank balances can be ascertained without interfering with the use of the ledger. The fact that they are separated from the ledger does not alter the fact that they are ledger accounts and form an integral part of the double entry system.

If the total of the bank column at the credit side exceeded the total of the bank column at the debit side, this would be a bank overdraft.

Assignment Exercises

10.1
Write up a two-column cash book from the following details, balance at the end of the month and bring down the balance(s).

Apr 1 Balance brought forward from last month: Cash £248; Bank £3,664.
   2 Paid rates by cheque (£140).
   3 Cash Sales (£175).
   4 M. Roberts paid the firm £469 by cheque.
   5 Banked £150 of the office cash.
   8 Paid motor expenses (£57) by cheque.
   9 Rent received from sub-tenant (£50) in cash.
  10 Cash sales paid direct into bank (£120).
  11 Cash purchases (£96).
  12 Paid wages in cash (£150).
  15 Withdrew £200 cash from the bank for business use.
  16 B. Stevens paid the firm £655 by cheque.
  17 Cash sales (£86).
  18 Received a cheque (£166) from C. Verity.
  19 Paid insurance (£85) in cash.
  22 Cash paid into bank (£250).
  25 Paid D. Shaw £750 by cheque.
  26 Bought office furniture (£175), paying by cheque.
  27 Received £55 in cash from B. Lord.
  28 Withdrew £200 cash from the bank for business use.
  29 Bought stationery (£28) in cash.

10.2
Write up the following transactions in a two-column cash book. Balance at the end of the month, and bring down the balance(s).

Jun 1 Started business with £6,000 in cash.
     2 Paid rent (£120) in cash.
     3 Bought goods (£495), paying in cash.
     4 Paid £5,000 cash into the bank.
     5 Cash sales (£220).
     8 Bought office equipment (£296), paying by cheque.
     9 Received £75 in cash from R. Trent.
    10 Cash purchases (£298).
    11 Paid rates (£120) by cheque.
    12 Cash drawings (£80).
    15 Paid wages in cash (£150).
    16 Withdrew £250 cash from bank for business use.
    17 Received refund of rates (£26) by cheque.
    18 Paid M. Timpson £45 in cash.
    19 Cash sales (£145).
    20 D. Chadwick lent the firm £500 by cheque.
    23 Paid £200 of the cash into the bank.
    24 Bought goods (£141), paying in cash.
    25 Paid E. Robinson £267 by cheque.
    26 M. Castle paid us £68 in cash.
    27 Paid insurance by cheque (£64).

10.3
Write up a two-column cash book to record the following transactions, balance at the end of the month, and bring down the balance(s).

Aug 2 Balances brought down from last month: cash £168; bank £2,998.
     3 Cash sales (£160).
     4 Bought display equipment (£248) by cheque.
     5 Paid £250 of the cash into the bank.
     6 Received £357 by cheque from S. Driver.
     9 Bought stationery (£34), paying in cash.
    10 Withdrew £250 cash from the bank for use in the business.
    11 Cash purchases (£128).
    12 Cash sales paid direct into bank (£146).
    13 Paid wages in cash (£90).
    17 B. Jones paid the firm £180 in cash.
    18 Paid £200 cash into the bank.
    19 Cash drawings (£55).
    20 Cash sales (£140).
    23 Received £196 by cheque from S. Ryder.
    26 Paid M. Dean £45 in cash.

27 Withdrew £150 in cash from the bank for business use.
28 Paid wages (£75) in cash.
29 Bought motor van (£950) paying by cheque.
30 Cash drawings (£120).

10.4
Record the following transactions in a two-column cash book. Balance at the end of the month, and bring down the balance(s).

Oct 1 Balances brought forward from previous month: cash £269; bank £3,086.
     2 Paid rent by cheque (£75).
     3 Received £294 by cheque from J. Kendall.
     4 Paid motor expenses in cash (£32).
     5 Paid £200 of the cash into the bank.
     8 Bought stationery (£18), paying in cash.
     9 M. Kaye paid £68 in cash.
    10 Withdrew £350 cash from the bank for use in the business.
    11 Cash purchases (£240).
    12 Cash drawings (£125).
    13 Bought machinery (£368), paying by cheque.
    14 Paid rates (£165) by cheque.
    17 Sold goods for £175 cash.
    18 Paid wages in cash (£80).
    19 Cash sales paid direct into bank (£226).
    20 Paid general expenses in cash (£42).
    21 Received commission (£67) by cheque.
    24 K. Waterman paid the firm £142 in cash.
    25 Paid a cheque to M. Hutton (£490).
    26 Cash sales (£160).
    27 Banked all the cash except for £50.
    28 Paid rates by cheque (£210).
    29 Bought office fixtures (£470), paying by cheque.

10.5
Record the following transactions in a two-column cash book. Balance at the end of the month, and bring down the balances.

Nov 1 Balances brought forward from previous month: cash £76; bank £2,641.
     2 Received £378 by cheque from D. Chadley.
     3 Cash sales (£150).
     4 Withdrew £250 cash from the bank for business use.
     5 Paid wages in cash (£145).
     6 Cash drawings (£125).
     7 M. Richardson paid the firm £192 by cheque.
     8 Bought goods (£72), paying in cash.
     9 Cash sales paid direct into bank (£278).
    10 Received £198 in cash from D. Crofton.

11 Paid £250 cash into the bank.
12 Bought stationery (£37), paying in cash.
13 Paid motor expenses (£98) by cheque.
14 Received £595 by cheque from R. Best.
15 Bought display fixtures (£278) by cheque.
16 Cash sales (£45).
17 Withdrew £200 cash from the bank for use in the business.
18 Bought goods (£62), paying in cash.
19 Cash drawings (£50).
20 Paid rates (£170) by cheque.
21 T. Bramley paid £98 in cash.
24 Paid insurance by cheque (£155).
26 Received rent (£45) in cash from sub-tenant.
28 Paid £200 of the cash into the bank.
29 B. Matthews paid the firm £165 by cheque.

10.6

Record the following transactions in a two-column cash book. Balance at the end of the month, and bring down the balances.

Jan 1 Balances brought down from previous month: cash £78; bank £2,649.
2 Paid rent by cheque (£95).
3 Withdrew £350 cash from the bank for business use.
4 Cash purchases (£226).
5 Bought motor van (£1,950), paying by cheque.
6 Sold goods for cash (£78).
7 Cash drawings (£50).
8 Paid J. Carson £165 by cheque.
9 Paid motor expenses (£25) in cash.
10 Cash sales (£168).
11 Paid £200 of the cash into the bank.
12 Sold surplus fixtures, receiving £165 by cheque.
13 Cash purchases (£65).
14 Received £798 by cheque from W. Powers.
15 Paid insurance (£69) by cheque.
16 Drawings by cheque (£50).
17 Withdrew £400 cash from the bank for business use.
18 Bought goods (£195), paying in cash.
19 Cash sales paid direct into bank £112.
20 Received commission in cash (£65).
21 L. Spencer paid the firm £268 in cash.
22 Paid motor expenses in cash (£35).
23 Paid £350 cash into the bank.
24 Bought display equipment (£425), paying by cheque.
25 Paid wages (£150) in cash.
26 Bought stationery (£46) by cheque.
27 Paid T. Norbury by cheque £550.

28 Cash sales (£158).
29 Cash drawings (£100).
30 Paid W. Freeman £478 by cheque.

11   Three-Column Cash Books and Cash Discounts

OBJECTIVES   To introduce and examine the double entry system for cash discounts and the three column cash book.

The three column cash book is simply the traditional two-column cash book with the addition of an extra column at each side. This extra column is used to record cash discounts: discount allowed column at the debit side, discount received column at the credit side. The discount columns are *not* accounts. They are memorandum columns only, where a note is made of the cash discount as it occurs.

Cash Discounts

The term 'cash discount' refers to an allowance or reduction of the price, offered as an inducement for prompt payment. The rate of cash discount is often quoted as a percentage. An example would be: 'subject to 5 per cent cash discount if the account is settled within one month from the date of invoice'. The rate of cash discount and the period in which payment is to be made are quoted on the invoice. It is still called 'cash discount' if the account is paid by cheque. Cash discounts are in two categories – discounts allowed and discounts received.

Discounts Allowed

On the debit side of the cash book the extra column is for 'discounts allowed', and the amounts of the discounts are entered into this column on the date they occur. These are cash discounts allowed to customers to encourage prompt payment. Consider the following example. On 1 October, sold goods on credit (£326) to T. Gregson, subject to 5 per cent discount if the account is settled within one month from date of invoice. The personal account of T. Gregson in the sales ledger would appear as follows:

T. Gregson Account

Oct	1 Sales	326.00	

On 22 October, T. Gregson pays his account by cheque for £309.70, having deducted 5 per cent discount. The personal account of T. Gregson in the sales ledger would now appear as follows:

T. Gregson Account

Oct	1	Sales	326.00	Oct	22	Bank	309.70
					22	Discount	16.30
			326.00				326.00

The debtor's account *must* be reduced by the full amount of the debt being settled. The firm has agreed to accept £309.70 in full settlement of the account, therefore the amount of the discount allowed, in this example £16.30, must also be credited to T. Gregson's Account to show the account is settled. In the cash book on 22 October the amount of the discount is entered in the discount allowed column; the amount of the cheque is entered in the bank column.

The entry in the three-column cash book, for this example, is illustrated in the fully worked example on page 79. The details of cash or cheque and discount are posted from the cash book to the respective individual personal accounts. The weekly or monthly total of the discount allowed column is posted to the debit side of the discount allowed account in the general ledger to complete the double entry.

Discounts Received

On the credit side of the cash book the extra column is for 'discounts received'; the amounts of the discounts are entered into this column as they occur. Discount received is the cash discount the firm receives from a supplier for prompt payment. Consider the following example. On 3 October, purchased goods on credit (£185) from S. Dyson, subject to 5 per cent cash discount if payment is received within 28 days from date of invoice. The personal account of S. Dyson in the Purchase ledger would appear as follows:

S. Dyson Account

				Oct	3	Purchases	185.00

On 25 October, the firm pays S. Dyson's account £175.75 by cheque, having taken advantage of the cash discount of £9.25 for prompt payment. The personal account of S. Dyson in the purchase ledger would now appear as follows:

Oct	25 Bank	175.75	Oct	3 Purchases	185.00
	25 Discount	9.25			
		185.00			185.00

The supplier's account *must* be reduced by the full amount of the debt being settled. S. Dyson has agreed to accept £175.75 in full settlement of the debt, therefore the amount of the discount received of £9.25 must also be taken to the debit side of the supplier's account to show the account is settled. In the cash book on 25 October the amount of the discount is entered in the discount received column; the amount of the cheque is entered in the bank column.

The entry in the three-column cash book, for this example, is illustrated in the fully worked example on page 79. The details of cash or cheque and discount are posted from the cash book to the respective individual personal accounts. The weekly or monthly total of the discount received column is posted to the credit side of the discount received account in the general ledger to complete the double entry.

POINTS TO REMEMBER

The term 'cash discount' refers to the allowance/reduction offered for prompt payment. It is still called cash discount even though payment may have been made by cheque.

To firms having sufficient resources to pay their accounts promptly, the discount offers an additional profit, and during the course of a year's trading could amount to a considerable sum.

The discount allowed column is placed at the debit side of the cash book. The discount received column is placed at the credit side of the cash book.

The 'discount' columns in the cash book are *not* part of the double entry system, they are merely lists of discounts, where a note is made of the discount as it occurs.

The cash account and the bank account columns are totalled and balanced, and the balances brought down. The discount columns are totalled but *never* balanced as they are memorandum columns only.

The following is a fully worked example of a three-column cash book for the month of October, 19–7.

Oct 1 Balances brought forward from previous month: cash £137; bank £3,921.
    2 Cash sales (£75).
    4 Received a cheque from J. Dickenson (£296.40), having deducted 5 per cent cash discount of £15.60.

6 Paid rent in cash (£125).

8 Withdrew £250 from bank for business use.

10 Paid B. Armitage in cash £85, having deducted £5 cash discount.

12 Cash purchases (£134).

15 R. Rhodes paid us by cheque £372.40 in full settlement of his account of £392 after deducting 5 per cent cash discount of £19.60.

18 Paid insurance by cheque (£68).

20 Cash sales (£245).

22 T. Gregson pays his account by cheque (£309.70 after deducting 5 per cent cash discount of £16,30).

24 Banked £250 of the cash.

25 Paid S. Dyson £175.75 by cheque, having deducted £9.25 cash discount.

30 Paid motor expenses in cash (£72).

There follows an illustration of the above transactions as they would appear in a three-column cash book. Take each item separately, in date order, and trace the item to where it appears in the three-column cash book.

At the end of the month, the total of the discount allowed column is posted to the debit side of the discount allowed account in the general ledger, as follows:

Discount Allowed Account

Oct 31 Total for month	51.50	

In the same way, at the end of the month, the total of the discount received column is posted to the credit side of the discount received account in the general ledger, as follows:

Discount Received Account

	Oct 31 Total for month	14.25

Assignment Exercises

11.1

Joseph Simpson is a trader who records his cash and bank transactions in a three-column cash book. From the following details write up his three-column cash book for the month of March 19–6. Balance at the end of the month and show the discount accounts as they would appear in the general ledger.

Mar 1 Balances brought down from previous month: cash £141; Bank £2,894.20.

2 Bought goods (£78), paying in cash.

Date	Particulars	F	Discount Allowed	Cash	Bank		Date	Particulars	F	Discount Received	Cash	Bank
19-7												
Oct 1	Balances b/d			137.00	3,921.00		Oct 6	Rent			125.00	
2	Sales			75.00			8	Cash				250.00
4	J. Dickenson	C	15.60		296.40		10	B. Armitage	C	5.00	85.00	
8	Bank			250.00			12	Purchases			134.00	
15	R. Rhodes		19.60		372.40		18	Insurance				68.00
20	Sales			245.00			24	Bank	C		250.00	
22	T. Gregson	C	16.30		309.70		25	S. Dyson		9.25		175.75
24	Cash				250.00		30	Motor Expenses			72.00	
							31	Balances c/d			41.00	4,655.75
			£51.50	707.00	5,149.50					£14.25	707.00	5,149.50
Nov 1	Balances b/d			41.00	4,655.75							

79

3 Received a cheque from G. Horsfall (£185.20) in full settlement of his account of £190.
5 Withdrew £300 from bank for use in the business.
6 Paid rent (£75) in cash.
7 Cash purchases (£152).
9 Paid M. Green £275 by cheque.
10 Paid by cheque L. Moore's account of £478.50 less 5 per cent cash discount.
12 Cash sales (£98).
14 Cash drawings (£150).
16 Withdrew £350 from bank for business use.
18 A. Thompson pays £121.50 in cash; this was in full settlement of debt of £128.75.
20 Purchased goods (£55), paying in cash.
22 Paid by cheque G. Strong's account, £296 less 5 per cent discount.
24 Received £386 in cash from J. Seymore. This was in full settlement of his account of £403.30.
26 Banked £250 of the cash.
27 Paid wages (£75) in cash.
28 R. Lewis pays £325.25 by cheque after deducting £17.50 cash discount.
30 Paid the following by cheque, in each case deducting 5 per cent cash discount: R. Morton £760.80; B. Pope £495.60; F. Mills £164.20; M. Stocks £230.50.

11.2
From the following details write up Harry Bairstow's three-column cash book for the month of May 19–8. Balance at the end of the month, bring down the balances. Write up the discount accounts as they would appear in the general ledger at the end of the month.

May 1 Balances brought down from previous month: cash £176; bank £1,823.33.
2 Cash sales paid direct into bank (£151).
3 Paid by cheque G. Binn's account (£312) less $2\frac{1}{2}$ per cent discount.
5 Drawings in cash (£75).
6 Cash purchases (£92).
7 Withdrew £200 from the bank for business use.
8 B. Thornton paid his account of £554 by cheque, less 5 per cent cash discount.
10 Paid wages in cash (£150).
12 Bought office equipment (£365), paying by cheque.
13 Cash sales (£185).
15 S. Vickers paid his account of £220 in cash less 5 per cent cash discount.
17 Banked £300 of the cash.
18 Paid motor expenses (£55) in cash.
20 Bought goods, paying by cheque for £416.
21 Cash drawn from bank for Bairstow's private use (£175).

22 T. Hunt paid his account of £465 by cheque, less 5 per cent cash discount.

24 Paid in cash R. Dobson's account of £94 less $2\frac{1}{2}$ per cent discount.

26 Withdrew £250 from bank for use in the business.

27 Paid rates (£160) by cheque.

28 Cash purchases (£126).

29 Paid by cheque R. Bates' account of £258, less 5 per cent discount.

30 Cash sales (£225).

31 Paid wages in cash (£150).

11.3

You are required to write up a three-column cash book for George Singer from the following details. Balance at the end of the month and bring down the balances. Show the discount accounts as they would appear in the general ledger at the end of the month.

Aug 1 Balances brought down from previous month: cash £217; bank overdraft £1,295.45.

2 Bought goods (£76), paying in cash.

3 Withdrew £200 from bank for use in the business.

4 P. Aston paid his account of £976 by cheque, less 5 per cent cash discount.

6 Cash sales paid direct into bank (£162).

8 Paid wages in cash (£125).

9 Paid rent by cheque (£65).

10 M. Miles paid £182 by cheque.

12 Cash sales (£278).

14 Cash drawings (£50).

15 Paid £300 cash into the bank.

17 Paid by cheque Newton Supplies' account of £520, less $2\frac{1}{2}$ per cent cash discount.

18 Received £20 in cash, rent from sub-tenant.

20 Paid insurance by cheque (£78).

21 D. Lawrence paid his account of £692 by cheque, less $2\frac{1}{2}$ per cent cash discount.

22 Singer drew cheque (£165) for private use.

23 Withdrew £250 from bank for use in the business.

24 Cash purchases (£145).

25 Paid motor expenses (£35) in cash.

26 Paid by cheque R. Tetley's account for £397, less 5 per cent cash discount.

28 Cash sales (£225).

30 Banked cash (£300).

31 Received £76 in cash from R. Gill.

11.4

Jean Jones opened a greengrocer's shop on 1 April 19–4. She had £1,000 cash, of which she placed £900 into a bank account. The transactions for the shop during the month of April were:

April			
3	Purchased goods from T. Duke on credit.		150.00
4	Paid half year's rent by cheque.		600.00
7	Cash sales for week.		685.40
	Cash drawings by J. Jones.		100.00
	Paid cash into bank.		500.00
8	Purchased goods from B. Prince on credit.		75.50
	Purchased goods from R. Knight on credit.		115.00
11	Paid T. Dukes a/c by cheque in full settlement.		135.00
14	Cash sales for week.		732.80
	Paid cash into bank.		600.00
	Cash drawings by J. Jones.		100.00
	Purchases from B. Prince on credit.		125.00
18	Paid B. Prince by cheque.		75.50
	Paid R. Knight by cheque on account.		50.00
19	Sales to J. Lord on credit.		30.00
21	Cash sales for week.		483.70
	Paid cash into bank.		500.00
23	Purchases from R. Knight on credit.		176.30
24	Bought cash register from ABC Ltd for credit.		172.00
25	J. Lord settled his account by cheque less (10 per cent discount).		?
28	Cash sales for week.		572.50
	Paid into bank.		700.00
	Drawings by cheque – J. Jones.		200.00

Note: Candidates should calculate the amount of the cheque paid by J. Lord on April 25.

From this information you are required to:

(a) record the appropriate transactions in a three-column cash book, and bring down the balances as at 30 April 19–4;
(b) write up the ledger accounts of T. Duke, B. Prince, R. Knight and J. Lord and bring down the balances as at 30 April 19–4.

(Joint Matriculation Board)

11.5

Cash Book (Credit side only)

Date 19–5			Discount £		Cash £		Bank £	
May	1	Balance					2,200	(. . .)
	10	J. Archer	20	(. . .)			380	(. . .)
	15	Bank			160	(. . .)		
	20	Purch- ases			95	(. . .)		
	27	Fixtures					750	(. . .)
	31	Balances			55	(. . .)	440	(. . .)
			20		310		3,770	

You are required to choose from the following statements the one which you feel best expresses the meaning of each entry shown in the cash book above. Enter the letter (A–M) representing your choice, in the space provided at the side of each entry (. . .).

A Discount allowed to a debtor for prompt payment.
B The balance in the firm's bank account.
C Discount allowed by a creditor.
D Cash paid into bank.
E The purchase of a typewriter.
F The amount of the bank overdraft.
G Cash withdrawn from bank for office use.
H Value of cheque received from a debtor.
J Cash paid for purchase of goods.
K The amount of cash held in the firm's office.
L Value of cheque paid to a creditor.
M The sale of a typewriter.

(Joint Matriculation Board)

12   Bank Cash Books

OBJECTIVES   To understand and gain practice in this modern development of the three-column cash book.

The bank cash book is a modernisation of the original three-column cash book and is used extensively in many businesses. The use and operation follows the rule that *all* money received, whether in cash or cheques, is to be paid into the bank intact, and that all payments are to be made by cheque. There are no 'contra entries' in a bank cash book. With regard to small payments in cash, which are necessary in business, these are made out of petty cash. The petty cash book and the Imprest System are fully described and covered in Module 13. The bank cash book has three columns at the debit side and three columns at the credit side, with the headings discount, details, bank.

At the debit side of the bank cash book the particulars are entered of all cash and cheques received and the individual details of the amounts received are itemised in the details column. The total amount paid into the bank is entered in the bank column. This amount should agree with the total paid into the bank as shown in the bank paying-in book. At the credit side of the bank cash book the particulars are recorded of all cheques drawn and the amount entered in the bank column. The details column is only used if one cheque is drawn to cover two or more payments, which will subsequently require posting to separate ledger accounts.

The bank columns are totalled and balanced in the usual way. The discount allowed column and the discount received column are totalled but *never* balanced.

The following is a typical example of the type of question set in recent examinations relating to a bank cash book. Brian Walsh pays all receipts into the bank and makes all payments greater than £10 by cheque. All small cash payments are made out of petty cash. You are required to write up Brian Walsh's bank cash book from the following details.

At the close of business on 28 February 19–8 Brian Walsh's balance at bank was £2,532.18. The counterfoils of his paying-in book for the next week were as follows:

Mar 2   Total paid in £621.65, consisting of cash from sales, £441.40, a cheque of £34 from L. Green and a cheque of £146.25 from G. Newton in full settlement of £150 owed by him.

     4   Total paid in £596.36, consisting of cash from sales, £298.20, a cheque of £50 from G. Lewis, and a cheque of £248.16 from M. Hobson in full settlement of £252 owed by him.

     6   Total paid in £225.57, consisting of cash from sales, £98, a cheque of £21 rebate of insurance which had been overpaid and a cheque of £106.57 from R. Coleman in full settlement of £109 owed by him.

During the week Brian Walsh drew the following cheques:

	£ p
Mar 2 Rent	100.00
3 S. Smythe in settlement of £450 owing	427.50
4 J. Martin in settlement of £676 owing	642.20
5 Drawings £150.00, petty cash £35.60	185.60
5 B. Binns in settlement of £120 owing	114.00

On page 86 there is a fully worked illustration of the above example question, completed as it would appear in a bank cash book. Look at each item carefully, in date order, and trace it to where it appears in the illustration of the bank cash book.

POINTS TO REMEMBER   The bank cash book is a modern development of the three-column cash book and is now widely used in business. It is favoured as a means of preventing discrepancies in the cash. Its operation follows the rule that *all* money received, whether in cash or cheques, is paid into the bank intact.

These types of questions appear regularly in examinations and are an effective test of a student's ability. In recent examination papers, with questions relating to the construction of a bank cash book, these have been combined with the additional requirement of the completion of an analytical petty cash book. In view of this development, there are a number of these types of questions from recent examination papers included in Module 13.

Assignment Exercises

12.1

You are a cashier for John Dawson and are required to write up his bank cash book. At the end of each day Mr Dawson pays all cash and cheques received into the bank. The balance at bank on 1 January 19–7 was £2,252.58.

Paying-in book counterfoils showed:

Jan 2 Paid in £547.20, being a cheque of £338.20 from S. Peters in full settlement of debt of £356, cash from sales (£142) and a cheque of £67 from J. Myers.

4 Paid in £352.80, being cash from sales (£167.80), a cheque for £137 from D. Adams in full settlement of his account of £150 and a cheque for £48 from M. Cliff.

5 Paid in £248.20, being a cheque for £92 from B. Groves, a cheque for £30 being commission received, and cash from sales (£126.20).

Date	Particulars	F	Discount Allowed	Details	Bank		Date	Particulars	F	Discount Received	Details	Bank
19-8												
Mar 1	Balance b/d				2,532.18		Mar 2	Rent				100.00
2	Sales			441.40			3	S. Smythe		22.50		427.50
2	L. Green			34.00			4	J. Martin		33.80		642.20
2	G. Newton		3.75	146.25	621.65		5	Drawings			150.00	
4	Sales			298.20			5	Petty Cash			35.60	185.60
4	G. Lewis			50.00			5	B. Binns		6.00		114.00
4	M. Hobson		3.84	248.16	596.36		6	Balance c/d				2,506.46
6	Sales			98.00								
6	Insurance			21.00								
6	R. Coleman		2.43	106.57	225.57							
			£10.02		3,975.76					£62.30		3,975.76
Mar 7	Balance b/d				2,506.46							

6 Paid in a total of £1,144.45. This consisted of cash sales (£238.95), a cheque for £750 from G. Spink who had purchased Dawson's old van, and a cheque for £155.50 from T. Denton in full settlement of £160 owed by him.

Cheques drawn during the week by Dawson were:

	£ p
Jan 2 D. Guy in full settlement of £120 debt.	114.40
3 Drew cheque for payment of : wages £350, petty cash £76.80, drawings £100.	526.80
4 S. Barnes.	127.00
5 Office equipment.	365.20
6 Rates.	125.00
6 B. Mills in full settlement of £480 debt.	456.00

12.2

Graham Dean banks all his business receipts daily. You are required to prepare his bank cash book from the following details. On 1 March 19–7 his balance at bank was £1,376.30.

Business cheque book counterfoils:

	£ p
Mar 2 Vehicle insurance.	150.00
2 W. Kay in full settlement of a debt of £220.	209.00
3 E. Franks.	76.60
4 Rent.	120.00
5 F. Peters in full settlement of his account of £450.	427.50
6 Petty cash £68.65 and for own use £150.	218.65

Paying-in book counterfoils showed:

Mar 2 £236.65 cash, all from sales.
   3 Total £456.55, being £276.55 cash sales, a cheque for £35 (rent from sub-tenant) and a cheque for £145 from C. Prince in full settlement of a £150 debt.
   4 Total £272.20, being a cheque for £150 from the sale of an old machine and £122.20 cash sales.
   6 Total £686.80, being a cheque for £347.50 from P. Timms in full settlement of a debt of £365.70, cash from sales (£178.80) and a cheque for £160.50 from J. Jacques in full settlement of his account of £166.76.

12.3

James McCann pays all his receipts into his bank account and makes all payments greater than £10 by cheque. On 5 February 19–7 his bank cash book showed a debit balance of £1,602.55. You are required to write up his bank cash book from the following details.

Paying-in book counterfoils showed:

Feb 6 £138.50 cash, all from sales.
   7 Total paid in £384.75, consisting of cash from sales £175.75 and a cheque from B. Moore for £209 in settlement of a debt of £220.50.
   8 Paid in £195.80 cash, from sales.
   9 Total paid in £318.25, consisting of a cheque of £55 from T. Warren, cash from sales (£67.75) and a cheque of £195.50 from M. Munro in full settlement of a debt of £209.
   10 Total paid in £321.55, consisting of cash from sales (£221.55) and a cheque for £100 from B. Andrews for old office equipment.

Cheque book counterfoils showed:

		£ p
Feb 6	Rent.	135.00
7	D. Spencer in full settlement of £220 owing to him.	214.50
8	Insurance.	67.50
9	Drawings (£75), wages (£150), petty cash (£37.90).	262.90
10	J. Black in full settlement of a debt of £295.	280.50

12.4

Charles Hargreaves pays all his receipts into his bank account and makes all payments greater than £20 by cheque. On 1st June 19–7 his balance in hand at the bank was £1,870.85.

From the following details, you are required to write up his bank cash book; the particulars column should show the name of the ledger account to be debited or credited in respect of each transaction.

Cheques drawn by Hargreaves during the week were as follows:

		£ p
Jun 2	W. Dyson (in settlement of £256 debt).	244.00
2	Bettisons Estate Agents, one quarter's rent.	215.00
3	D. Stead (in settlement of £128.40 debt).	123.00
3	Larkshire Council for rates.	58.90
4	G. Barker (in settlement of £178 debt).	169.10
4	Post Office (vehicle tax).	100.00
5	A. Paul (in settlement of £68.50 debt).	66.00
5	Petty cash (£47.60); Hargreaves' own use (£150); wages (£450).	647.60
5	Stylax Ltd – new office desk.	196.50

The counterfoils of his paying-in book showed:

Jun 2 Total paid in £511.25, consisting of a cheque of £126.25 from J. Larkin in full settlement of £130 owed by him; cash from sales (£235) and a cheque of £150 from D. Mawson who purchased Hargreaves' old adding machine.

3 Total paid in £658.40, consisting of cash from sales (£236.40), a cheque of £68 from S. Senior in full settlement of £70.50 owed by him, a cheque of £15 refund of insurance overpaid and a cheque of £339 from C. Masters in full settlement of £345.50 owed by him.

4 Total paid in £195.80, all cash from sales.

5 Total paid in £324.54, consisting of a cheque of £40 from George Lewis, a sub-tenant of Hargreaves, a cheque of £49.14 from M. Griffin in full settlement of debt of £50.40, cash from sales (£98.90) and a cheque for £136.50 from Joseph Plumb in full settlement of debt of £140.

13   The Analytical Petty Cash Book and the Imprest System

OBJECTIVES   To gain an understanding of the use and functions of the analytical petty cash book and the imprest system.

In Module 12, which covered the bank cash book, the advantages of paying all cash and cheques into the bank intact were evident. In a business operating this type of cash book, small cash payments are usually made out of petty cash. These small cash payments are recorded in a separate book, known as a petty cash book. The person appointed to carry out the duties of handling and recording the petty cash is usually a junior member of staff known as the petty cashier.

The Analysed or Columnar Petty Cash Book

This type of petty cash book is ruled with suitable analysis columns to show the expenditure in each type of expense. The type of expenditure made through the petty cash generally falls into the following main categories: travelling, postage and stationery, cleaning, motor expenses and ledger accounts.

There are other categories of petty cash expenditure, and these would be adapted, as required, to the special needs of a particular business. A column is kept for each type of expense, and the headings correspond with the expense accounts in the general ledger. The end or last column is usually chosen as a ledger column. Expenditure entered into this column will require posting to a ledger *other than* the general ledger. This would occur if a purchase ledger account was settled out of petty cash, or if a refund was made out of petty cash to a customer who had overpaid his account. The receipts column only represents the debit side of the petty cash book.

The entries on the credit side of the petty cash book are first entered into the totals column, and are then extended and entered into the appropriate expense column. At the end of the period, all the columns are totalled, making sure that the total of the totals column equals the sum of the other expense columns. To complete the double entry, the total of each expense column is debited to the relevant expense account in the general ledger.

Vouchers

The petty cashier is usually instructed that a receipt should be obtained for each individual expense. When a payment is made out of petty cash, the person receiving the money will be required to fill out a voucher, showing exactly what the expense was, and will be required to sign the voucher acknowledging receipt of the amount.

The entries for each expense are first made in the total column, and are then extended into the appropriate expense column. The voucher number is placed alongside, in the relevant column.

The Imprest System

Under the imprest system of keeping petty cash a specific sum of money is given to the petty cashier as a 'float'. The 'imprest' is the original amount of cash which is established to meet the requirements of the small cash payments. This is a sufficient sum to cover the petty cash expenditure for a period of time, which could be a week or a month. At the end of the period, the petty cashier is reimbursed with the amount spent, which restores the petty cash balance to the original amount. This is referred to as 'restoring the imprest'.

Thus whatever is spent is received back by the petty cashier. For example, a sum of £50 is handed over to the petty cashier, this will be the 'imprest'. During the following week the expense payments total £35.56. At the end of the week the petty cashier will receive £35.56, the amount spent, to restore the imprest to the original sum.

POINTS TO REMEMBER The receipts column only represents the debit side of the petty cash book. Note that each item of expense in the petty cash book is shown both in the total column and in the appropriate analysis column, and the voucher number is placed alongside the entry. The totals of the combined analysis columns should agree with the addition of the main total column. This amount is the total of petty cash expenditure for the period, and when deducted from the original imprest will leave the balance of petty cash in hand. At the end of the period, the total of each individual expense column is debited to the relevant expense account in the general ledger.

The following is a worked example to illustrate the compilation of an analytical petty cash book. James Fisher, a sole trader, keeps his petty cash on the imprest system and the imprest amount is £100. The petty cash transactions for the first week of March 19–7 were as follows:

Receipts	Date	Details	Voucher No.	Total Payments	Travelling	Cleaning	Postage & Stationery	Folio	Ledger
	19 – 7								
21.67	Mar 1	Balance b/d							
78.33	Mar 1	Cash							
	Mar 2	Train fares	21	16.60	16.60				
	Mar 3	Postage stamps	22	5.50			5.50		
	Mar 4	Window cleaner	23	10.50		10.50			
	Mar 5	Envelopes	24	9.85			9.85		
	Mar 5	Bus fares	25	2.80	2.80				
	Mar 6	G. Mortimer	26	23.18					23.18
				68.43	19.40	10.50	15.35		23.18
	Mar 6	Balance c/d		31.57					
100.00				100.00					
31.57	Mar 7	Balance b/d							

92

Mar 1 Petty cash in hand £21.67.
    1 Petty cash restored to imprest amount.
    2 Train fares £16.60.   (Voucher No. 21)
    3 Postage stamps £5.50.   (Voucher No. 22)
    4 Window cleaner £10.50.   (Voucher No. 23)
    5 Envelopes £9.85.   (Voucher No. 24)
    5 Bus fares £2.80.   (Voucher No. 25)
    6 G. Mortimer, a creditor, £23.18.   (Voucher No. 26)

Assignment Exercises

13.1

Mark Alexander is a sole trader who keeps his petty cash on the imprest system, the imprest amount being £100. The following are his petty cash transactions for the month of February, 19–8:

Feb 1 Petty cash in hand £15.62.
     1 Petty cash restored to imprest amount.
     2 Paid wages (£16.10).
     4 Bought postage stamps (£3.44).
     8 Paid G. Newman, a creditor, £12.40.
   10 Car sponge and car polish (£5.65).
   12 Paid wages (£18.20).
   15 Envelopes (£2.25).
   17 Bought rear light reflector for van (£14.55).
   18 Postage on parcel (£1.70).
   21 Paid wages (£12.50).
   24 Stationery (£3.45).

You are required to draw up a petty cash book to record the above transactions and also give the entry on 1 March 19–8, restoring the petty cash to the imprest amount.

    Your analysis columns shall be for (a) wages, (b) postage, (c) stationery, (d) motor expenses, (e) ledger.

13.2

John Beaumont uses an analysed petty cash book with columns for travelling, motor expenses, postage and stationery, ledger accounts. At the close of business on 31 March 19–8 his cash in hand stood at the imprest amount of £200. You are required to write up the petty cash book for the month of April, 19–8.

		Voucher	£ p
Apr	1 Petrol.	34	10.50
	2 Postage stamps.	35	6.90
	3 Van tyre.	36	18.30
	4 Envelopes.	37	2.50
	5 Train fares.	38	7.20
	8 Paper clips.	39	1.35
	9 Car polish.	40	2.80
	10 Petrol and oil.	41	12.90
	11 Bus fares.	42	1.40
	12 George Seal, a creditor.	43	18.50
	15 Stationery.	44	3.30
	16 Postage on parcel.	45	2.60
	17 Train fares.	46	6.50
	18 Petrol.	47	14.00
	19 Postage stamps.	48	5.80
	22 M. Smith, a creditor.	49	15.40
	24 Typing paper.	50	2.30
	25 Van seat covers.	51	12.60
	26 Bus fares.	52	1.20
	29 James Jones, a creditor.	53	8.50
	30 Taxi fare.	54	4.00

13.3

Jennifer Peterson is a florist who keeps her petty cash on the imprest system, the imprest amount being £100. The following are her petty cash transactions for the month of August, 19–8.

		£ p
Aug	1 Petty cash in hand.	12.60
	1 Petty cash restored to imprest amount.	
	2 Bus fares.	1.20
	3 Window cleaner.	2.50
	4 F. Harrison, a creditor.	9.70
	5 Postage stamps.	4.60
	6 Petrol and oil.	10.00
	8 Train fares.	3.40
	9 Cleaning materials.	4.75
	10 Self-adhesive labels.	1.25
	11 Postage – air mail.	2.60
	12 Window cleaner.	2.50
	14 Taxi fare.	3.50
	15 Cards and envelopes.	1.75
	16 A. Ford, a creditor.	6.20
	17 Petrol.	12.00
	18 Cleaning lady.	10.00
	21 Locking petrol cap.	5.95

22	Felt-tip pens.	2.20
24	Train fares.	4.60
28	E. Morgan, a creditor.	4.80
30	Postage stamps.	2.65

Required: Draw up a petty cash book to record the above transactions and also give the entry on 1 September, restoring the petty cash to the imprest amount. Your analysis columns shall be for: cleaning, motor expenses, travelling, postage and stationery, ledger accounts.

These types of questions frequently appear on examination papers, and recently have been combined with a question requiring the construction of a bank cash book. The exercises which follow, which are taken from recent examination papers, illustrate this requirement, that is, the construction of a petty cash book and a bank cash book.

13.4

George Mainwaring maintains a petty cash book for all payments less than £20. The imprest of £100 is restored at the end of each week. Other payments are made by cheque, and all receipts are paid into the bank. At the start of business on Monday 3 March 19–6 his bank cash book showed a balance in hand at the bank of £1,468.12.

For the week which followed his bank paying-in book counterfoils showed the following:

4 March   Total paid in £402.55, consisting of cash from sales (£280.80), a cheque for £97.50 from C. Godfrey in full settlement of £100 debt, and a cheque for £24.25 from M. Square, representing commission due.

6 March   Total paid in £503.30, consisting of cash sales (£488.30) and a cheque for £15 from H. Blewitt who had bought Mainwaring's old typewriter.

7 March   Total paid in £272.90, all from cash sales.

During the same week Mainwaring drew the following cheques:

4 March	For own use.	£250.00
6 March	Warmington Council (rates).	£315.30
6 March	M. Fox (in full settlement of an account of £800.00).	£780.00
7 March	Petty cash.	£ ?

Payments out of petty cash were:

		Voucher No.	
3 March	Petrol.	501	£16.80
3 March	A. Yeatman (a creditor).	502	£18.10
4 March	Cleaning lady.	503	£11.40
5 March	Stationery.	504	£4.30
5 March	Train fares.	505	£10.10
6 March	Postage stamps.	506	£15.20
7 March	Window cleaner.	507	£5.50

You are required to write up:

(a) The petty cash book, with analysis columns for travelling, cleaning, postage and stationery and ledger accounts.
(b) The bank cash book. The 'particulars' column should clearly name the ledger account to be debited or credited in respect of each transaction.

(Royal Society of Arts)

13.5

Doug Wigby pays all receipts into his bank account and makes all payments greater than £15 by cheque. All other cash payments are made out of petty cash, and at the end of each week the petty cashier is given a cheque to restore the imprest.

At 5 January 19–7 Doug Wigby's balances were as follows:

	£
Bank	620.78 (Debit)
Petty cash	40.00

Enter these balances in his bank cash book and petty cash book. Paying-in book counterfoils showed:

Jan 5 Cheque of £106.39 from Ian Tait.
  6 Total paid in £293.22, consisting of cash from sales (£195.72) and a cheque from Martin Quantrill for £97.50 in settlement of a debt of £100.
  8 Paid in £160.58 from sales.
  9 Total paid in £383.03, consisting of cash from sales (£248.03) and a cheque for £135 from Bridget Rogers for an old typewriter surplus to requirements.

Cheque book counterfoils showed:

Jan 5 West Loamshire County Council, for rates, £350.
  7 £114 to David Hunter in settlement of £120 owing to him.
  8 Drawings £75.

9 Petty cash £29.

9 Midland Motors Ltd £1,500 for second-hand delivery van.

Petty cash payments were as follows:

		£
Jan 5	Postage stamps.	5.80
6	Travelling expenses.	4.70
7	George Lingard, a creditor.	12.00
8	Stationery.	6.50

In addition Doug Wigby was informed on 9 January that the cheque from Ian Tait for £106.39 paid in on 5 January had been returned marked R/D ('refer to drawer'). You are required to write up:

(a) The bank cash book, and
(b) The petty cash book, using analysis columns for postages and stationery, travelling expenses and ledger accounts, and balance both books on 9 January 19–7;
(c) Open the ledger accounts and complete the double entry for each of the petty cash analysis columns.

(Joint Matriculation Board)

13.6

Martin Brice makes all payments of under £25 through his petty cash book. At the end of each week he restores its imprest of £100. All other payments are made by cheque, and all receipts are paid into the bank. At the start of business on Monday 15 December 19–6 his bank cash book showed an overdrawn bank balance of £86.34.

In the following week his payments out of petty cash were:

		Voucher No.	
15 December	Stationery.	811	£11.86
16 December	Bus fares.	812	£ 1.36
16 December	Postage stamps.	813	£21.20
17 December	Cleaning.	814	£12.50
18 December	F. Woodbridge, (a creditor).	815	£24.72
18 December	Window cleaner.	816	£ 6.25
19 December	Train fares.	817	£13.90

His payments into the bank were:

15 December   £435.60 cash, all from sales.
17 December   Total £387.54; being £229.54 cash sales, a cheque for £60 (rent from the flat over his shop), and a cheque for £98 from T. Cooper in full settlement of a £100 debt.
19 December   Total £612.88; being a cheque for £200 from the sale of Brice's old van, and £412.88 cash sales.

During that week Brice drew the following cheques:

Date	Particulars	Amount
16 December	For Housekeeping.	£80.00
18 December	Deposit on new van.	£1,000.00
18 December	A. Paterson (in settlement of a debt for £500).	£487.50
19 December	Petty cash (restoring imprest).	£?

You are required to write up:

(a) The petty cash book, making use of the analysis columns, travelling, cleaning, postage and stationery, ledger accounts;
(b) The bank cash book. The name of the ledger account to be debited or credited in respect of each transaction should appear in the 'particulars' column.

(Royal Society of Arts)

14   The Sales Day Book

OBJECTIVES   To consider invoices, trade discount and the sales day book.

In a great many businesses a considerable proportion of the sales and the purchases will be made on a credit basis (to be paid for at a future date), and when the credit sales and the credit purchases become very numerous, as they are in fairly large firms, a sales day book and a purchases day book are used to record the daily details.

Invoices

On each occasion that goods are sold on credit a document known as an invoice is made out. It is made out by the seller, and at least one copy is sent to the buyer. The invoice will display the seller's full name and address, the customer's full name and address, the invoice number and full details of the goods sold, the prices of the goods and any trade discount.

The top copy will be sent to the purchaser, and becomes his accounting record, and is subsequently entered, with any other purchase invoices, in his purchases day book. The second copy stays with the seller, and becomes his accounting record, and is subsequently entered in his sales day book. The design and layout of the invoices will vary from business to business, each having its own 'house style' design.

Trade Discount

Trade discount is a reduction, usually quoted as a percentage of the list or catalogue price, allowed by a manufacturer or wholesaler to a retailer in the same trade. Not all businesses use trade discount and, as trade discount is merely a way of calculating sales prices, no entry for trade discount should be made in the double entry records. The calculation of trade discount and its display on the invoice will usually be as shown in the example invoice set out below:

SALES INVOICE

Invoice No. 7876

Demland Supplies

Sandmore Lane

BRIGHOUSE BX16 8ER

Your Order No | 4346

Tax Point and Date | 1 November 19–7

Grove & Sons
Bridge Croft
LEEDS LS56 1PR

VAT Registration No. 987654321

Quantity	Description	£
6	Electric Kettles at £19.50 each	117.00
3	Electric Toasters at £18.75 each	56.25
		173.25
	Less Trade Discount at 20%	34.65
		138.60

The Sales Day Book

Because of the considerable number of daily entries required in the sales account, in a business with a large number of invoices the sales account would soon become overloaded with entries. It is necessary, therefore, to organise and reduce the number of entries which must be made. In order to do this, a system of books of original entry has been developed. It provides a system whereby certain classes of transactions are grouped together and summarised before entries are made in the double entry accounts. The sales day book is the book of original entry for all sales on credit.

It is from the copies of the sales invoices that the seller enters the details in the sales day book. This book is a list, in date order, of each sales invoice, showing the date, the name of the firm to whom the goods have been sold, the number of the invoice, and the net amount of the invoice.

The entries are made in the sales day book from the copy invoices, and continue day by day for a certain period, usually one month. At the end of the month the posting from the sales day book will be to the double entry accounts, that is, the customers' individual personal accounts in the sales ledger, and the total of the sales day book for the period will be transferred to the credit side of the sales account in the general ledger.

The following is an illustration of a sales day book for the month, commencing with the example invoice:

Sales Day Book

Date			Invoice No.	F	£ p
Nov	1	Grove & Sons	7876	SL	138.60
	9	M. Dean	7877	SL	120.20
	18	G. Parkinson	7878	SL	176.80
	25	J. Spencer	7879	SL	237.10
	30	T. Gill	7880	SL	142.20
		Transferred to Sales Account		GL	814.90

The 'posting' of the sales day book to the double entry accounts would be as follows:

Sales Ledger

Grove & Sons Account

Nov	1	Sales	138.60	

M. Dean Account

Nov	9	Sales	120.20	

G. Parkinson Account

Nov	18	Sales	176.80

J. Spencer Account

Nov	25	Sales	237.10

T. Gill Account

Nov	30	Sales	142.20

General Ledger

Sales Account

	Nov 30 Total for month	814.90

The practice of copying the full details of the invoices into the sales day book was discontinued in favour of the more modern approach, with less detail.

With regard to cash sales, these are *never* entered in the sales day book. The book of original entry for all cash sales is the cash book, the double entry being debit the cash account and credit the sales account.

POINTS TO REMEMBER
Invoices do not all look the same; each business will have its own preference for layout and design.

Trade discount is only a way of calculating sales prices; no entry for trade discount should be made in the double entry records, or in the sales day book – trade discount *never* enters a ledger account of any kind, at any time.

Alternative names for the sales day book include the sales journal; the word 'journal' is a French word, meaning 'daily record'. It is also known as the sales book and in examinations is sometimes referred to as a subsidiary book.

Occasionally in examination questions the examiners will request that 'full details of the invoices should be entered in the sales day book'. The student should, of course, comply with any such requirement.

Slip System

The method of collecting together information with the use of day books is, in some businesses, being superseded by more modern methods which save time and labour. One of these is the slip system.

The slip system is an alternative method of dealing with the numerous sales on credit. With this system the copy invoices are kept together, in date order, in a file. At the end of the period, this may be a week or a month, these are added up and the total is entered at the credit side of the sales account in the general ledger. To complete the double entry, the net amount of each individual copy invoice is entered in the customers' personal account in the sales ledger.

The slip system can also be used for purchase invoices and for returns inwards and returns outwards – credit notes and debit notes – as some businesses file all original documents, in date order, so that a permanent and full record is kept of all original information.

POINTS TO REMEMBER REGARDING THE SLIP SYSTEM	This system is a saving of time and labour. There are said to be fewer errors, as much of the copying of details is dispensed with and quick reference is available between the ledger and the original documents.

Assignment Exercises

14.1
James Dickson of 34 Kingsway, Leeds LS16 8ER is the proprietor of a small business. His sales on credit for the month of May, 19–7 were as follows:

May   2   G. A. Coleman, 2 Parkfield, Nottingham:
       6 garden chairs at £4.50 each,
       10 deck chairs at £3.75 each,
       6 patio furniture sets at £26 each.
       All less trade discount 15 per cent.

May   9   Kota Supplies, 2 Deansgate, Bradford:
       10 deck chairs at £3.75 each,
       10 patio furniture sets at £26 each,
       10 luxury garden chairs at £12.50 each.
       All less trade discount 20 per cent.

May 15   B. Newton, 66 Cross Green Road, Bridlington:
       3 garden chairs at £4.50 each,
       3 patio furniture sets at £26 each,
       6 deck chairs at £3.75 each.
       All less trade discount 15 per cent.

May 22   Moss Linton, 46 The Ridgeway, Castleford:
       6 luxury garden chairs at £12.50 each,
       6 patio furniture sets at £26 each,
       6 sun loungers at £7.50 each.
       All less trade discount 25 per cent.

May 30 L. Gibson & Son, 58 The Causeway, Scarborough:
      25 deck chairs at £3.75 each,
      20 luxury garden chairs at £12.50 each,
      15 sun loungers at £7.50 each.
      All less trade discount $33\frac{1}{3}$ per cent.

Draw up a sales invoice for each of the above sales. Write up the sales day book for the month of May, 19–7. Post to the personal accounts in the sales ledger and transfer the total to the sales account in the general ledger.

14.2

Speed electrics of 2 High Street, Huddersfield is a wholesale electrical business. During the month of June 19–7 the following sales are made:

June 1 To James McMillan, 2 Spring Lane, Bradford:
      3 electric kettles, list price £19.50 each;
     10 electric toasters, list price £18.75 each;
      3 electric knives, list price £15.50 each.
     All less trade discount 25 per cent.
June 5 To J. Sanderson, 34 Knights Court, York:
      6 electric coffee makers, list price £14.95 each;
      6 electric knives, list price £15.50 each.
     All less trade discount 20 per cent.
June 12 To B. Sinclair, 67 Beech Terrace, Denby Dale:
     10 electric kettles, list price £19.50 each;
      4 electric coffee makers, list price £14.95 each.
     All less trade discount 15 per cent.
June 19 To T. Matthews. 1 Kingsway, Nottingham:
      5 electric toasters, list price £18.75 each;
      5 electric knives, list price £15.50 each;
      5 electric coffee makers, list price £14.95 each.
     All less trade discount $33\frac{1}{3}$ per cent.
June 30 To L. Booth, 4 Richmond Lane, Manchester:
      2 electric kettles, list price £19.50 each;
      6 electric knives, list price £15.50 each;
      6 electric can openers, list price £6. each;
      3 electric toasters, list price £18.75 each.
     All less trade discount 20 per cent.

You are required to show your calculations for each of the above sales. Enter each of the sales in the sales day book and post to the personal and nominal accounts in the ledger.

14.3

Martin Greendale, 8 Parkside, Darlington, owns a garden accessories business. During the month of August 19–7 his sales on credit were as follows:

Aug 1 Adel Garden Shop, The Heathway, Adel, Leeds:
　　　3 lawn mowers, list price £55 each;
　　　6 garden forks, list price £6.50 each;
　　　3 garden spades, list price £7.50 each;
　　　4 ornamental garden gnomes, list price £3.50 each.
　　　All less trade discount 15 per cent.

Aug 4 George Riley, High Ash Croft, Mansfield.
　　　6 lawn mowers, list price £55 each;
　　　6 rotary mowers, list price £95 each;
　　　6 garden shears, list price £9.50 each;
　　　6 garden spades, list price £7.50 each.
　　　All less trade discount 25 per cent.

Aug 8 T. Newbury, 8 Longdon Close, Nuneaton:
　　　15 garden forks, list price £6.50 each;
　　　10 ornamental garden gnomes, list price £3.50 each;
　　　6 garden shears, list price £9.50 each;
　　　5 lawn sprinklers, list price £5.50 each.
　　　All less trade discount 20 per cent.

Aug 14 B. J. Lacey, 2 Crosby Court, Chester:
　　　2 rotary mowers, list price £95 each;
　　　5 lawn mowers, list price £55 each;
　　　6 garden spades, list price £7.50 each;
　　　5 garden tool sets, list price £8. per set.
　　　All less trade discount 15 per cent.

Aug 20 S. Stocks, 57 Dunbar Lane, Beverley:
　　　5 garden shears, list price £9.50 each;
　　　10 garden spades, list price £7.50 each;
　　　6 ornamental garden gnomes, list price £3.50 each;
　　　10 garden tool sets, list price £8. per set.
　　　All less trade discount 25 per cent.

Aug 25 H. Crossley, 34 High Street, Dewsbury:
　　　5 rotary mowers, list price £95 each;
　　　4 lawn mowers, list price £55 each;
　　　20 garden forks, list price £6.50 each;
　　　15 garden spades, list price £7.50 each.
　　　All less trade discount $33\frac{1}{3}$ per cent.

Aug 31 Thornton Supplies, 33 Main Street, Birmingham:
　　　15 garden spades, list price £7.50 each;
　　　10 ornamental garden gnomes, list price £3.50 each;
　　　4 garden shears, list price £9.50 each;
　　　6 garden tool sets, list price £8. per set;
　　　5 lawn sprinklers, list price £5.50 each.
　　　All less trade discount 20 per cent.

You are required to:
(a) Draw up a sales invoice for each of the above sales.
(b) Write up the sales day book for the month of August, 19–7.
(c) Post to the personal accounts in the sales ledger and show the transfer to the sales account in the general ledger.

14.4
James Sellars, 34 High Street Bradford is a textile wholesaler. During the month of September 19–8 he made the following sales:

White cotton pillow cases, list price 45p each;
White cotton sheets, list price £2.50 each;
Grey mixture blankets, list price £5.75 each;
White wool blankets, list price £7.50 each.
Sept 1 To: G. Miller,
        10 white cotton pillow cases, 6 grey mixture blankets, 15 white wool blankets. All less trade discount 25 per cent.
Sept 5 To: T. Bennett,
        10 white cotton sheets, 10 grey mixture blankets, 5 white wool blankets. All less trade discount 20 per cent.
Sept 8 To: B. Watkinson,
        20 white cotton pillow cases, 10 white cotton sheets. All less trade discount 10 per cent.
Sept 14 To: L. Roberts,
        15 grey mixture blankets, 20 white wool blankets, 20 white cotton sheets. All less trade discount 25 per cent.
Sept 22 To: A. Dixon,
        30 white cotton pillow cases, 25 white cotton sheets, 20 white wool blankets. All less trade discount 15 per cent.
Sept 30 To: D. Hewitt,
        25 white cotton pillow cases, 6 grey mixture blankets, 6 white wool blankets. All less trade discount 20 per cent.

You are required to:
(a) Show your calculations for each of the above sales.
(b) Enter up the sales day book and post to the personal and nominal accounts in the ledger.

15 The Purchases Day Book

OBJECTIVES   To consider and examine the Purchases Day Book which is the book of original entry for the purchase of goods on credit; to emphasise the necessity of the checking procedures for purchase invoices.

The purchases day book is used to record all the purchase invoices for goods and services supplied on credit to the firm. In modern business a considerable proportion of the purchases will be made on a credit basis (the goods are received immediately, but payment is made at a later date). When a business buys goods on credit an invoice will be made out by the supplier showing full details of the goods supplied, the prices of the goods, and any trade discount. This is a purchase invoice.

The following will then be checked as a means of verifying the invoices:

(a) The goods were ordered.
(b) The goods have actually been received in conformity with the terms of the order.
(c) The prices charged on the invoice are correct.
(d) The trade discounts are correct.
(e) The calculations on the supplier's invoice are correct.

When the checking procedure has been carried out the purchase invoices are entered in the purchases day book. It is very convenient to use a separate book to keep a daily record of the purchases; this also avoids burdening the purchases account with the detail of each individual transaction. The purchases day book is the book of original entry for all purchases on credit. Each purchase invoice is entered up daily, showing the date, the name of the firm who has supplied the goods, the number of the invoice, and the net amount of the invoice (*after* the deduction of any trade discount).

The entries continue day by day, for a certain period of time, usually one month. At the end of the month the posting from the purchases day book will be to the double entry accounts, that is, at the credit side of the suppliers' individual personal accounts in the purchase ledger, and the total of the purchases day book for the period will be transferred to the debit side of the purchases account in the general ledger.

The following is an illustration of a purchases day book for the month:

Purchases Day Book

Date		Invoice No.	F	£ p
May 2	F. Craig	79801	PL	380.50
May 6	B. Johnson	102/J	PL	252.65
May 12	V. Porter & Son	P.90412	PL	455.10
May 18	Grice Bros.	G.9337	PL	185.90
May 24	W. Nelson	517683	PL	519.40
May 30	Stephenson & Son	2813	PL	288.20
	Transferred to Purchases Account		GL	2,081.75

The 'posting' of the purchases day book to the double entry accounts would be as follows:

Purchase Ledger

F. Craig Account

	May 2 Purchases	380.50

B. Johnson Account

	May 6 Purchases	252.65

V. Porter & Son Account

	May 12 Purchases	455.10

Grice Bros. Account

	May 18 Purchases	185.90

W. Nelson Account

	May 24 Purchases	519.40

Stephenson & Son Account

	May 30 Purchases	288.20

General Ledger

Purchases Account

May 31 Total for month	2,081.75	

The practice of copying the full details of the invoices into the purchases day book has been discontinued in favour of the more modern style with less detail. However, occasionally in examination papers the question may state 'full details of the purchase invoices should be entered in the purchases day book'. The student should, of course, comply with any such requirement.

Cash purchases are *never* entered in the purchases day book. The book of original entry for all cash purchases is the cash book, the double entry being credit the cash account and debit the purchases account.

POINTS TO REMEMBER

In accounting terms *purchases* are goods bought with the intention of selling. For example, in an electrical business, the firm would buy various types of electrical products for resale. If a firm buys something else, for instance office equipment, this will not be regarded as purchases, as the office equipment was bought for use within the business, and would be an asset, and not for resale and would *not* be entered in the purchases day book. Similarly, 'sales' in accounting terms applies to the goods in which the firm normally deals, as in the example of an electrical business. The sale of an old typewriter, for instance, would *not* be entered in the sales day book.

Each purchase invoice will vary in appearance; each supplier will have its own particular layout and design.

No entry for trade discount should be made in the double entry accounts.

The slip system can also be used for purchase invoices. The purchase invoices would be kept together in a file, in date order.

The name 'purchases day book' indicates that it contains a daily record of the purchases; it is also known as: the purchases journal, the purchases book, the bought day book, and in examination papers is sometimes referred to as a subsidiary book.

Assignment Exercises

15.1
Bryan Forbes, a sole trader, has the following purchases on credit for the month of February, 19–8.

Feb 2 General Supplies Ltd:
       12 electric razors, list price £19.70 each;
        5 electric clocks, list price £7.50 each.
       All less trade discount 10 per cent.

Feb 7 Jones Manufacturing Ltd:
   100 lamps, 100w, list price 65p each;
   50 lamps, 75w, list price 55p each;
   25 lamps, 60w, list price 45p each;
   15 lamps, 40w, list price 35p each;
   10 lamps, 15w, list price 30p each.
   All less trade discount 20 per cent.
Feb 15 General Supplies Ltd:
   10 electric clocks, list price £7.50 each;
   15 hairdryers, list price £9.90 each.
   All less trade discount 10 per cent.
Feb 22 Thomas Dean Ltd:
   25 battery torches B.65, list price £1.75 each;
   20 battery torches B.50, list price £1.50 each;
   10 battery torches B.45, list price £1.25 each.
   All less trade discount 25 per cent.
Feb 28 Peter Simmonds:
   5 electric heaters, model S107, list price £22.50 each;
   6 electric heaters, model S227, list price £35 each.
   All less trade discount 15 per cent.

You are required to:

(a) Show your calculations of the net amount to be invoiced by each supplier.
(b) Enter each in the purchases day book for the month of February, 19–8.
(c) Post to the suppliers' personal accounts and transfer the total to the purchases account in the general ledger.

15.2
John Haines is the proprietor of a retail business. His purchases on credit during the month of March 19–8 were as follows:

Mar 2 Kenneth Ingram:
   20 cassette tapes C120, list price £1.30 each;
   50 cassette tapes C 90, list price 95p each;
   30 cassette tapes C 60, list price 75p each.
   All less trade discount 15 per cent.
Mar 4 Graham Clifton.
   6 hand blenders, list price £9.90 each;
   10 food processors, list price £35.50 each;
   6 food mixers, list price £22.50 each;
   5 liquidizers, list price £10.25 each;
   6 electric knives, list price £12.00 each.
   All less trade discount 20 per cent.
Mar 8 Stewart Brothers:
   20 packs HP16 batteries, list price £1.20 per pack;
   50 packs EP12 batteries, list price £1.50 per pack;

25 packs HP18 batteries, list price £1.75 per pack.

All less trade discount 25 per cent.

Mar 16 Frederick Rycroft:

10 men's digital watches, list price £5.90 each;

5 ladies' digital watches, list price £4.90 each.

All less trade discount 10 per cent.

Mar 24 Robert Linton:

10 cassette recorders, list price £12.50 each;

6 radio cassette recorders, list price £27.25 each;

6 pocket radios, list price £3.50 each;

15 model 'S' radios, list price £15.80 each.

All less trade discount $33\frac{1}{3}$ per cent.

Mar 30 Vincent Hood:

20 steam irons, list price £18.20 each;

15 steam spray irons, list price £22.50 each;

10 travel irons, list price £7.70 each.

All less trade discount 20 per cent.

You are required to:

(a) Show clearly your calculations of the net amount to be invoiced by each supplier.

(b) Write up the purchases day book for the month and post to the personal and nominal accounts concerned.

15.3

William Giles owns a retail store. During the month of May, 19–8 the following transactions took place:

May 2 Sold goods on credit (£282) to F. Spencer.

4 Sold goods on credit (£247) to R. Gordon.

5 Purchased stock on credit from Harold Tyler, list price £340, subject to trade discount of 20 per cent.

9 Sold goods on credit (£225) to E. Nelson.

10 Sold goods on credit (£190) to J. Stokes.

12 Purchased stock on credit from B. Hobson, list price £360. Allowed trade discount of 15 per cent.

13 Sales on credit (£414) to T. Marshall.

15 Purchases on credit from Harold Tyler, list price £220, subject to trade discount 20 per cent.

17 Sales on credit (£350) to F. Spencer.

18 Purchased stock on credit from J. Douglas, list price £570, subject to trade discount of $33\frac{1}{3}$ per cent.

20 Sold goods on credit (£174) to J. Marple.

22 Sold goods on credit (£195) to R. Gordon.

24 Purchases on credit from B. Hobson, list price £290, subject to trade discount of 15 per cent.

25 Purchased stock on credit from A. Sylvester, list price £416. Allowed a trade discount of 25 per cent.

26 Sales on credit (£255) to C. Barnes.

28 Purchases on credit from J. Douglas, list price £318, subject to trade discount of $33\frac{1}{3}$ per cent.

30 Sales on credit (£124) to F. Spencer.

31 Purchased stock on credit from T. Norman, list price £280, subject to trade discount of 10 per cent.

You are required to write up:

(a) The sales day book and the purchases day book for the month of May, 19–8.
(b) The personal accounts and nominal accounts as they would appear in the ledgers of William Giles.

16 The Returns Day Books

OBJECTIVES To introduce and examine the documents concerned with the returning of goods, and to consider the importance of internal credit control.

The Credit Note

A credit note is a business document made out whenever one person returns goods to another. It is usually printed in red, to distinguish it from an invoice and, like an invoice, is made out by the seller of the goods, who is now receiving them back again. In the course of business it is expected that some customers will inevitably return goods for valid reasons. The most common reasons for the return of goods are that the goods supplied are: the wrong size; wrong colour; not up to specification; imperfect in some way or damaged.

Another example would be if the goods supplied are unsatisfactory for some reason but are not returned because of the inconvenience and cost involved. The purchaser may be prepared to keep the goods if the seller will make an allowance. This is done by sending a credit note for a mutually agreed amount. This is called an allowance.

Also, where an error has been made on an invoice and a customer has been overcharged (for example, an invoice sent to a customer for £950 is checked and found to be incorrectly calculated: the sum should have been £850) a credit note would be required to correct the overcharge.

In all of these circumstances the document used is a credit note. It is made out by the seller (the original supplier of the goods) and at least one copy is sent to the customer giving full details of the goods returned, the prices of the goods, or the allowance, or overcharge and any trade discount. The top copy is sent to the customer; the copies of the credit notes are subsequently entered in the returns inwards day book. There is an illustration of a credit note on the next page.

CREDIT NOTE

Demland Supplies
Sandmore Lane
BRIGHOUSE BX16 8ER

10 November 19–7

Grove & Sons
Bridge Croft
LEEDS LS56 1PR

Quantity	Description	£
1	Electric Kettle at £19.50 each	19.50
	Less Trade Discount at 20%	3.90
		£15.60

The credit note takes its name from the fact that the customer's personal account will be credited so as to reduce the amount owing by him.

The Returns Inwards Day Book

The seller enters the details from the copies of the credit notes in the returns inwards day book. This book is kept in exactly the same way as the other day books. At the end of the period, usually one month, the posting from the returns inwards day book will be to the double entry accounts, that is, to the credit side of the customers' individual personal accounts in the sales ledger, and the total of the returns inwards day book for the period will be transferred to the debit side of the returns inwards account in the general ledger.

The following is an illustration of a returns inwards day book for the month, commencing with the example credit note:

Returns Inwards Day Book

Date			Credit Note No.	F	£ p
Nov	10	Grove & Sons	D/3741	SL	15.60
	15	W. James	D/3742	SL	22.80
	21	G. Parkinson	D/3743	SL	18.20
	29	J. Spencer	D/3744	SL	21.40
		Transferred to Returns Inwards Account		GL	78.00

The 'posting' of the returns inwards day book to the double entry accounts would be as follows:

Sales Ledger

Grove & Sons Account

	Nov 10 Returns Inwards 15.60

W. James Account

	Nov 15 Returns Inwards 22.80

G. Parkinson Account

	Nov 21 Returns Inwards 18.20

J. Spencer Account

	Nov 29 Returns Inwards 21.40

General Ledger

Nov 30 Total for month	78.00

Alternative names for the returns inwards day book are: returns inwards book, returns inwards journal, sales returns book, and it is also referred to as a subsidiary book.

Debit Notes

A debit note is a document made out whenever a purchaser returns goods, advising the supplier that the goods have been despatched and informs the supplier of the particulars of the goods and the reason for their return. The term 'debit note' originates from the fact that the supplier's personal account must be debited so as to show a reduction in the amount owing.

A debit note could also be used to cover an allowance made in respect of damaged or faulty goods, or if for any reason goods have been undercharged.

The Returns Outwards Day Book

The top copy of the debit note is sent to the supplier. The copies of the debit notes are subsequently entered in the returns outwards day book. This book is kept in the same way as the other day books. At the end of the period, usually one month, the posting from the returns outwards day book will be to the double entry accounts, that is to the debit side of the supplier's personal accounts in the purchase ledger, and the total of the returns outwards day book for the period will be transferred to the credit side of the returns outwards account in the general ledger.

The following is an illustration of a returns outwards day book for the month of May 19–8:

Returns Outwards Day Book

Date			Debit Note No.	F	£ p
May	5	F. Craig	D/1922	PL	26.70
	16	V. Porter & Son	D/1923	PL	15.50
	22	Grice Bros.	D/1924	PL	22.80
	30	W. Nelson	D/1925	PL	38.60
		Transferred to Returns Outwards Account		GL	103.60

The 'posting' of the returns outwards day book to the double entry accounts, would be as follows:

116

Purchase Ledger

F. Craig Account

May 5 Returns Outwards 26.70	

V. Porter & Son Account

May 16 Returns Outwards 15.50	

Grice Bros. Account

May 22 Returns Outwards 22.80	

W. Nelson Account

May 30 Returns Outwards 38.60	

General Ledger

Returns Outwards Account

	May 31 Total for month 103 60

Alternative names for the returns outwards day book are: returns outwards book, returns outwards journal, purchase returns book, and it is also referred to as a subsidiary book.

Statements

At the end of each month a statement is sent to each customer. This is a document showing full details of the transactions, in date order, which have taken place during the month. The statement commences with the balance outstanding (if any) brought forward from the previous month, and continues by listing, in date order, the total of each sales invoice, each credit note, and any cash and cheques received from the debtor; the final figure is the amount outstanding at the end of the month.

A monthly statement also acts as a reminder to the debtor that payment is due, and will show the date by which payment should be made. The debtor will use the statement to check and reconcile his own accounting records.

Internal Credit Control

It is the responsibility of this department of the business to monitor the volume of credit allowed to customers and to ensure that it is kept within the capabilities of the firm. When an order is received by the firm, the customer's credit worthiness must be checked. For each debtor a maximum credit limit is usually set. In many instances this will depend on the firm's previous dealings with the debtor and his ability to pay his debts promptly within the period of time allowed. In the case of a new customer caution should be observed. A new customer may be required to provide trade references, the names and addresses of businessmen or companies with whom he has previously conducted business, and a reference from his banker.

Some firms would also require a new customer to sign a 'customer undertaking'. This is a printed document setting out the terms and conditions under which the credit facilities would be granted. An example of this would be: 'assuming credit facilities are granted I herewith confirm that payment will be made in accordance with your terms of credit, and settlement in the month following delivery'. Some or all of these measures should be taken in order to ascertain a potential customer's credit worthiness. The risk of non-payment by some debtors will always exist, therefore it is extremely important to be cautious with new customers, and to act quickly when a slow or bad payer is identified, in order to prevent the losses involved being too great.

POINTS TO REMEMBER

The returns day books are the books of original entry for all the returning of goods, and the information comes from the original documents. The definition of 'goods' applies to the merchandise in which the firm normally deals.

Care should be taken with regard to trade discount in connection with a return of goods; the same percentage of the trade discount deducted from any original invoice *must* also be deducted from the gross value of any returns. It would be incorrect to give a customer a credit note for the full catalogue or list price of the goods if the original invoice was subject to a trade discount.

Trade discount is a percentage reduction on the catalogue or list price and *never* enters a ledger account, at any time.

Credit notes are usually printed in red so that they are easily distinguishable from invoices.

The slip system can also be used for returns inwards and returns outwards; the copies of the credit notes and debit notes will be kept, in date order, in a file.

Statements are sent to customers at the end of each month showing full details of all the transactions which have taken place during the month.

Assignment Exercises

16.1

During the month of June, 19–8 John Mortimer's credit transactions were as follows:

June 1 Sales on credit to G. Spink (£218); J. Goodall (£127); Scott Bros. (£92).
June 5 Sales on credit to B. Moss (£117); L. Gibson (£138); P. Andrews (£242); F. Benn (£189).
June 8 Goods returned by J. Goodall (£21); Scott Bros. (£17).
June 11 Sales on credit to F. Myers (£233); B. Moss (£186).
June 14 Goods returned by L. Gibson (£28); P. Andrews (£32).
June 20 Sales on credit to J. Goodall (£149); F. Benn (£256).
June 23 Sales on credit to K. Williams (£212); G. Spink (£306).
June 27 Goods returned by F. Benn (£37).
June 30 Sales on credit to B. Moss (£290); E. Nelson (£135).

You are required to:

(a) Write up John Mortimer's sales day book and returns inwards day book for the month of June, 19–8.
(b) Post to the relevant personal accounts in the sales ledger and show the transfers to the general ledger.

16.2

Prepare the purchases day book and the returns outwards day book for the month of August, 19–8 from the following details. At the end of the month post to the personal and nominal accounts in the ledger.

Aug 1 Purchased goods on credit from W. Lawrence (£258).
     4 Credit purchases from the following: J. Barrymore (£316); T. Groves (£192); H. Roper (£257); D. Passmore (£168).
     8 Goods returned to W. Lawrence (£17).
    10 Purchased goods on credit from T. Groves (£388); P. Armstrong (£219); H. Roper (£242); W. Jones (£312).
    12 Goods returned to the following: J. Barrymore (£56); D. Passmore (£35).
    18 Credit purchases from W. Lawrence (£280); M. Hardy (£116).
    20 Goods returned to T. Groves (£28).
    24 Purchased goods on credit from J. Barrymore (£185).
    28 Goods returned to M. Hardy (£15).
    30 Credit purchases from F. King (£395).

16.3

During the month of October 19–8 James Garrett's credit transactions were as follows:

Oct 1 Purchases from E. Smythe (£326), subject to 20 per cent trade discount.
      3 Sales to B. Marsh (£126); L. Young (£65); D. Davey (£38).
      5 Purchases from R. Chalker (£543), subject to 25 per cent trade discount.
      9 Goods returned by L. Young (£14).
   14 Sales to W. Preston (£124); M Dyson (£273).
   16 Returned goods to R. Chalker with a list price of £48.
   18 M. Dyson returned goods (£36).
   20 Purchases from M. Trenholme (£450), subject to 15 per cent trade discount.
   22 Sales to B. Marsh (£212).
   24 Returned goods to M. Trenholme with a list price of £50.
   26 Sales to V. Reedman (£173).
   28 Goods returned by B. Marsh (£28).
   29 Purchases from C. Hemingway (£398), subject to a 10 per cent trade discount.
   30 Sales to W. Preston (£78); J. Jackson (£132).

You are required to:

(a) Write up Garrett's sales, purchases, sales returns and purchase returns day books for the month of October 19–8.
(b) Post the items to the personal and nominal accounts in the ledger.

16.4

The following account appears in the ledger of Dawn Gwinnett:

Dr.			Denise Hathersmith				Cr.
19–6			£	19–6			£
Jan	1	Balance b/d	500	Jan	7	Bank	475
	12	Goods	1,800		7	Discount	25
					20	Returns	40
					31	Balance c/d	1,760
			2,300				2,300
Feb	1	Balance b/d	1,760				

Answer the following questions relating to the above account:

(a) On 1 January was Denise Hathersmith a debtor or a creditor of Dawn Gwinnett?
(b) On 12 January did Denise Hathersmith purchase or sell goods?
(c) Who received the cheque on 7 January?
(d) What rate per cent of discount was allowed on 7 January?

(e) Was the discount on 7 January trade or cash?

(f) Does Denise Hathersmith regard the returns on 20 January as returns inwards or returns outwards?

(g) If the debt owing on 1 February was settled on 9 February, less $2\frac{1}{2}$ per cent discount, what was the amount of the cheque?

(Joint Matriculation Board)

16.5

State briefly the checking procedures you would follow before authorising payment of an invoice received from a supplier.

(The Royal Society of Arts)

16.6

		STATEMENT				
In account with						
		J. Hunt				
		24 Coventry Road				
		Nuneaton C4				
Mr R. J. Cook						
14 Thorn Street						
Derby DE3						
			£	£	£	31 March 19–4
February	1	Balance			130.42	
	6	Invoice 512	140.64		271.06	
	8	Cheque		127.16		
		Discount		3.26	140.64	
	12	Returns		16.30	124.34	
	26	Invoice 540	184.42		308.76	
	28	Undercharge	3.60		312.36	

Study the statement above.

(a) Name the person who is supplying goods.

(b) Explain in simple terms the meaning of each item in the statement from February 1–26 and state the document used for the item on February 28 and the names of the sender and the receiver.

(c) Give the names of the debtor and the creditor and the amount owed on 28 February 19–4.

(The Royal Society of Arts)

16.7

A trader informs you that he does not use conventional day books to record his credit transactions. He posts direct to the ledger from invoices or copy invoices and from debit or credit notes.

(a) State what system of book-keeping the trader is using.

(b) List the advantages of this system.

16.8

The basic principle of double-entry book-keeping is that 'for every debit entry there must be a corresponding credit entry'.

Explain how this statement is followed when posting from:

(a) The purchases day book.

(b) The sales returns book.

(c) The cash book.

Give an example of each to illustrate your answer.

(The Royal Society of Arts)

16.9

(a) You have been newly appointed as a clerk in your company's credit control department and an order from an old established customer has been passed to you for clearance. What procedure would you follow before passing the order to the sales department for completion?

(b) In what way would the procedure be different if the order was for a new customer?

(The Royal Society of Arts)

17 Value Added Tax

OBJECTIVES To examine Value Added Tax and to gain experience and proficiency in the recording of VAT in the double entry accounts.

Value Added Tax is a tax on the supply of goods and services which is eventually borne by the final customer, but it is collected at each stage of the production and distribution chain. Value Added Tax, which is generally abbreviated to VAT, is charged on the supply both of goods and of services by firms who are registered and taxable for VAT.

The government authority which administers VAT in the United Kingdom is the Customs and Excise Department. VAT is an indirect tax charged as a percentage of the selling price on certain services and commodities. The percentage rate is set by the government and is changed from time to time via the Budget.

When VAT was first introduced into the United Kingdom there were two separate percentage rates of VAT levied, certain classes of goods being subject to a higher percentage rate. At the present time, there is one standard percentage rate of 15 per cent which applies to all taxable goods and services. It is the responsibility of the taxable trader or firm making the sale, at each stage of production, to charge and collect the VAT from the customer. Most goods and services are subject to VAT but there are exceptions:

(1) There are some services and certain classes of goods which are completely exempt from VAT.
(2) Some classes of goods are not taxed and are said to be zero rated. This in effect means that, at the present time, these goods or services are not subject to VAT, but in the future changes may take place and VAT could be applicable.
(3) There are certain traders or providers of services whose taxable turnover (sales) is under a certain amount; this figure is referred to as the taxable 'threshold'. The 'threshold limit' is the figure, set by the government, to be used as a margin; traders whose turnover is below this figure are not required to register for VAT. The amount of the 'threshold limit' is usually reviewed and increased each year. Any traders or providers of services who are not registered for VAT cannot charge VAT to their customers, nor can they recover the amount of VAT paid on their purchases.

Registration for VAT is compulsory for persons and firms whose turnover is in excess of the 'threshold limit'. The vast majority of traders and businesses are taxable and registered for VAT. A taxable firm selling goods or services must collect the Value Added Tax from the customer; this is known as output tax. A business will also have to pay VAT to its suppliers; this is known as input tax.

Output Tax

Output tax is the amount of VAT which a taxable firm will charge and add to the value of the sales invoices on the goods or services it sells to its customers. This is based on the amount of the invoice *after* any trade discount and/or any cash discount has been deducted.

Input Tax

Input tax is the amount of VAT a taxable firm must pay on the goods or services it purchases from its suppliers. This is based on the amount of the invoice *after* any trade discount and/or any cash discount has been deducted. For each VAT accounting period, which is currently every three months, if the VAT on outputs (sales) is greater than VAT on inputs (purchases) the firm will have to pay the difference between these amounts to the Customs and Excise Department.

If VAT on inputs is greater than VAT on outputs the business will collect the difference from the Customs and Excise Department. The business, therefore, simply acts as a tax collector for the government. The amount of VAT charged on all invoices should always be shown separately for accounting purposes.

The VAT percentage rate levied by the government changes over a period of time, and in view of this many examination boards set questions assuming a VAT percentage rate of 10 per cent. For this reason, the examples and illustrations used in this Module will assume a VAT rate of 10 per cent throughout.

Sales on Credit – Sales Invoices

A trader or firm which is registered and taxable for VAT will be required to add VAT to the value of the sales invoices after any trade discount has been deducted. The calculation of VAT and its display on the sales invoice will usually be as shown in the following example invoice:

SALES INVOICE

Demland Supplies

Sandmore Lane

BRIGHOUSE BX16 8ER

Your Order No | 4346

Tax Point and Date | 1 March 19–8

Grove & Sons
Bridge Croft
LEEDS LS56 1PR

VAT Registration No. 987654321

Quantity	Description	£
10	Electric Kettles at £19.50 each	195.00
20	Electric Toasters at £18.75 each	375.00
		570.00
	Less Trade Discount at 20%	114.00
		456.00
	Add VAT at 10%	45.60
		501.60

From the copies of the sales invoices the seller enters the details in the sales day book. It is extremely important that the entries for VAT are made in the sales day book, and to facilitate this requirement the day books will have additional extra columns. The following is an illustration of a sales day book for the month, commencing with the example invoice.

Sales Day Book

Date			In-voice No.	F	Total £	Net £	VAT £
19–8							
Mar	1	Grove & Sons	8674	SL	501.60	456.00	45.60
	8	G. Parker	8675	SL	173.80	158.00	15.80
	18	J. Oliver	8676	SL	376.20	342.00	34.20
	27	M. Reynolds	8677	SL	296.45	269.50	26.95
	31	B. Conway	8678	SL	135.08	122.80	12.28
					1,483.13	1,348.30	134.83

At the end of the month the posting from the sales day book will be to the double entry accounts, that is, to the customers' individual personal accounts in the sales ledger, and to the sales account and the value added tax account in the general ledger. The customers' personal accounts are entered with the *total* amount of each invoice, *including VAT*, as follows:

Sales Ledger

Grove & Sons Account

Mar	1 Sales	501.60	

G. Parker Account

Mar	8 Sales	173.80	

J. Oliver Account

Mar	18 Sales	376.20	

M. Reynolds Account

Mar	27 Sales	296.45	

B. Conway Account

Mar	31 Sales	135.08	

126

To complete the double entry the amount of the sales *content* only (without VAT) is transferred to the credit side of the sales account in the general ledger, as this is the true amount of the sale. The amount of VAT is entered and recorded at the credit side, in the Value Added Tax account; the posting of these accounts would appear as follows:

General Ledger

Sales Account

	Mar 31 Total for the month 1,348.30

Value Added Tax Account

	Mar 31 Total S.D.B. Content 134.83

Purchases on Credit – Purchase Invoices

In business a considerable proportion of the purchases will be made on a credit basis. When a firm buys goods on credit an invoice will be made out by the supplier showing full details of the goods supplied, the prices of the goods and the deduction of any trade discount. The supplier will then have to add the amount of VAT to the invoice.

When the necessary checking procedures have been carried out the purchase invoices are then entered in the purchases day book. The following is an illustration of a purchases day book for the month of March 19–8:

Purchases Day Book

Date			In- voice No.	F	Total £	Net £ .	VAT £ .
19–8							
Mar	2	S. Barnsdale	34275	PL	385.00	350.00	35.00
	6	R. Carlton	8125	PL	214.50	195.00	19.50
	17	M. Lane	L/6517	PL	187.55	170.50	17.05
	25	G. Stewart	44368	PL	405.35	368.50	36.85
	31	J. Silverwood	S/355	PL	133.10	121.00	12.10
					1,325.50	1,205.00	120.50

At the end of the month the posting from the purchases day book will be to the double entry accounts, that is to the suppliers' individual personal accounts in the purchase ledger, and to the purchases account and Value Added Tax account in the general ledger. The suppliers' personal accounts are entered with the *total* amount of each invoice, *including VAT*, as follows:

Purchase Ledger

S. Barnsdale Account

	Mar 2 Purchases	385.00

R. Carlton Account

	Mar 6 Purchases	214.50

M. Lane Account

	Mar 17 Purchases	187.55

G. Stewart Account

	Mar 25 Purchases	405.35

J. Silverwood Account

	Mar 31 Purchases	133.10

To complete the double entry the amount of the purchases *content* only (excluding VAT) is transferred to the debit side of the purchases account. This is the true amount the goods are costing the firm. The amount of the VAT is entered and recorded at the debit side of the Value Added Tax account. The posting of these accounts is now completed, as follows:

General Ledger

Purchases Account

Mar 31 Total for the month 1,205.00		

Value Added Tax Account

Mar 31 Total P.D.B.	Mar 31 Total S.D.B.	
Content 120.50	Content 134.83	

128

Cash Sales and Cash Purchases

The Value Added Tax account will summarise *all* items of input tax and output tax. It will be necessary, therefore, to enter and record the VAT on cash transactions.

Cash sales and cash purchases are not entered in the day books. The book of 'original entry' for all cash transactions is the cash book. The amount of VAT should be calculated at the appropriate percentage on each of the cash sales and cash purchases, and then entered with the amount of VAT recorded in a separate column in the cash book.

The posting of the cash sales from the cash book will be to the sales account and the Value Added Tax account; the amount of the sales content only will be taken to the credit side of the sales account. The amount of VAT is transferred to the credit side of the Value Added Tax account.

Similarly, with cash purchases, the posting of the cash purchases from the cash book will be to the purchases account and the Value Added Tax Account; the amount of the purchases content only, will be taken to the debit side of the purchases account. The amount of VAT is transferred to the debit side of the Value Added Tax account.

VAT – Returns Inwards and Returns Outwards

The returns day books will also have additional extra columns to record the entries involving VAT.

Returns Inwards Day Book

The details are entered in the returns inwards day book, with the amount of VAT in a separate VAT column. At the end of the month the posting from the returns inwards day book to the double entry accounts is as follows: the total amount of each individual transaction (including VAT) is taken to the credit side of the customer's personal account in the sales ledger, the total amount of the goods returned column is posted to the debit side of the returns inwards account, and the total of the VAT column is posted to the debit side of the Value Added Tax account.

Returns Outwards Day Book

Similarly, the details are entered in the returns outwards day book, with the amount of VAT in a separate VAT column. At the end of the month the posting from the returns outwards day book to the double entry accounts is as follows: the total amount of each individual transaction (including VAT) is taken to the debit side of the supplier's personal account in the purchase ledger, the total amount of the goods returned column is posted to the credit side of the returns outwards account, and the total of the VAT column is posted to the credit side of the Value Added Tax account.

VAT on Expenses and Assets

Value Added Tax is an indirect tax charged on the majority of goods and services. During the course of business a firm will be charged VAT on expenses such as telephone and stationery and the firm will also be charged VAT on the purchase of assets for use in the business; examples of these could be furniture, machinery, computers or typewriters. The amount of the VAT on expenses and items purchased for use in the business can also be re-claimed. As a result of this, the amount of VAT charged on these items will be entered at the debit side of the Value Added Tax account.

Even in a relatively small business a typical Value Added Tax account could contain any or all of the following:

At the debit side: the amounts of VAT charged by the suppliers on all the purchases (these are the goods in which the firm normally deals, and are bought with the intention of resale); the amounts of VAT from the returns inwards day book; the amounts of VAT charged on certain expenses and the VAT charged on items purchased for use in the business.

At the credit side: The amounts of VAT charged on all the sales; and the amount of VAT from the returns outwards day book.

VAT and the Balance Sheet

At the end of the financial year when the final accounts of a business are prepared, any amount of VAT owing to the Customs and Excise Department would appear as a creditor on the balance sheet; any amount of VAT owing to the business would appear as a debtor on the balance sheet.

POINTS TO REMEMBER

Value Added Tax, which is generally abbreviated to VAT, is charged on the supply both of goods and of services by firms who are registered and taxable for VAT. The government authority which administers VAT in the United Kingdom is the Customs and Excise Department.

The detailed recording of input and output tax on invoices is extremely important, and it is therefore necessary to include additional extra columns in the day books.

Posting the sales day book – the customers' personal accounts are entered with the *total* amount of each invoice, *including VAT*; to complete the double entry the amount of the sales *content* only is transferred to the credit side of the sales account, the amount of VAT is entered and recorded at the credit side of the Value Added Tax account.

Posting the purchases day book – the suppliers' individual personal accounts are entered with the *total* amount of each invoice, *including VAT*; to complete the double entry the amount of the purchases *content* only is transferred to the debit side of the purchases account, the amount of VAT is entered and recorded at the debit side of the Value Added Tax account.

The amount of VAT on expenses incurred by the business, and items purchased for use in the business can be reclaimed. The amount of VAT charged on these items will be entered at the debit side of the Value Added Tax account.

The Value Added Tax account is a summary of *ALL* the VAT inputs and outputs during each VAT accounting period; the balance, which is the difference between the two sides of the Value Added Tax account, is the amount payable in the case of a credit balance, to the Customs and Excise Department, or, in the case of a debit balance, remitted by the Customs and Excise Department.

Assignment Exercises

17.1

Joseph Stephenson is a trader. During the month of April 19–8 sales on credit were made to the following:

19–8			£
April	2	Sales to J. Wilson.	250
	5	Sales to K. Allen.	178
	10	Sales to F. Stones.	490
	15	Sales to R. Lockwood.	155
	22	Sales to B. McKenzie.	212
	30	Sales to M. Newman.	364

The above transactions are subject to VAT at 10 per cent. You are required to:

(a) Write up the sales day book for the month of April 19–8 and
(b) post the sales day book to the personal accounts and the nominal accounts in the ledgers to complete the double entry.

17.2

During the month of May 19–8 Cyril Sanderson's purchases on credit were as follows:

19–8

May 1 Purchases from M. Booth (£296), subject to 20 per cent trade discount.
4 Purchases from J. Price (£492), subject to 25 per cent trade discount.
8 Purchases from B. Ramsden (£184), subject to 15 per cent trade discount.
14 Purchases from L. Nelson (£273), subject to 20 per cent trade discount.
20 Purchases from M. Senior (£158), subject to 15 per cent trade discount.
25 Purchases from D. Rawdon (£332), subject to 25 per cent trade discount.

All the above transactions are subject to VAT at 10 per cent. You are required to:

(a) Write up the purchases day book for the month of May 19–8.
(b) Post the purchases day book to the personal accounts and nominal accounts in the ledgers.

17.3
W. Gascoigne is a wholesaler. During the month of June 19–8 the following transactions took place.

19–8

June 1 Purchased stock on credit from A. Singer, list price £250. He was allowed trade discount of 20 per cent.
5 Purchased stock on credit from N. Peters, list price £190. He was allowed trade discount of $33\frac{1}{3}$ per cent.
8 Sold goods on credit (£280) to B. Booth.
12 Purchased a new typewriter on credit from Office Supplies (£220). This was for use in the firm's office.
18 B. Booth returned goods having a list price of £30.
22 Sent a cheque to A. Singer in full settlement of his account.
27 Returned goods, list price £30, to N. Peters as being unsuitable.
29 Received a cheque from B. Booth in full settlement of his account.

The above transactions are subject to VAT at 10 per cent. You are required to write up the nominal accounts, the personal accounts, the bank account and the Value Added Tax Account as they would appear in the ledger of W. Gascoigne.
NB *Day books are not required.*

17.4
You are employed by Anderson and Littlewood, 22 Grange Street, Hull HN5 7BZ, suppliers of office equipment and materials. On 29 February your firm had supplied the following goods to T. Woodward of 44 Market Cross, Driffield, North Humberside YO16 4NL. The invoice number is 66161. VAT Registration number 23456789.

100 reams of A4 paper at £4 per ream.
200 bottles of correction fluid at 48p per bottle.
150 boxes of address labels at 80p per box.
1 four-drawer metal filing cabinet at £120.
VAT is charged at 10 per cent on all items.

You are required to prepare the invoice to be sent to T. Woodward.

(Royal Society of Arts)

17.5

(a) Clearly distinguish between VAT inputs and VAT outputs.
(b) A. Wise made the following purchases and sales on credit during the three
months ended 31 December 19–1.

Purchases
19–1	October	£6,000 + VAT
	November	£8,000 + VAT
	December	£9,000 + VAT

Sales
	October	£9,000 + VAT
	November	£10,000 + VAT
	December	£15,000 + VAT

VAT is to be taken at the rate of 10 per cent.

Prepare the VAT account of A. Wise for the three months ended 31 December
19–1. Any outstanding amount payable to the Customs and Excise should be
remitted by cheque on 31 December 19–1.

(Royal Society of Arts)

17.6

D. Withers is a wholesaler. The following *credit* transactions took place during
the month of May 19–2. Enter each transaction in the appropriate book of
original entry, total for the month and post to the purchases, sales, returns and
value added tax accounts in the ledger.

All amounts given are before the addition of value added tax, which is to be
taken at 10 per cent. All trade purchases are allowed a trade discount of 20 per
cent, not yet taken into account in the figures given below. Trade discount is not
allowed on any sales.

19–2		£
May	1 Purchased stock from T. Smithers Ltd.	400
	3 Sold stock to W. Wilkin.	350
	4 Sold stock to T. Wilson.	300
	11 Returned stock bought on 1 May 19–2 to T. Smithers Ltd.	50

12	Purchased stationery for office use from Paper Co. Ltd.	150
14	Purchased office furniture from Office Supplies Ltd.	400
20	T. Wilson returned stock.	20
29	Sold stock to W. Wilkin.	170
29	Purchased stock from T. Smithers Ltd.	150

(Royal Society of Arts)

17.7

During the month of September 19–5 Oliver Stanley's credit transactions were as follows:

Sept 2	Sales to E. Cowan.	£182
4	Sales to R. Douglas.	£357
5	Purchases from H. Pearce.	£440, subject to 20 per cent trade discount.
10	Sales to N. Eddie.	£225
12	Returns from E. Cowan.	£14
13	Purchases from P. Stokes.	£360, subject to 25 per cent trade discount.
17	Sales to T. Galloway.	£412
23	Purchases from P. Stokes.	£250, subject to 30 per cent trade discount.
24	Received credit note from H. Pearce in respect of goods with list price (excluding VAT) of £50.	
26	Sales to R. Douglas.	£383
30	Returns from T. Galloway.	£33

Note: All purchases, sales and returns are subject to Value Added Tax at 10 per cent.

You are required to write up Stanley's sales, purchases, sales returns and purchases returns day books for the month of September 19–5.

(Royal Society of Arts)

17.8

The following sales and purchases were made by Smithers during the month of May 19–6:

May 5 Sold 3 desks the list price of which was £150 each on credit to Ace Furnishings. Trade discount was given at the rate of $33\frac{1}{3}$ per cent.

May 10 Sold 2 dining suites, list price £360 each, less trade discount of 25 per cent on credit to Comfy Chair Co.

May 18 Purchased the following goods on credit from The Top Woodworkers:

24 kitchen chairs, list price £12.00 each, trade discount 25 per cent;
12 wall cupboards, list price £10 each, trade discount 20 per cent.

134

All transactions are subject to the Value Added Tax at 10 per cent and cash discount is neither given nor received.

In addition to the above, Smithers received an invoice for £110 on 20 May from Jones. This was for shop fittings supplied for use within the business and included Value Added Tax at 10 per cent.

You are required to:

(a) Calculate the net value of the invoice in each of the four instances mentioned above.
(b) To write up the sales account, purchases account, shop fittings, VAT account and relevant personal accounts for the month of May. Your VAT account should show the amount owing to/by the Customs and Excise as at 31 May 19–6.

(Royal Society of Arts)

18 Sales and Purchase Analysed Day Books

OBJECTIVES To examine the need to make more detailed information available to firms dealing in different commodities or several departments.

A business may deal in several different products, or may be divided into a number of departments. The information already available may not be adequate to enable the business to discover whether each product or department is contributing its share to the profitability of the business. It may require additional information giving the details of the sales and purchases for each commodity or department. This information can most simply and readily be obtained by using analysis columns in the subsidiary books (day books) where a continuous analysis can be made as the original entries are recorded.

In order to ensure that the accounts give the information required the analysis must be in continuous form throughout the trading period. This will enable the business to compare the trading results for each commodity or department, and discover if each department is contributing its share to the profitability of the business.

For the business to obtain this important and useful information it will be necessary to create a system of analysis of the purchases, sales, returns inwards and returns outwards. This is achieved by adding extra columns in the day books, one for each commodity or department. There will be a total column in which the total amount of each document is entered and there will usually be as well as those for each commodity or department, a column for VAT. At the end of the month, or other period selected, all the columns are totalled. The total amount of the totals column should equal the sum of all the other analysis columns.

Trade Discount, if any, is deducted, and any other calculations which may be required are carried out before the entries are made in the analysed day books. This is particularly relevant in examinations questions, as the student is very often required to carry out the calculation of the invoices. This should be completed before entering the details of the invoices in the analysed day books.

The practice of copying the full details of the documents into the analysed day books has been discontinued in favour of the more modern style, with less detail. However, the question may state: 'It is the firm's policy to enter and record in the day books full details of the items bought and the total of each invoice'. In this situation, the student should of course comply with the requirement.

For example, a business which deals in three main commodities, namely; televisions, video recorders and personal computers, may use an analysed sales day book, ruled and set out as illustrated below.

NB: As many of the examination boards set questions assuming a VAT percentage rate of 10 per cent, the examples shown in this Module are calculated at that rate.

Analysed Sales Day Book

Date			F	Total	Televisions	Video Recorders	Personal Computers	VAT
19–8				£	£	£	£	£
Mar	1	F. Briggs	SL	935.00	850.00			85.00
	6	M. King	SL	1,089.00		600.00	390.00	99.00
	9	B. Franks	SL	1,034.00	590.00	350.00		94.00
	15	D. Grice	SL	1,406.90	420.00	299.00	560.00	127.90
	23	W. Newton	SL	715.00			650.00	65.00
	31	M. Dyson	SL	1,199.00	730.00		360.00	109.00
				6,378.90	2,590.00	1,249.00	1,960.00	579.90

Posting the Analysed Day Books

The personal accounts in the sales ledger and the purchase ledger are not affected in any way, by the analysis. The total amount of each invoice (including VAT where applicable) is taken to each individual personal account. The following is an illustration of the posting of the example analysed sales day book:

Sales Ledger

F. Briggs Account

Mar	1 Sales	935.00	

M. King Account

Mar	6 Sales	1,089.00	

B. Franks Account

Mar	9 Sales	1,034.00	

D. Grice Account

Mar 15 Sales	1,406.90	

W. Newton Account

Mar 23 Sales	715.00	

M. Dyson Account

Mar 31 Sales	1,199.00	

In order to make full use of the information given in the analysed day books it is necessary to extend the analysis to the accounts in the nominal ledger. This is successfully achieved by having analysed accounts, one for each commodity or department. The following is an illustration of the posting to the nominal accounts, in the example analysed sales day book:

Nominal Ledger

Sales Account – Televisions

	Mar 31 Total for the month	2,590.00

Sales Account – Video Recorders

	Mar 31 Total for the month	1,249.00

Sales Account – Personal Computers

	Mar 31 Total for the month	1,960.00

Value Added Tax Account

	Mar 31 Total S.D.B. Content	579.90

Alternatively, one analysed sales account could be used, with separate columns for each commodity or department. However, where there are several different products or departments, it may be difficult to have sufficient additional columns in the ledger accounts without causing the ledger to be exceedingly cumbersome in size. In the majority of instances separate accounts for each of the products or departments is preferred.

Similar analysed or columnar day books would be kept for purchases, returns inwards and returns outwards.

The following is an illustration of an analysed purchases day book for the month of June 19–7 for a firm which has divided its retail business into three main departments.

Analysed Purchases Day Book

Date		F	Total	Carpet Dept.	Furniture Dept.	Electrical Dept.	VAT
19–7			£	£	£	£	£
Jun	1 D. Smythe	PL	638.00		580.00		58.00
	5 H. Benson	PL	413.60	230.00		146.00	37.60
	12 F. Parker	PL	635.80	158.00	420.00		57.80
	21 P. Ellis	PL	409.20			372.00	37.20
	30 G. Wilson	PL	778.80	286.00	422.00		70.80
			2,875.40	674.00	1,422.00	518.00	261.40

The posting of the above analysed purchases day book to the double entry accounts would be as follows:

Purchase Ledger

D. Smythe Account

	Jun	1 Purchases	638.00

H. Benson Account

	Jun	5 Purchases	413.60

F. Parker Account

	Jun	12 Purchases	635.80

P. Ellis Account

	Jun	21 Purchases	409.20

G. Wilson Account

	Jun	30 Purchases	778.80

Nominal Ledger

Purchases Account – Carpet Department

Jun	30	Total for the month	674.00	

Purchases Account – Furniture Department

Jun	30	Total for the month	1,422.00	

Purchases Account – Electrical Department

Jun	30	Total for the month	518.00	

Value Added Tax Account

Jun	30	Total P.D.B. Content	261.40	

POINTS TO REMEMBER

The keeping of analysed or columnar day books by a firm will provide the business with useful and important information relating to each particular commodity or department.

It is extremely important when posting from the columnar day books to the individual personal accounts to post the total amount of each invoice (including VAT where applicable). When posting to the nominal accounts, the information given in the columnar day books must be extended to the nominal accounts. A separate account will be required for each commodity or department. When VAT is charged, the amount of VAT is transferred to the Value Added Tax account.

No entry for trade discount should be made in the double entry accounts.

Assignment Exercises

The following assignment exercises are all taken from past examination papers.

18.1

'Handyman' is a local 'Do-it-Yourself' store which divides its purchases of stock into two main departments: General Household and Garden Accessories.
Purchases on credit during the month of April 19–3 were:

April 2 Self Paste Ltd.
     Wallpaper supplies at list price £1,040, less trade discount 20 per cent;
     Emulsion paint at list price £1,600, less trade discount 15 per cent.
April 15 Green Fingers Ltd.
     12 patio furniture sets at list price £20 each, less trade discount 20 per cent;
     10 lawn mowers at list price £90 each, less trade discount 10 per cent.
April 20 G. A. Coleman & Son.
     Plasterboard supplies at list price £220, less trade discount 10 per cent.

None of these suppliers allows any cash discount for prompt payment and all transactions are subject to Value Added Tax at 10 per cent.
   You are required to:
(a) Write up the purchases day book for the month and post the relevant totals to the personal and nominal accounts concerned.
(b) Show clearly your calculations of the net amount to be invoiced by each supplier.

(Royal Society of Arts)

18.2

John Dickenson is the proprietor of a retail business which he has divided into two departments: Furniture and Electrical Goods. His purchases on credit during the month of May 19–3 were:

May 5 Overland Furniture Co. Ltd.
     3 dining suites, list price £250 each, less trade discount 20 per cent;
     4 double beds, list price £150 each, less trade discount $33\frac{1}{3}$ per cent.
May 13 Pelican Co. Ltd.
     25 electric kettles, list price £20 each;
     5 electric toasters, list price £15 each;
     5 electric knives, list price £15 each;
     all these purchases less trade discount 20 per cent.
May 25 Overland Furniture Co. Ltd.
     24 dining chairs, list price £20 each, less trade discount 25 per cent.

All transactions are subject to Value Added Tax at 10 per cent. Neither supplier allows cash discount.
   You are required to:
(a) Show your calculations of the net amount to be invoiced by each supplier.
(b) Rule up a purchase day book with four columns. Column 1 is for the totals, column 2 for furniture department purchases, column 3 for electrical goods department purchases and column 4 for value added tax.

(c) Write up the day book for the month of May and post to the personal and nominal accounts in the ledger.

(Royal Society of Arts)

18.3
K. E. Stevens has divided his business into three departments: camping, sports and garden furniture. His purchases on credit during the month of May 19–6 were:

May 3 H. O. Land.
> 3 garden suites, list price £400 each, less trade discount 20 per cent.

May 12 Fairfield and Co.
> 12 lightweight tents, list price £60 each, less trade discount 25 per cent.

May 28 Outdoor Supplies.
> 6 tennis racquets, list price £15 each;
> 9 camping stoves list price £50 each;
> 24 pairs training shoes list price £10 per pair;
> all less trade discount at 15 per cent.

On May 30 he returned one camping stove and one pair of training shoes to Outdoor Supplies and one garden suite to H. O. Land, all these goods having been found to be damaged on receipt.

You are required to:

(a) Rule up a purchase day book with four columns; Column 1 is for the totals, Column 2 is for camping department purchases, Column 3 is for sports department purchases and Column 4 is for garden furniture department purchases.

(b) Rule up a suitable purchases returns day book.

(c) Write up the day books for the month of May and post to the departmentalised nominal accounts in the ledger.

NB: (i) Personal accounts are not required.
     (ii) Ignore VAT.

(Royal Society of Arts)

18.4
C. Berry, a retailer, divides his business into three departments: Kitchen Hardware, Electrical and Garden. During the month of June 19–6 he bought the following goods on credit:

4 June	Grofast Seeds Ltd	1,200 packets of garden seeds costing £5 per 100.
6 June	E. Gaze	Various kitchen utensils for £240 list price, less 20 per cent trade discount.
16 June	Light & Shade Ltd	70 electric light shades at £5 each.
20 June	E. Gaze	50 frying pans at £4 each.
		200 peat flower pots for a total of £25.

| 26 June | Lightning Wire Company | 100 yards of electric wire at £120 list price, less 10 per cent trade discount. |
| 29 June | The Rich Loam Company | 60 bags of garden compost at £6 per bag. |

Required
(i) Write up the purchases day book of C. Berry for the month of June 19–6, using the following columnar ruling:

Date	Name of Supplier	Ledger Folio	Total	Kitchen Hardware	Electrical	Garden

Note: Details of invoices need not be entered.
(ii) Post the totals of the columns to the appropriate ledger accounts.

(London Chamber of Commerce and Industry)

18.5
M. and P. Harris have divided their retail business into two departments, china and cutlery. All items of stock are bought on credit. Their purchases and purchase returns for October 19–6 were:

6 October Coghlin Supplies
            10 china tea sets, list price £12 each, less trade discount 20 per cent.
14 October Simmonds Services
            6 canteens cutlery, list price £30 each, less trade discount 25 per cent.
16 October Jenson Ltd
            6 bone china dinner services, list price £25 each, less trade discount 15 per cent.
18 October Coghlin Supplies
            1 china tea set, invoiced on 6 October, returned damaged.

All purchases are subject to Value Added Tax at 10 per cent.
    You are required to:
(1) Rule up appropriate day books to record the above transactions with columns headed:

Date	Name and details	List price less trade discount £ £	Value Added Tax	Total

(2) Write up the day books giving full details of each transaction.
(3) Complete the double entry, posting the day books to all of the necessary accounts in the ledger.

(Royal Society of Arts)

143

18.6

Paul Jones, the proprietor of Midland Radio and Television Services, has divided his business into two departments, Commercial sales and Servicing. His transactions for the week beginning 26 May 19–6, all of which are subject to the addition of value added tax (VAT) at 15 per cent, are as follows:

Credit purchases for resale

				£
May	26	G. Armstrong	television sets and radios	1,760
	27	S. Brown	spare parts for servicing	160

Credit sales

May	28	U. Nijam	radios	200
	29	H. Carr	television sets	1,340

Returns outwards

May	30	S. Brown	spare parts	40

Returns inwards

May	31	U. Nijam	radios	60

(a) You are required to show
   (i) the entries in the purchases, sales and returns analysed day books.
   (ii) the entries in the purchases, sales and nominal ledgers.
Note: the value added tax account is kept in the nominal ledger.
(b) What is the meaning of your balance brought down in the value added tax account?

(Joint Matriculation Board)

18.7

The Leafy Service Station has separate sections selling car tyres and exhaust systems. Credit purchases for the month of February 19–5 were:

4 February Ace Tyres Ltd. Invoice No. AT 1714
   40 tyres size 145 × 10 list price £15 each, less trade discount 25 per cent.
   30 tyres size 155 × 13 list price £20 each, less trade discount $33\frac{1}{3}$ per cent.
14 February Fast Exhausts Ltd. Invoice No. FE 762
   5 exhausts type MIN list price £20 each.
   10 exhausts type CAV list price £40 each.
   6 exhausts type DAT list price £50 each.
   All exhausts less trade discount 40 per cent.
25 February Ace Tyres Ltd. Invoice No. AT 1783
   50 tyres size 165 × 13 list price £24 each, less trade discount 25 per cent.
All transactions are subject to Value Added Tax at 10 per cent.
The suppliers do not allow any cash discount.

You are required to:
(a) Prepare a purchases day book with four columns, headed as follows:
   (1) Totals; (2) Tyres; (3) Exhausts; (4) Value Added Tax.
(b) Write up the day book for the month of February. It is the firm's policy to make entries in the book as and when each invoice is received, and to record there full details of the items bought and the total of each invoice.
(c) Post the items to the personal and nominal accounts in the ledger.

(Royal Society of Arts)

19 Trading and Profit and Loss Accounts and Balance Sheets

OBJECTIVES To understand the use and function of the trading and profit and loss accounts and balance sheets in providing the information from which the profits or losses made by a business are calculated. To consider the unsold stock of goods at the end of the accounting period and the classification of assets and liabilities on a balance sheet.

The Trading Account

The trading period or 'accounting period' of a business may cover any length of time, but it is generally one year. It is essential that the length of the accounting period should remain the same, otherwise the business cannot properly compare one period's achievements and results with another.

The trading account is a 'collecting together account', bringing together information from other accounts specifically for the purpose of ascertaining the gross profit (or loss) made by the business during the accounting period of trading. The gross profit is the amount by which the selling price exceeds the buying price of the merchandise in which the business normally deals.

The information required to draw up a trading account is contained in the nominal accounts in the general ledger, commencing with the purchases account and sales account. At the end of the accounting period, when the information has been transferred to the trading account, these accounts have served their purpose and are closed; new accounts are opened for the purchases and sales for the next trading period.

The double entry from the purchases account and the sales account to the trading account is carried out as follows:

Purchases Account

19–8		£	19–8		£
Dec 31 Balance b/d		3,350.00	Dec 31 Transfer to trading A/c		3,350.00

The purchases account has been closed by the credit entry – Transfer to Trading A/c; the debit entry will be in the trading account.

Sales Account

19–8			£	19–8			£
Dec	31	Transfer to Trading A/c	4,500.00	Dec	31	Balance b/d	4,500.00

The sales account has been closed by the debit entry – Transfer to Trading A/c; the credit entry will be in the trading account.

The full definition of gross profit in a business is, 'the amount by which, in a given period, the value of sales is greater than the cost of goods sold, without taking note of any expenses for selling, distribution or administration. It is represented by a credit balance in the trading account'.

However, the purchases will only equal 'the cost of goods sold' if all the goods purchased had been sold by the end of the accounting period, in this example, 31 December, 19–8. This is unlikely: generally there would be a stock of unsold goods. In order to calculate 'the cost of goods sold' the value, in money, of the stock of unsold goods must be found. The way to find the accurate value of the stock of unsold goods, is to carry out a stock-taking, after the close of business on a specific day. Stock-taking is the physical counting of all the stock of goods remaining on hand, after which it must be valued. Accountants follow the accounting convention of conservatism when valuing stock. This convention or rule requires accountants to be 'conservative' or cautious in their valuation; stock should be valued at a price which results in the lowest gross profit. For example, if the cost price of an article is £5.00 and the market price is £5.75, the stock will be valued at the cost price. The stock is thus valued at the lowest price. At this point a stock account is opened, and the amount of the value of unsold goods is placed at the debit side, as follows:

Stock Account

19–8			£		
Dec	31	Trading Account	500.00		

The debit balance remains on the Stock Account until the end of the next accounting period. It is then included in that year's trial balance and subsequently will become the opening stock for that year's trading and profit and loss accounts.

In order to calculate the gross profit, the amount of the value of the closing stock is required to be transferred to the trading account. To complete the double entry, the credit entry for the closing stock is in the trading account, as shown in the following example:

Trading Account for the Year Ended 31 December 19–8

	£		£
Purchases	3,350	Sales	4,500
Gross Profit c/d	1,650	Closing stock	500
	5,000		5,000
		Gross Profit b/d	1,650

The gross profit is the amount of the difference between the two sides of the Trading Account, but is not referred to as 'the balance'. Thus, £5,000 less £3,350 = £1,650 – gross profit.

In modern accounting methods the entry of the closing stock is shown as a deduction from the purchases at the debit side of the trading account, thus clearly showing 'the cost of goods sold'. The revised trading account would appear as follows:

Trading Account for the Year Ended 31 December 19–8

	£		£
Purchases	3,350	Sales	4,500
Less Closing Stock	500		
Cost of Goods Sold	2,850		
Gross Profit c/d	1,650		
	4,500		4,500
		Gross Profit b/d	1,650

Although the closing stock is now on the debit side of the trading account it is still the credit entry for the £500 on the stock account, because this item is now a deduction. This is an example of an important accounting principle: if an item on one side of an account is transferred for any reason to the other side it becomes an amount to be subtracted.

It is usual for the trading and profit and loss accounts to be shown under one combined heading, the trading account being the top section as illustrated above, and the profit and loss account being the lower section, commencing with the gross profit b/d.

Profit and Loss Account

Gross profit is the amount of profit the business has gained in the buying and selling of goods. However, during the period of trading many expenses will have been incurred, such as wages, rent, rates, insurance, telephone, electricity and so on. The profit when all of the expenses have been taken into consideration is the *net profit*.

Every transaction is recorded in a ledger account. Therefore, to find out the net profit or net loss, as the case may be, the information required is to be found in the remaining nominal accounts. At the end of the accounting period these accounts are closed, and the information is transferred to the profit and loss account. The profit and loss account commences with the gross profit from the trading account.

The double entry to close the nominal accounts and transfer to the profit and loss account is carried out as follows:

Wages Account

19–8		£	19–8		£
Dec 31	Balance b/d	325.00	Dec 31	Profit & Loss A/c	325.00

The wages account has been closed by the credit entry – Profit and Loss A/c; the debit entry will be in the profit and loss account. In the same way the remaining expense accounts are closed as follows:

Rent Account

19–8		£	19–8		£
Dec 31	Balance b/d	120.00	Dec 31	Profit & Loss A/c	120.00

Telephone Account

19–8		£	19–8		£
Dec 31	Balance b/d	66.00	Dec 31	Profit & Loss A/c	66.00

Motor Expenses Account

19–8		£	19–8		£
Dec 31	Balance b/d	85.00	Dec 31	Profit & Loss A/c	85.00

Electricity Account

19–8		£	19–8		£
Dec 31	Balance b/d	112.00	Dec 31	Profit & Loss A/c	112.00

Examine carefully the following illustration of the completed trading and profit and loss account.

Trading and Profit and Loss Account for the Year Ended 31 December 19–8

	£		£
Purchases	3,350	Sales	4,500
Less closing stock	500		
	———		
Cost of goods sold:	2,850		
Gross profit c/d	1,650		
	———		———
	4,500		4,500
	═══		═══
Wages	325	Gross profit b/d	1,650
Rent	120		
Telephone	66		
Motor expenses	85		
Electricity	112		
Net profit	942		
	———		———
	1,650		1,650
	═══		═══

The net profit is calculated by deducting the total of all the expenses for the accounting period from the gross profit – in the above example, the expenses total £708; when this figure is deducted from the gross profit of £1,650. There is a balance of £942, which is the net profit. If, however, the total amount of the expenses for the period had been greater than the amount of gross profit, the result would have been a net loss.

The procedures carried out in making these transfers have strictly observed the rules of double entry, namely, for every debit entry there is a corresponding credit entry – the credit entry for the net profit is made in the capital account. Net profit increases the capital of the proprietor; a net loss decreases the capital of the proprietor.

At 1 January 19–8 the Capital Account appeared as follows:

Capital Account

		19–8	£
		Jan 1 Cash	2,300

Any withdrawals by the proprietor, whether in cash or in goods, during the year are recorded in a separate drawings account. At 31 December 19–8 the drawings account appeared as follows:

Drawings Account

19–8	£		
Dec 31 Balance b/d	800		

Drawings reduce the capital. Therefore at the end of the accounting period the drawings account is closed and the total of the drawings for the period, will be transferred to the debit side of the capital account as follows:

Drawings Account

19–8			£	19–8			£
Dec	31	Balance b/d	800	Dec	31	Transfer to Capital	800

Capital Account

19–8			£	19–8			£
Dec	31	Drawings	800	Jan	1	Cash	2,300

The completed capital account for the year ending 31 December 19–8 is as follows:

Capital Account

19–8			£	19–8			£
Dec	31	Drawings	800	Jan	1	Cash	2,300
Dec	31	Balance c/d	2,442	Dec	31	Net Profit	942
			3,242				3,242
				19–9			
				Jan	1	Balance b/d	2,442

The trading and profit and loss accounts are prepared at the end of the trading period after the arithmetical accuracy of the books has been ascertained by the extracting of a trial balance. The following trial balance extracted on 31 December 19–8 has been used in the illustrations and examples already shown in this Module:

	Dr. £	Cr. £
Capital		2,300
* Sales		4,500
* Purchases	3,350	
* Wages	325	
* Rent	120	
* Telephone	66	
* Motor Expenses	85	
* Electricity	112	
Fixtures	700	
Debtors	620	
Creditors		890
Bank	1,474	
Cash	38	
Drawings	800	
	7,690	7,690

Stock at 31 December 19–8 was £500

In the above trial balance the 'balances' already used to draw up the trading and profit and loss account are marked by an asterisk. The remaining balances on the trial balance are now used to draw up a balance sheet.

The Balance Sheet

A balance sheet is a list of balances remaining on the accounts after the trading and profit and loss account have been completed. It is important to note that the balance sheet is a financial statement; it is *not* part of the double entry system, it is a classified summary listing the outstanding balances. All these remaining balances are arranged separately according to whether they are asset balances, liability balances or capital balances on a balance sheet. There are various ways in which a balance sheet can be presented, however, in most Stage I examinations, the conventional form of layout is most often used. This form of presentation is also known as the horizontal layout, the assets being listed at the left-hand side and the capital and liabilities listed at the right-hand side. A balance sheet must always be dated.

Classification of Assets

Fixed Assets

Fixed assets are for long-term use in the business and will remain the property of the business for long periods of time: the general rule for a fixed asset is more than one year.

Examples of fixed assets are premises, land, machinery, fixtures, furniture and fittings, motor vehicles. Fixed assets are listed and displayed in the order of 'permanence'; the most enduring item is entered first, successive items are positioned in decreasing order of permanence.

Current Assets

These are also called 'circulating assets' as they are assets which are continually being turned over and replaced: the general rule for a current asset is that it is to be kept by the business for less than one year. The word 'current' is derived from the French word 'courant' which means 'running'.

Examples of current assets are stock (closing stock at the end of the trading period), debtors, bank and cash. These are listed in the order of 'permanence' for realisation into cash.

Classification of Liabilities

Capital

The capital is the original investment in the business, by the owner of the business, and is contained in his capital account. The balance sheet will indicate how the balance on the capital account has been calculated: that is the capital at the start of the trading period, plus the net profit (or less a net loss), less the drawings, equals the capital at the end of the trading period. This is the net worth of the business and is known as the owner's equity.

Long-term Liabilities

These are usually formal loans of money from a bank, building society, private investor or a finance company. These types of liabilities are evidenced by a formal agreement or contract, stating (a) the amount of the loan, (b) the terms of repayment, (c) the rate of interest, and (d) the period of time – number of years of repayment. Examples of long-term liabilities are bank loans, private loans and mortgages.

Current Liabilities

These are amounts owed by the business in respect of debts, which are short-term, to be repaid in the near future. Examples of current liabilities are creditors and bank overdrafts.

A Balance Sheet has five main sections or subdivisions. The items and the amounts in each section are listed, and inset, under their respective headings. The total amount for each section is then extended. The conventional form of layout for the balance sheet is shown as follows:

	£	£		£	£
Fixed Assets			Capital at		
Fixtures		700	1 January 19–8	2,300	
			Add Net Profit	942	
Current Assets				3,242	
Stock	500		Less Drawings	800	2,442
Debtors	620				
Bank	1,474		*Current Liabilities*		
Cash	38	2,632	Creditors		890
		3,332			3,332

Points to Remember

Headings which are clear and concise are an essential requirement; they must also state the date of the period covered by the trading and profit and loss account and the balance sheet.

Gross profit is calculated in the trading account; this is the amount of the difference between 'the cost of goods sold' and the net sales figure. The 'cost of goods sold' is also known as 'the cost of sales'.

Net profit (or net loss) is calculated in the profit and loss account. Net profit increases the amount of the proprietor's capital in the business; net loss decreases it. In the case of a net loss, this would be made evident by the fact that the total amount of the expenses for the period would be greater than the amount of gross profit.

Any 'opening stock', which is the stock on hand at the start of the trading period, will be listed in the trial balance and dated for the first day of the new trading period. In the trading account any opening stock is entered as the first item; for example, opening stock plus the purchases, less closing stock. Each 'balance' contained within the trial balance is used *once* only in preparing the trading and profit and loss account and the balance sheet. The closing stock at the end of the trading period is *never* included within the trial balance; it is always shown separately. This figure is used in the trading account and also on the balance sheet, listed as the first of the current assets.

A balance sheet is not an account, it is an important financial statement, prepared to show the overall financial position of the business at the end of the accounting period, and is *not* part of the double entry system. The balances on these accounts are assets, liabilities or capital. These accounts are not closed; the balances are carried forward to the next accounting period.

When drawing up a Balance sheet, special attention is required with regard to a bank overdraft. If the bank account is overdrawn at the end of the accounting period, the amount of the overdraft would appear in the credit column of the trial balance. In this situation, it is not a current asset of the business. The amount by which the bank is overdrawn would appear on the balance sheet, under the heading of current liabilities, as it is an amount owing to the bank at the end of the accounting period.

The term 'final accounts' is sometimes used by examiners and means, collectively, the trading and profit and loss account and the balance sheet.

Assignment Exercises

19.1

From the following trial balance, taken from the books of Sandra Ramsden at 31 December 19–6, after one year's trading, prepare a trading and profit and loss account and a balance sheet as at that date.

Trial Balance as at 31 December 19–6

	Dr. £	Cr. £
Sales		20,662
Purchases	15,269	
Rent	650	
Insurance	155	
Motor Expenses	545	
Wages	2,568	
Equipment	2,850	
Motor Vehicle	1,100	
Debtors	2,350	
Creditors		1,682
Cash at Bank	1,864	
Cash in hand	68	
Drawings	925	
Capital		6,000
	28,344	28,344

Closing Stock 31 December 19–6 was £2,868.

19.2

From the following trial balance, taken from the books of Michael Seymour after one year's trading, draw up a trading and profit and loss account and a balance sheet for the year ending 31 December 19–7.

Trial Balance as at 31 December 19–7

	Dr. £	Cr. £
Capital		18,000
Cash at Bank	1,646	
Cash in Hand	122	
Debtors	2,865	
Creditors		1,926
Purchases	14,650	
Sales		18,874
Motor Vehicle	3,900	
Drawings	1,250	
Premises	7,700	
Fixtures & Fittings	1,750	
Rates	720	
General Expenses	490	
Wages and Salaries	3,105	
Motor Expenses	382	
Insurance	220	
	38,800	38,800

Stock on hand at 31 December 19–7 was £3,235.

19.3

The following trial balance was extracted from the books of Pauline Ellis. You are required to prepare the trading and profit & loss account for the year ended 31 May 19–7 and a balance sheet as at that date.

Trial Balance as at 31 May 19–7

	Dr. £	Cr. £
Capital		20,508
Debtors	3,670	
Creditors		2,018
Stock at 1 June 19–6	2,342	
Sales		27,974
Purchases	23,308	
Rent	760	
Lighting and Heating Expenses	520	
Salaries and Wages	2,950	
Fixtures and Fittings	2,500	
Cash at Bank	4,438	
Cash in Hand	170	
Insurance	280	
Motor Vehicles	6,750	
Motor Expenses	612	
Drawings	2,200	
	50,500	50,500

Stock at 31 May 19–7 was £5,995.

19.4

From the following trial balance, taken from the books of Frederick Allen, draw up a trading and profit and loss account for the year ending 31 October 19–7 and a balance sheet as at that date.

Trial Balance as at 31 October 19–7

	Dr. £	Cr. £
Sales		35,650
Purchases	28,452	
Stock at 1 November 19–6	5,425	
Premises	15,000	
Fixtures and Fittings	5,600	
Motor Vehicles	8,800	
Loan: T. Wiseman		6,000
Debtors	4,926	
Creditors		4,124
Rates	970	
Electricity	644	
General Expenses	933	
Salaries and Wages	3,850	
Insurance	617	
Drawings	2,450	
Bank Overdraft		2,326
Cash in Hand	338	
Motor Expenses	795	
Capital		30,700
	78,800	78,800

Stock at 31 October 19–7 was £4,965.

19.5

The figures of the following trial balance were extracted from the books of James Conway, a sole trader, as on 31 March 19–8.

Trial Balance as at 31 March 19–8

	Dr. £	Cr. £
Capital		38,200
Cash at Bank	13,326	
Cash in Hand	234	
Debtors	15,808	
Creditors		13,864
Stock at 1 April 19–7	16,940	
Motor Van	7,000	
Sales		45,736
Purchases	28,435	
Telephone	672	
Insurance	593	
Premises	12,000	
Rates	764	
Loan: J. Graham		5,000
General Expenses	316	
Wages	4,800	
Motor Expenses	412	
Drawings	1,500	
	102,800	102,800

Stock at 31 March 19–8 was £15,420.

You are required to prepare a trading and profit and loss account for the year ended 31 March 19–8, and a balance sheet as at that date.

20   Further Trading and Profit and Loss Accounts

OBJECTIVES   To consider further trading and profit and loss accounts. With an examination of returns inwards, returns outwards, carriage inwards and carriage outwards.

It has already been established that, during the course of business, goods are returned. The two ledger accounts which are concerned with the returning of goods are the returns inwards account and the returns outwards account. Any balances remaining on these accounts will need to be transferred to the trading account in order to calculate the net purchases and net sales figures.

Carriage inwards is the cost of transport incurred in delivering the goods purchased. This means a charge has been made for the conveyance of the goods purchased, and this charge will increase the price of those goods, therefore any carriage inwards must be added to the total purchases in the trading account. Carriage outwards is the cost incurred by the business in delivering the goods to its customers.

Returns Inwards

The 'turnover' of a business is the 'net sales figure'. 'Net' means 'remaining after necessary deductions'. In order to calculate the true net sales figure the value of any returns inwards (goods which have been returned by customers) should be deducted from the total sales. In the trading account the sales are shown less the value of any sales returns, as illustrated below:

Trading and Profit and Loss Account for the Year Ending 31 December 19–7

Sales	19,500	
Less Returns Inwards	350	19,150

Returns Outwards

'Purchases' in an ordinary business denotes the total of the cash and credit purchases of goods for resale. Returns outwards are goods which have been returned to the suppliers. The value of any purchase returns should be shown as a deduction from the total purchases in the trading account, to give the true and net figure for the purchases. This is carried out as follows:

Trading and Profit and Loss Account for the Year Ending 31 December 19–7

Opening Stock		3,495	Sales	19,500	
Purchases	12,120		Less Returns Inwards	350	19,150
Less Returns Outwards	436	11,684			
		15,179			

Carriage Inwards

Carriage inwards is the carriage paid on purchases (the goods for resale) coming into the business. Goods are sold either: (1) carriage paid, or (2) carriage forward. In the first case the seller pays the carriage; the goods are bought with carriage paid, and the transport costs are included in the purchase price. In the second case the cost of the carriage has to be paid by the buyer.

These costs are called carriage inwards and are kept in a separate ledger account. Carriage inwards is an additional cost to the purchases and consequently increases the cost of the goods purchased. It is an addition to the net purchases figure in the trading account. Carriage inwards is an expense, but as it is a direct cost related to the goods purchased and represents an increase in the purchase price, any carriage inwards increases the cost of the goods bought.

The completed trading account would appear as follows:

Trading and Profit and Loss Account for the Year Ending 31 December 19–7

Opening Stock		3,495	Sales	19,500	
Purchases	12,120		Less Returns Inwards	350	19,150
Less Returns Outwards	436	11,684			
		15,179			
Carriage Inwards		285			
		15,464			
Less Closing Stock		3,860			
		11,604			
Cost of Goods Sold:-		11,604			
Gross profit c/d		7,546			
		19,150		19,150	
			Gross profit b/d	7,546	

161

Carriage Outwards

The gross profit as shown by the trading account is carried down to the profit and loss account, and all the expenses incurred in the accounting period of trading are set against the gross profit in order to calculate net profit or net loss. Carriage outwards is an expense of selling and distribution and is *always* entered and debited in the profit and loss account.

Trading Account Expenses

As already illustrated, the cost of carriage inwards is an additional expense which increases the price of the goods purchased; similarly any costs incurred in bringing goods into a saleable condition may be required to be charged to the trading account. Such costs may include: warehouse costs, packing costs, labour or wages costs.

Under normal circumstances wages will appear in the profit and loss account. However, in examination questions you may be required to apportion part of the wages costs to the trading account; for example, one-quarter of the wages costs are to be charged to the trading account and three-quarters to the profit and loss account. Calculate the amounts by dividing the figure given for wages by four, to obtain one quarter. The amount should then be *added* in the trading account immediately before deducting the closing stock. The remaining three-quarters will appear at the debit side in the profit and loss account. Usually a specific instruction will be given if any part of labour, wages or any other item of expense is to be apportioned or included in the trading account.

Final Accounts of Non-traders

If the final accounts being prepared are for people who are *not* trading in goods, such as, for example, accountants, hairdressers, bookmakers and business consultants, there *will not* be a trading account, because goods are not bought and sold. The final accounts for providers of services will consist of a profit and loss account and a balance sheet. The profit and loss account will contain all items of revenue received at the credit side and all items of revenue expense at the debit side. The balance sheet will be *exactly* the same as for traders.

Revenue Received Accounts

All accounts which are expenses of the business are closed at the end of the accounting period by transfer to the trading account or to the profit and loss account. Similarly, any accounts which are revenues received by the business are closed at the end of the accounting period by transfer to the profit and loss account. The revenues received by the business are recognized by the word 'received' and include: rent received, commissions received, interest received and discounts received. These items will increase the profit and, therefore, are brought into the profit calculations as part of the profit and loss account. Any revenue received items are entered at the credit side of the profit and loss account.

The following trial balance, extracted on 31 December 19–7, has been used in the illustrations and examples already shown in this Module:

Trial Balance as at 31 December 19–7

	Dr.	Cr.
Stock at 1 January 19–7	3,495	
Sales		19,500
Purchases	12,120	
Returns Inwards	350	
Returns Outwards		436
Carriage Inwards	285	
Carriage Outwards	357	
Wages	3,260	
Rates	350	
Motor Expenses	475	
Electricity	586	
General Expenses	214	
Discount Allowed	248	
Discount Received		368
Premises	7,500	
Loan: D. Kent		3,000
Motor Vehicles	4,800	
Debtors	5,740	
Creditors		3,536
Cash at Bank	2,892	
Cash in Hand	378	
Drawings	1,450	
Capital		17,660
	£44,500	£44,500

Stock at 31 December 19–7 was £3,860.

The fully worked and completed trading and profit and loss account for the year ending 31 December 19–7 and a balance sheet as at that date is as follows:

Trading and Profit and Loss Account for the Year Ended 31 December 19-7

Opening Stock		3,495	Sales	19,500	
Purchases	12,120		Less Returns Inwards	350	19,150
Less Returns Outwards	436	11,684			
		15,179			
Carriage Inwards		285			
		15,464			
Less Closing Stock		3,860			
Cost of Goods Sold		11,604			
Gross Profit c/d		7,546			
		£19,150			£19,150
Carriage Outwards		357	Gross Profit b/d	7,546	
Wages		3,260	Discounts Received	368	7,914
Rates		350			
Motor Expenses		475			
Electricity		586			
General Expenses		214			
Discounts Allowed		248			
Net Profit		2,424			
		£ 7,914			£ 7,914

Balance Sheet as at 31 December 19-7

Fixed Assets			Capital	17,660	
Premises	7,500		Net Profit	2,424	
Motor Vehicles	4,800	12,300		20,084	
			Less Drawings	1,450	18,634
Current Assets					
Stock	3,860		*Long Term Liabilities*		
Debtors	5,740		Loan: D. Kent		3,000
Bank	2,892				
Cash	378	12,870	*Current Liabilities*		
			Creditors		3,536
		25,170			25,170

**POINTS TO
REMEMBER**

When the final accounts are being prepared 'after one year's trading' (this means it is the first year a person or firm has been in business trading) there will not be a figure in the trial balance for the 'opening stock'. The trading account will commence with the figure for 'purchases'. In subsequent years the trading account will commence with the figure of the 'opening stock'.

The 'turnover' of a business is the 'net sales figure'.

Returns inwards are goods which have been returned by customers. The value of any returns inwards should be deducted from the sales figure in the trading account.

Returns outwards are goods which have been returned to the suppliers. The value of any returns outwards should be deducted from the 'purchases' figure in the trading account.

Carriage inwards is a direct additional cost on purchases and, therefore, increases the price of the purchases. Carriage inwards is an expense on purchases and is debited in the trading account.

Carriage outwards is a selling expense and is *always* entered and debited in the profit and loss account. (Carriage inwards and carriage outwards are both expenses; both are 'debit balances' in the trial balance.)

Any 'balances' on the trial balance which are revenues received by the business will increase the profit. Any revenue received items are entered at the credit side of the profit and loss account.

Assignment Exercises

20.1

The following trial balance was extracted from the books of William Dyson on 31 December 19–7.

Trial Balance as at 31 December 19–7

	Dr.	Cr.
Capital		30,200
Debtors	14,950	
Creditors		10,735
Returns Inwards	562	
Returns Outwards		415
Cash at Bank	4,620	
Cash in Hand	513	
Stock: at 1 January 19–7	21,190	
Rent	1,855	
Wages and Salaries	9,890	
Carriage Outwards	251	
Insurance	365	
Carriage Inwards	204	
Sales		98,650
Purchases	76,990	
Motor Vehicle	5,500	
Motor Expenses	932	
Furniture and Fittings	4,420	
Drawings	2,330	
Loan: D. Conway		5,000
General Expenses	428	
	£145,000	£145,000

Stock at 31 December 19–7 was £22,560.

You are required to prepare the trading and profit and loss account for the year ended 31 December 19–7 and a balance sheet as at that date.

20.2

David Allen, a sole trader, extracted the following trial balance from his books at the close of business on 30 September 19–7

	Dr.	Cr.
Sales		69,480
Purchases	45,612	
Stock: 1 October 19–6	9,842	
Salaries and Wages	7,838	
Insurance	556	
Returns Inwards	872	
Returns Outwards		684
Rent and Rates	740	
Carriage Inwards	485	
Carriage Outwards	414	
Motor Expenses	526	
Discount Received		452
Discount Allowed	322	
Motor Vehicles	7,500	
Fixtures and Fittings	2,900	
Drawings	2,500	
Debtors	10,765	
Creditors		8,984
Cash at Bank	5,628	
Capital		16,900
	£96,500	£96,500

Stock at 30 September 19–7 was £8,975.

You are required to prepare the trading and profit and loss accounts for the year ended 30 September 19–7, together with a balance sheet as at that date.

20.3

John Roberts is a retail trader. From the following information prepare a trading and profit and loss account for the year ended 30 April 19–5 and a balance sheet on that date.

Trial Balance as at 30 April 19–5

	Dr.	Cr.
Capital on 1 May 19–4		24,640
Furniture and Equipment	9,400	
Sales		46,800
Postage and Stationery	1,680	
Returns Inwards	1,320	
Rates	760	
Insurance	450	
Wages and Salaries	7,480	
Purchases	27,510	
Drawings	5,000	
Trade Creditors		2,580
Carriage Inwards	270	
Cash in Hand	180	
Bank Balance		3,480
Sundry Expenses	430	
Stock: 1 May 19–4	6,560	
Loan from City Bank		3,000
Freehold Premises	16,500	
Trade Debtors	2,960	
	£80,500	£80,500

Stock at 30 April 19–5 was valued at £6,740.

20.4

The following trial balance was extracted from the books of James Giles on 31 December 19–6

	Dr.	Cr.
Capital		25,090
Equipment	6,000	
Furniture and Fittings	3,700	
Sales		36,000
Purchases	27,500	
Drawings	4,800	
Carriage Outwards	490	
Trade Creditors		5,980
Sundry Expenses	322	
Cash in Hand	170	
Cash at Bank	3,792	
Returns Outwards		1,250
Carriage Inwards	430	
Wages	5,880	
Printing and Stationery	390	
Trade Debtors	9,700	
Rent	550	
Insurance	226	
Commissions Received		480
Stock at 1 January 19–6	4,850	
	£68,800	£68,800

Stock on 31 December 19–6 was valued at £6,500.

You are required to prepare the trading and profit and loss account for the year ended 31 December 19–6 and a balance sheet as at that date.

20.5

Nicholas Davidson is a retail trader. From the figures below prepare his trading and profit and loss account for the year ended 30 September 19–7 and a balance sheet on that date.

	Dr.	Cr.
Salaries	8,250	
Rent and Rates	1,500	
Cash in Hand	120	
Bank balance		2,890
Debtors	8,810	
Creditors		5,650
Returns Inwards	580	
Sundry Expenses	256	
Stock at 1 October 19–6	5,995	
Carriage Outwards	397	
Discounts Received		842
Motor Vehicles	9,400	
Insurances	564	
Telephone	290	
Sales		38,800
Purchases	28,640	
Capital: 1 October 19–6		25,218
Vehicle Expenses	768	
Fixtures and Fittings	8,500	
Drawings	4,330	
Loan from City Bank		5,000
	£78,400	£78,400

Stock at 30 September 19–7 was £6,870.

20.6

Brian Stone, a sole trader, extracted the following trial balance from his books at the close of business on 31 October 19–7

	Dr.	Cr.
Freehold Land and Buildings	25,000	
Motor Van	3,500	
Purchases	62,880	
Sales		84,600
Cash at Bank	2,990	
Cash in Hand	520	
Stock at 1 November 19–6	4,740	
Debtors	7,500	
Creditors		4,950
Carriage Inwards	675	
Carriage Outwards	890	
Motor Expenses	465	
Rates	750	
Sundry Expenses	390	
Sales Returns	820	
Drawings	3,500	
Stationery and Printing	376	
Purchase Returns		982
Discounts Allowed	246	
Discounts Received		378
Wages and Salaries	9,058	
Capital at 1 November 19–6		33,390
	£124,300	£124,300

Stock at 31 October 19–7 was valued at £7,650.

You are required to prepare the trading and profit and loss account for the year ended 31 October 19–7 and a balance sheet as at that date.

21 Calculating Depreciation for Fixed Assets

OBJECTIVES   To consider the reasons and the necessity for depreciation and to examine in detail the two main methods used in its calculation.

Initially when considering depreciation it is important to recognise the reasons for depreciation, as these are directly concerned with establishing the 'accurate value' of the fixed assets which are shown on the balance sheet.

It has been emphasised earlier that a balance sheet is an important classified financial statement, and it should always represent a 'true and fair view' of the financial position of a business. This 'true and fair view' is applied to all the information contained on the balance sheet. It is essential therefore, that the fixed assets which have been acquired by a business should be expressed on the balance sheet, as close as possible to their 'true value'.

The fixed assets acquired by a firm are primarily intended for long-term use in the business, and will usually remain the property of the business for some considerable time. During their continuous use, over a number of years, the fixed assets earn profits for a business, but, with the exception of land, they do not last indefinitely, and most fixed assets suffer from deterioration.

Some fixed assets, such as machinery or motor vehicles, are being used continuously over a period of time, and consequently have a limited productive life. The market value of these fixed assets will inevitably decrease. Each year, in order to determine the true monetary value of a fixed asset, the amount of its decrease in value should be taken into consideration, otherwise the true value would be overstated on the balance sheet.

Depreciation is a reduction in value, due usually to normal wear and tear. By calculating the anticipated amount of the depreciation each year, a business can effectively reduce the value of a fixed asset. Depreciation is a means of 'spreading the cost' of a fixed asset over its estimated life and period of use by a business. This is achieved by calculating and deducting an estimated amount each year, which will give an appreciation of the fixed asset as close as possible to its true value.

Depreciation can be defined as the part of the cost of the fixed asset which is 'used up' during its period of use by the business. It is an expense, in the same way as costs for such items as wages, rent, insurance and so on. The amount calculated for the cost of depreciation is an expense of the business, and at the end of the financial year it will need to be charged to the profit and loss account.

The double entry accounting for depreciation is covered in detail in Module 22.

Calculating depreciation involves three important considerations:

(a) The original cost.
(b) The anticipated life of the fixed asset.
(c) The estimated disposal value (if any).

The original cost is the expenditure involved in acquiring the fixed asset. The anticipated life of the fixed asset is an estimate of the period of time it will be kept and used by the business. The estimated disposal value is an estimate of its approximate monetary value to the business, at the end of its period of use. Such 'value' is also referred to as the 'residual value', which is sometimes abbreviated to 'RV'. This 'forecast of its life' is determined by, and usually based upon, the previous experience of similar types of fixed assets.

Methods of Calculating Depreciation

There are several ways of calculating the depreciation charge, and the method selected will invariably depend upon the circumstances and the type of fixed asset. The two main methods are the straight line method and the reducing balance method.

The Straight Line Method

This is the most widely used method for calculating depreciation. By this method the cost of the fixed asset, less any estimated disposal value, is divided equally by the number of years' use. For example, a motor vehicle cost £15,000; it is anticipated it will be kept for three years; and it has an estimated disposal value of £3,000. This may be expressed as follows:

Cost: £15,000 less £3,000 (disposal value) = £12,000 divided by 3 = £4,000, which is the depreciation charge for each of the 3 years.

The calculations would be as follows:

(£15,000 − £3,000 = £12,000, divided by 3 = £4,000) or, expressed as a fraction:

$$\text{Annual Depreciation} = \frac{£15,000 - £3,000}{3} = £4,000$$

	£
Cost	15,000
Depreciation 1st year	4,000
	11,000
Depreciation 2nd year	4,000
	7,000
Depreciation 3rd year	4,000
Disposal value	3,000

173

With this method the charge for depreciation is the same each year. It is also known as the fixed instalment method.

The Reducing Balance Method

By this method the fixed asset is depreciated by a fixed percentage. The fixed percentage is deducted in the first year, and in subsequent years the same percentage is taken, but of the reduced balance.

Consider the following example. A business buys a machine costing £7,500. It will be kept for four years and then sold for an estimated figure of £1,800. The depreciation is to be calculated on the reducing balance method at a rate of 30 per cent. The calculations to the nearest pound, would be as follows:

	£
Cost	7,500
1st year – depreciation at 30% (of £7,500)	2,250
	5,250
2nd year – depreciation at 30% (of £5,250)	1,575
	3,675
3rd year – depreciation at 30% (of £3,675)	1,103
	2,572
4th year – depreciation at 30% (of £2,572)	772
Estimated disposal value	1,800

Using the reducing balance method the effect will be evident, in that much higher amounts are charged for depreciation in the early years of the assets life, and considerably less during the later years. The reducing balance method is also known as the diminishing balance method.

The purpose of depreciation is effectively to spread the original cost of the fixed asset, less any disposal value, over its expected useful life.

It is important to note that depreciation does NOT provide a reserve fund for the replacement of the fixed assets at the end of their life, it is merely a way of spreading the cost over a period of time.

Depreciation Charge for Part of a Year

Fixed assets can be bought or sold at any time during the year. However, calculating the charge for depreciation usually takes place at the end of the financial year, before the preparation of the final accounts. When a fixed asset is bought or sold during an accounting period this can create a problem.

In practice the normal procedure is to provide for a full year's depreciation in the year of purchase, and make no charge for depreciation in the year of sale.

In examination questions, however, unless it is otherwise indicated, the student will be expected to calculate and determine the depreciation charge for the part of the year of ownership, and apportion the charge on a monthly basis. In other words, in the first year, it would be necessary to calculate the actual number of months of ownership; the charge for depreciation is then made on the basis of each month's ownership.

Consider the following example: a business which prepares its accounts annually to 31 December purchased a new motor van costing £15,000 on 1 July 19–4. It is anticipated that the van will be kept for four years and it is decided to calculate depreciation at the rate of 40 per cent on the reducing balance method. You are required to show the calculations of depreciation for each year, from the year of purchase to the year ending 31 December 19–7.

Solution: The motor van was purchased on 1 July 19–4. The charge for depreciation for the year ending 31 December 19–4 should be for six months (the number of months of ownership). This is calculated as follows: 40 per cent of £15,000 is £6,000, divided by 12 = £500 per month. This figure is then multiplied by six, the number of months of ownership, which gives £3,000. This is the depreciation charge for the year 19–4.

The calculations would be shown as follows:

	£
Cost	15,000
19–4 Depreciation at 40% (six months)	3,000
	12,000
19–5 Depreciation at 40%	4,800
	7,200
19–6 Depreciation at 40%	2,880
	4,320
19–7 Depreciation at 40%	1,728
Disposal value	2,592

POINTS TO REMEMBER   Depreciation means a reduction in value, due usually to normal wear and tear.

The purpose of depreciation is to reduce the original cost of the fixed asset, in order to show its accurate value.

The straight line method of depreciation reduces the original cost of the fixed asset by the same amount for each year. This is expressed as: the original cost, less any disposal value, divided by the number of years' use.

The reducing balance method is calculated by using a fixed percentage. The original cost is reduced by the fixed percentage. In subsequent years the same percentage is taken, but of the reduced balance. This method gives a higher depreciation charge in the early years of the assets life, and less in the later years. This is sometimes an advantage, as the cost of repairs often increases towards the end of the expected working life.

Assignment Exercises

All calculations to the nearest pound.

21.1

A packing machine is purchased for £20,000. The business plans to use it for five years, and it is estimated that at the end of that time it will have a disposal value of £5,000. The depreciation is to be calculated by the straight line method. You are required to calculate the amount of depreciation for each year.

21.2

John Preston purchased a delivery van costing £8,000 on 1 January 19–7. He anticipated he would keep it for three years; it would then be sold for an estimated figure of £2,744. He decided to calculate depreciation on the delivery van at the rate of 30 per cent per annum, by the reducing balance method. Show the depreciation calculations for each of the three years.

21.3

A fork-lift machine is purchased for £10,500. It is anticipated it will be kept for four years and at the end of that time its residual value is estimated to be £2,520. You are required to show your calculations of the figures for depreciation for each of the four years using (a) the straight line method and (b) the reducing balance method at a rate of 30 per cent.

21.4

A firm purchased a machine costing £3,000 in July 19–7. It is estimated it will have a life of five years, and a disposal value at the end of this time of £712. Accounts are prepared to 31 December in each year and a full year's depreciation is provided in the year of purchase. You are required to show your calculations of the figures for depreciation for each of the five years, using (a) the straight line method and (b) the reducing balance method at a rate of 25 per cent.

21.5

D. Armstrong's accounts are prepared to 31 December each year. He provides for depreciation of his motor vehicles at the rate of 20 per cent per annum on the diminishing balance method. On 1 January 19–5 Armstrong bought a new motor van at a cost of £6,500. On 1 April 19–6 Armstrong purchased a further delivery van at a cost of £7,500.

You are required to show your calculations for depreciation, for each vehicle, for the years to 31 December 19–7.

21.6

A business which prepares its accounts annually to 30 June depreciates all its machinery at the rate of 30 per cent per annum, on the reducing balance method. The details of the machines and the dates of purchase are as follows:

	£
Machine Type 'M' purchased on 1 August 19–5 cost	3,000
Machine Type 'D' purchased on 1 January 19–6 cost	4,000
Machine Type 'W' purchased on 1 June 19–6 cost	5,000
Machine Type 'B' purchased on 1 March 19–7 cost	6,000

You are required to show your calculations of depreciation for each machine, for each year, from the year of purchase to the year ending 30 June 19–8.

22 The Double Entry System for Depreciation

OBJECTIVES To consider the entries required in recording the depreciation charges in the double entry accounts, the sale of fixed assets and the collecting together of the relevant information.

The accounting records are exactly the same for both the straight line method and the reducing balance method of calculating the charges for depreciation. It is the *amounts* which vary according to the method chosen.

In Module 21 it was established that the charges made for depreciation reduce the value of the fixed asset. The amount of the depreciation charge each year is an expense of the business, and is set against the profits earned by the business, at the end of the financial year. There are two methods of recording the depreciation in the double entry accounts.

Method 1 Direct Depreciation

By this method the depreciation is shown in the fixed asset account, reducing the value of the asset each year, and in a depreciation expense account. The double entry is: debit the depreciation expense account; credit the fixed asset account.

Consider the following example: on 1 January 19–6 a firm bought a new motor van costing £8,000. It is to be depreciated at the rate of 25 per cent per annum, using the reducing balance method. The double entry accounts for the year ending 31 December 19–6 would appear as follows:

Motor Van Account

19–6			£	19–6			£
Jan	1	Bank	8,000.00	Dec	31	Depreciation	2,000.00
					31	Balance c/d	6,000.00
			8,000.00				8,000.00
19–7							
Jan	1	Balance b/d	6,000.00				

Depreciation Account

19–6		£		
Dec	31 Motor Van	2,000.00		

Depreciation is an expense, and at the end of the accounting period will need to be charged to the profit and loss account. The double entry to close the depreciation account and transfer to the profit and loss account is carried out as follows:

Depreciation Account

19–6		£	19–6		£
Dec	31 Motor Van	2,000.00	Dec	31 Profit & Loss A/c	2,000.00

The depreciation account has been closed by the credit entry – Profit and Loss A/c. The debit entry will be in the profit and loss account, as follows:

Profit and Loss Account for the Year Ended 31 December 19–6

Depreciation	2,000.00	

On the balance sheet the value of the fixed asset, in this example the motor van, is shown at its original cost in the first year, less the depreciation charges to date. The balance sheet entry for the year ending 31 December 19–6 would appear as follows:

Balance Sheet as at 31 December 19–6

Fixed Assets			
Motor Van	8,000.00		
Less Depreciation	2,000.00	6,000.00	

In subsequent years the value of the fixed asset, in this example the motor van, is decreased in the ledger account and appears on the balance sheet at the reduced figure.

The following is an illustration of the completed ledger accounts, using the same example, for the first three years, 19–6, 19–7 and 19–8

Motor Van Account

19–6		£	19–6			£
Jan	1 Bank	8,000.00	Dec	31 Depreciation		2,000.00
				31 Balance c/d		6,000.00
		8,000.00				8,000.00
19–7			19–7			
Jan	1 Balance b/d	6,000.00	Dec	31 Depreciation		1,500.00
				31 Balance c/d		4,500.00
		6,000.00				6,000.00
19–8			19–8			
Jan	1 Balance b/d	4,500.00	Dec	31 Depreciation		1,125.00
				31 Balance c/d		3,375.00
		4,500.00				4,500.00
19–9						
Jan	1 Balance b/d	3,375.00				

Depreciation Account

19–6		£	19–6		£
Dec	31 Motor Van	2,000.00	Dec	31 Profit & Loss A/c	2,000.00
19–7			19–7		
Dec	31 Motor Van	1,500.00	Dec	31 Profit & Loss A/c	1,500.00
19–8			19–8		
Dec	31 Motor Van	1,125.00	Dec	31 Profit & Loss A/c	1,125.00

The entries in the profit and loss accounts for the three years would appear as follows:

Profit and Loss Account for the year Ending 31 December 19–6

Depreciation	2,000.00	

Profit and Loss Account for the Year Ending 31 December 19–7

Depreciation	1,500.00

Profit and Loss Account for the Year Ending 31 December 19–8

Depreciation	1,125.00

The balance sheet entries for the years 19–6, 19–7 and 19–8 would appear as set out below.

Note: The fixed asset, the motor van, is shown at its original cost in the first year, in the later years at the *reduced* value, as shown in the ledger account.

Balance Sheet as at 31 December 19–6

Fixed Assets		
Motor Van	8,000.00	
Less Depreciation	2,000.00	6,000.00

Balance Sheet as at 31 December 19–7

Fixed Assets		
Motor Van	6,000.00	
Less Depreciation	1,500.00	4,500.00

Balance Sheet as at 31 December 19–8

Fixed Assets		
Motor Van	4,500.00	
Less Depreciation	1,125.00	3,375.00

Method 2   Providing for Depreciation

With this method the fixed asset account remains at its original cost, and no entries for depreciation are made in the fixed asset account. Instead the amount of depreciation deducted each year is accumulated in a separate account called a provision for depreciation account.

The Companies Act 1948 introduced the requirement for companies that the assets must be shown on the balance sheet at 'cost price less accumulated depreciation to date'. At the present time this is not a legal requirement for sole traders but it is rapidly becoming normal practice for most businesses to conform with this requirement.

This method of providing for depreciation in a separate account facilitates matters by making the required information readily available, and therefore has generally replaced the former practice of reducing the value of the fixed asset account. The double entry is: debit the profit and loss account; credit the provision for depreciation account – with the amount of the depreciation charge for the year.

Using the same example, to assist comparison, the following is an illustration, showing the double entry accounts using Method 2. On 1 January 19–6 a firm bought a new motor van costing £8,000. It is to be depreciated at the rate of 25 per cent per annum, using the reducing balance method. The double entry accounts for the years ending 31 December 19–6, 19–7 and 19–8 would appear as follows:

Motor Van Account

19–6			£				
Jan	1 Bank		8,000.00				

Provision for Depreciation Account – Motor Van

19–6			£	19–6			£
Dec	31 Balance c/d		2,000.00	Dec	31 Profit & Loss A/c		2,000.00
19–7				19–7			
Dec	31 Balance c/d		3,500.00	Jan	1 Balance b/d		2,000.00
				Dec	31 Profit & Loss A/c		1,500.00
			3,500.00				3,500.00
19–8				19–8			
Dec	31 Balance c/d		4,625.00	Jan	1 Balance b/d		3,500.00
				Dec	31 Profit & Loss A/c		1,125.00
			4,625.00				4,625.00
				19–9			
				Jan	1 Balance b/d		4,625.00

The entries in the profit and loss accounts for the three years would appear as follows:

Profit and Loss Account for the Year Ending 31 December 19–6

Depreciation	2,000.00	

Profit and Loss Account for the Year Ending 31 December 19–7

Depreciation	1,500.00	

Depreciation	1,125.00	

Note: With this method the balance sheet entry always shows the original cost of the fixed asset, as recorded in the fixed asset account, less the balance on the provision for depreciation account.

The balance sheet entries for the three years would appear as follows:

Balance Sheet as at 31 December 19–6

Fixed Assets		
Motor Van at cost	8,000.00	
Less Depreciation	2,000.00	6,000.00

Balance Sheet as at 31 December 19–7

Fixed Assets		
Motor Van at cost	8,000.00	
Less Depreciation		
to date . . .	3,500.00	4,500.00

Balance Sheet as at 31 December 19–8

Fixed Assets		
Motor Van at cost	8,000.00	
Less Depreciation		
to date . . .	4,625.00	3,375.00

A balance sheet should always represent a 'true and fair view'; with this method the fixed asset is shown at its accurate value, that is, the original cost price less the total amount of depreciation charges to date. This value is called its *net book value*. For each individual fixed asset account there should also be a separate provision for depreciation account.

This method is now generally preferred and is used extensively in many businesses. The accounting principles for both methods of depreciation have been fully covered in this module to accommodate the syllabus requirements of the various Examination Boards.

Selling an Asset

The annual charge made for the depreciation of a fixed asset is an estimate of its fall in value during each year's use by the business. The disposal or residual value is an estimate of its value when it is sold. Only when the fixed asset is scrapped or sold will the true accuracy of the estimates be ascertained.

When the fixed asset is sold, the amount received (if any) may not be exactly the same as the net book value. It may be sold for more than its net book value, in which case there would be a profit on disposal. Similarly the fixed asset may be sold for less than its net book value, in which case there would be a loss on disposal. The difference is, in fact, an over-/or an under-depreciation charge in the estimates.

Consider the following example: on 1 February 19–9 the motor van was sold for £3,500. The net book value of the motor van is £3,375. This would give a gain or profit on the sale of £125.

The accounting entries required for the disposal of a fixed asset are as follows:

(a) Open a fixed asset disposals account – a debit entry with the original cost price of the fixed asset – motor van £8,000.

Motor Van – Disposal Account

19–9		£		
Jan	1 Motor Van	8,000.00		

The credit entry is in the motor van account, showing the original cost price of the motor van.

Motor Van Account

19–6		£	19–9		£
Jan	1 Bank	8,000.00	Feb	1 Disposal Account	8,000.00

(b) A debit entry in the provision for depreciation account – motor van, to transfer the accumulated depreciation.

Provision for Depreciation Account – Motor Van

19–9		£	19–9		£
Feb	1 Disposal Account	4,625.00	Jan	1 Balance b/d	4,625.00

The credit entry is in the Motor Van Disposal Account.

Motor Van – Disposal Account

19–9		£	19–9		£
Feb	1 Motor Van	8,000.00	Feb	1 Prov. Depreciation	4,625.00

For the remittance received on disposal: a debit entry in the bank account:

Cash Book – (Bank column)

19–9		£	
Feb	1 Motor Van	3,500.00	

The credit entry for the remittance is in the motor van – disposal account.

Motor Van – Disposal Account

19–9		£	19–9		£
Feb	1 Motor Van	8,000.00	Feb	1 Prov. Depreciation	4,625.00
			Feb	1 Bank	3,500.00

When the fixed asset is over-depreciated and sold for a sum greater than the estimated disposal value, this profit will be transferred, at the end of the financial year, to the profit and loss account. The completed entries, showing the transfer at the end of the financial year are as follows. The debit entry would appear in the motor van disposal account:

Motor Van – Disposal Account

19–9		£	19–9		£
Feb	1 Motor Van	8,000.00	Feb	1 Prov. Depreciation	4,625.00
Dec	31 Profit & Loss A/c	125.00		1 Bank	3,500.00
		8,125.00			8,125.00

The credit entry would appear in the Profit and Loss Account as follows:

Profit and Loss Account for the Year Ending 31 December 19–9

	Profit on sale of Motor Van	125.00

Examine now the situation when the fixed asset is under-depreciated and sold for a sum less than the estimated disposal value. For example, if the motor van was sold on 1 February 19–9 for £3,000 and the net book value of the motor van is £3,375, this would result in a loss on the sale of £375.

The amount of the remittance received from the sale of the motor van, in this situation would be £3,000. The accounting entries now required in the motor van disposal account, and the corresponding entry in the profit and loss account, would appear as follows. A credit entry on 31 December 19–9 in the motor van disposal account:

Motor Van – Disposal Account

19–9		£	19–9			£
Feb	1 Motor Van	8,000.00	Feb	1	Prov.	4,625.00
					Depreciation	
				1	Bank	3,000.00
			Dec	31	Profit & Loss A/c	375.00
		8,000.00				8,000.00

A debit entry in the Profit and Loss Account, the vehicle was under-depreciated, a loss on the sale:

Profit and Loss Account for the Year Ending 31 December 19–9

Loss on sale of Motor Van	375.00	

The 'fixed asset – disposal account' is a 'collecting together' account which effectively brings together all the information relevant to the disposal of the fixed asset.

The accumulating balance on the provision for depreciation account does *not* represent putting aside sums of money; it is the part of the cost of the fixed asset which is used up during its period of use by the business.

POINTS TO REMEMBER

The two main ways of calculating the amount of depreciation to be charged are the straight line method and the reducing balance method.

Whichever method is adopted, or requested in examinations, the double entry records are the same – it is the *amounts* which vary according to the method used.

Depreciation is an expense, and, as with all expenses, the depreciation charge for each year will need to be transferred to the profit and loss account. Method 1 – Direct Depreciation: the depreciation charges are shown in the fixed asset's account, reducing its value each year, and in a depreciation expense account. On the balance sheet the fixed asset is shown at its reduced value.

Method 2 – Providing for depreciation: This is the more modern method and generally preferred. By this method the amount of the depreciation is calculated each year and entered in a provision for depreciation account. The depreciation accumulates in this account each year. On the balance sheet the fixed asset is shown at the original cost price, less the total amount of all the depreciation charges to date. This amount is called the 'net book value'.

When a fixed asset is sold, all the information relevant to the particular fixed asset is brought together in the disposal account.

Assignment Exercises

22.1
Graham Dyson purchased machinery for £3,000 in April 19–3. It is expected to have an effective working life of five years and its estimated disposal value at the end of this period is £712.

You are required to show the machinery and the provision for depreciation of machinery accounts for the five years, calculating depreciation at a rate of 25 per cent per annum on the reducing balance method. Accounts are prepared annually to 31 December and a full year's depreciation is provided in the year of purchase.

22.2
David Allen purchased a vehicle costing £23,000 on 1 January 19–3. Its life is anticipated to be five years. At the end of this time it is estimated to be worth £3,000. A provision for depreciation is to be established and depreciation charges calculated on the fixed instalment method. Accounts are prepared to 31 December each year.

You are required to prepare the vehicle account and the provision for depreciation account for the five years to 31 December 19–7, and to show the balance sheet entry at the end of each year.

22.3
Brian Tate purchased machinery costing £25,000 in March 19–5. It is the firm's policy to depreciate machinery by direct depreciation on the machinery account, using the reducing balance method at a rate of 20 per cent per annum. The financial year ends on 30 September and a full year's depreciation is charged in the year of purchase.

You are required to show the entries for three years, 19–5, 19–6 and 19–7, on the machinery account, the depreciation account, the profit and loss account and the relevant balance sheet entries.

22.4
James Clayton purchased a motor van for £10,800, paying by cheque on 1 June 19–5. It was estimated he would keep it for three years, providing depreciation at a rate of $33\frac{1}{3}$ per cent per annum by the diminishing balance method. On 1 June

19–8 the van was sold for £3,000 cash. The final accounts are prepared to 31 May each year.

You are required to write up for the years 19–5, 19–6, 19–7, 19–8 and 19–9

(a) (i) the motor van account
    (ii) the provision for depreciation account
   (iii) the disposal account
(b) the relevant extract entries in the profit and loss accounts;
(c) the relevant extract entries of the balance sheets.

22.5

The financial year end of William Evans, a sole trader, is 31 December each year. On 4 January 19–5 he purchased machinery costing £15,500, paying by cheque. Evans plans to use the machinery for four years and estimates that at the end of that time its residual value will be £3,000.

A provision for depreciation was established and depreciation was calculated on the fixed instalment method. On 3 January, 19–9 the machinery was sold for £3,250.

You are required to draw up for the years 19–5, 19–6, 19–7, 19–8 and 19–9:

(a) The machinery account;
(b) the provision for depreciation account;
(c) the disposal account;
(d) the relevant extracts for each year including the year of sale, in the profit and loss account and the balance sheet.

22.6

(i) What is meant by depreciation and why is it important that a businessman should provide for depreciation in his accounts?
(ii) On 1 January 19–6 A. Swain, a haulage contractor, purchased three tipper lorries for £4,800 each. Mr Swain estimated that his lorries would have an effective working life of five years with a disposal value of £300 each. The straight line method of depreciation is to be used. The financial year ends on 31 December. One of the lorries kept breaking down and was sold on 1 January 19–8 for £2,500.

You are required to show the relevant entries for the years 19–6, 19–7 and 19–8 in the following ledger accounts:

(a) Lorries.
(b) Lorries disposal.
(c) Provision for depreciation on lorries.

All workings are to be shown.

(Royal Society of Arts)

22.7

The financial year end of Hodgson (Builders Merchants) Ltd is 31 December. The company's policy is to depreciate its motor vans at 20 per cent per annum, using the straight line method, and to calculate a full year's depreciation on the assets in existence at the end of the financial year, regardless of when they were purchased or sold. The company's vans were purchased and sold as follows:

			£
1 January 19–9	Purchased	AB 101 T	2,500
1 July 19–0	Purchased	CD 202 V	3,000
31 March 19–1	Purchased	EF 303 W	2,000
31 March 19–1	Sold	AB 101 T	1,000
1 April 19–2	Purchased	GH 404 X	3,500
31 August 19–2	Sold	CD 202 V	2,000

You are required to draw up for the years 19–9, 19–0, 19–1 and 19–2:

(a)   (i) the motor van account,
    (ii) the provision for depreciation of motor vans account,
    (iii) the disposal of motor vans account;
(b) extracts of the profit and loss acounts;
(c) extracts of the balance sheets.

(Joint Matriculation Board)

23 Bad Debts and the Provision for Bad and Doubtful Debts

OBJECTIVES To understand that bad debts are debts which are likely never to be paid, and how these matters are dealt with using the double entry system. With regard to the provision for bad and doubtful debts, to consider the providing of a reserve fund to guard against the possibility of some debtors failing to pay their accounts, by setting aside money from the profits of the business.

Bad Debts

Most transactions in business are conducted on a credit basis, and the majority of customers do meet their obligations. Credit is not usually given to customers until references have been obtained regarding their ability to pay their debts and their creditworthiness. However, occasionally it may happen that a customer, sometimes through no fault of his own, is not in a position to pay his account. A debtor who cannot pay his debt is called a 'bad' debtor, and the debt owing is referred to as a 'bad debt'. Usually many attempts will have been made in an effort to recover the outstanding amount but, whatever the reason or circumstances, if a debtor cannot pay what is owed and the amount becomes irrecoverable, it is a business loss, and must be treated in the same way as other losses and expenses.

Consider the following example of a debt which is entirely bad: On 1 July 19–7 Edward Hemingway is a debtor for the sum of £95. He is declared bankrupt on 8 July 19–7 and we are informed the amount will not be paid. It is decided to write the debt off as a bad debt. Edward Hemingway's account in the sales ledger would appear as follows:

Edward Hemingway Account		
July 1 Balance b/d	95.00	

When it becomes necessary for a bad debt to be written off, the procedure is as follows: Open a bad debts account; debit the bad debts account with the amount of the bad debt – this is the amount outstanding on the debtor's account.

Bad Debts Account

July 8 Edward Hemingway 95.00	

To complete the double entry, and close the debtor's account, the corresponding credit entry will appear at the credit side of Edward Hemingway's Account, as follows:-

Edward Hemingway Account

July 1 Balance b/d 95.00	July 8 Bad Debts A/c 95.00

There is no point or advantage in continuing to maintain the debtor's account in the ledger; it is no longer an asset, and therefore it is closed. The debtor's account in the sales ledger would be clearly marked *bad debtor*, to prevent any further credit being made available in the future.

The bad debts account is a 'collecting together' account of all the bad debts incurred during the accounting period. *Only* at the end of the accounting period is the bad debts account totalled and the total transferred, by means of a credit entry, to the debit side of the profit and loss account. Bad debts are an expense, and are taken, with the other expenses incurred during the financial year, to the profit and loss account. At the end of the financial year 31 December 19–7 the bad debts account would appear as follows:

Bad Debts Account

July 8 Edward Hemingway 95.00	Dec 31 Profit & Loss 95.00

The entry in the Profit and Loss Account would appear as follows:

Profit and Loss Account for the Year Ending 31 December 19–7

	£		£
Bad Debts	95.00	Gross Profit b/d	3,688.00

In certain circumstances, if a debtor is declared bankrupt or goes into voluntary liquidation he (or perhaps in the case of a bereavement, the estate of the debtor) will only be able to pay a 'composition' or dividend of so much in the pound of the outstanding debt. (This is an agreement to settle the debt by payment of a lesser amount.) In these cases the amount received will be debited in the bank account or cash account, and the same amount credited to the debtor's personal account. The balance remaining on the debtor's account is a bad debt and clearly should be written off.

Consider the following example of a debt which is partially bad: on 1 August 19–7 Brian Forbes is a debtor for goods supplied for £268. He goes into voluntary liquidation, and after negotiation the firm agrees to accept a payment of 50 pence in the pound in full settlement of the debt. A cheque is received on 22 August 19–7. The Brian Forbes account in the sales ledger would appear as follows:

Brian Forbes Account

Aug 1 Balance b/d	268.00	

A cheque for £134 is received. This will be debited in the bank account:

Bank Account

Aug 22 Brian Forbes	134.00	

The credit entry will appear in the Brian Forbes account:

Brian Forbes Account

Aug 1 Balance b/d	268.00	Aug 22 Bank	134.00

The balance remaining of £134 on the Brian Forbes account is a bad debt and should be written off. The debit entry is made in the bad debts account, the credit entry is in the Brian Forbes account:

Bad Debts Account

Aug 22 Brian Forbes	134.00	

Brian Forbes Account

Aug 1 Balance b/d	268.00	Aug 22 Bank	134.00
		22 Bad Debts A/c	134.00
	268.00		268.00

There are three possible situations which can arise with regard to bad debts, these are (a) a debt that is entirely bad; (b) a debt which is partially bad; (c) a bad debt which is recovered at a later date, with interest.

A bankrupt is a debtor who has been declared by a bankruptcy court to be insolvent, that is, unable to pay his debts in full. A company unable to pay its debts cannot be made bankrupt; instead it can be put into liquidation, that is, its assets are sold for cash, which is used to settle its debts.

A certificated bankrupt is a bankrupt person who, on being discharged from bankruptcy, has been given a certificate of misfortune by the court, stating that his bankruptcy was caused by misfortune and not by any wrongful act of the bankrupt. An undischarged bankrupt is a bankrupt who has not been discharged, that is, released by the court from the limits placed upon him under the law. While a bankrupt he may not obtain much credit, nor own any property (except the tools of his trade); nor may he be a company director; he is barred from holding most public offices; and his right to enter into contracts is severely limited.

Because of the bankruptcy laws and the limitations imposed, some bankrupts do their best to pay off their debts. This can often take a considerable time, but cases are recorded of people paying their debts many years after their bankruptcies. In such cases it is usual for interest to be charged on the amount of the original debt.

Consider the following example of a bad debt recovered: K. Stead, whose account of £68 was written off as a bad debt two years ago, pays £74.80 by cheque in full settlement of the debt, on 8 October 19–7. K. Stead's account was closed two years ago, in 19–5, and has been removed from the sales ledger. The amount of the outstanding debt was £68, which, with interest at 5 per cent, per year amounts to £74.80. The procedure in this instance is as follows. The amount of the cheque, £74.80, would be debited in the bank account:

	Bank Account	
Oct 8 K. Stead 74.80	

The amount of £68, being the bad debt recovered, may be placed at the credit side of a special bad debts recovered account, or at the credit side of the bad debts account where it will offset any bad debts that occur during the current financial year. The amount of £6.80 representing interest on the original debt is profit and should be credited to an interest received account. These entries would appear as follows:

Bad Debts Recovered Account	
	Oct 8 Bank 68.00

Interest Received Account	
	Oct 8 Bank 6.80

It is important to note that no entry is made in the debtor's 'dead' account.

Provision for Bad and Doubtful Debts

A balance sheet should present a 'true and fair view' of the debtors. Accountants know from experience that there will always be a proportion of the debtors who will be unable to pay their debts during an accounting period. Some businesses

193

therefore, consider it prudent to set aside a certain sum of money, to create a reserve or provision to guard against the likelihood of some debtors failing to pay their accounts. Practically every business suffers a proportion of bad debts, but a good businessman will know, from experience, approximately what percentage of bad debts is normal for his type of business. Therefore a provision should be made to cover the estimated amount of the bad debts. The amount of the provision set aside is usually quoted as a percentage of the total debtor's figure. This amount is placed at the credit side of a special account called the provision for bad debts account.

Consider the following example: on 31 December 19–6, S. Ramsden's total debtors amounted to £15,000. It is estimated that 4 per cent of the debts (£600) will eventually prove to be bad debts, and S. Ramsden decides to make a provision for this amount out of his profits for the year. The accounts would appear as follows:

Profit and Loss Account for the Year Ended 31 December 19–6

	£		£
Provision for Bad Debts	600	Gross Profit b/d	5,678

Provision for Bad Debts Account

			£
	19–6		
	Dec 31 Profit & Loss		600

The credit balance on the provision for bad debts account will remain in the ledger until the end of the next accounting period. It will appear in the credit column of the trial balance for the next financial period. Any adjustment to the provision, increase or decrease, will be made on this account.

On the balance sheet as at 31 December 19–6 the amount of the provision set aside for eventual bad debts is shown as a deduction from the total debtors figure. This is done in order to show the estimated 'true and fair' value of the debtors.

Balance Sheet as at 31 December 19 –6 (Extract)

Current Assets		£
Debtors	15,000	
Less Provision		
for Bad Debts	600	14,400

Increasing the Provision in Subsequent Years

Consider the following: the provision made by S. Ramsden in the above example will remain at £600 until it is adjusted. At the end of the following year, 31 December 19–7, the provision may be required to be increased. This would arise because the total debtors had increased for example to £18,000 and the provision was still estimated at 4 per cent. If the provision is to be increased, the provision for bad debts account should be credited with the amount of the increase (£120) and the profit and loss account should be debited with the same amount – the amount of the *increase only*. The total of the provision which is now required is 4 per cent of £18,000, which is £720, less existing provision of £600, which equals £120, the amount of the *increase* in the provision.) On 1 January 19–7 the provision for bad debts account would appear as follows:

Provision for Bad Debts Account

19–6			£	19–6			£
Dec	31	Balance c/d	600	Dec	31	Profit & Loss	600
				19–7			
				Jan	1	Balance b/d	600

The provision for bad debts account should be totalled and the balance brought down at the end of each financial year. The entries to adjust the amount of the provision for the year ending 31 December 19–7 would appear as follows:

Provision for Bad Debts Account

19–6			£	19–6			£
Dec	31	Balance c/d	600	Dec	31	Profit & Loss	600
19–7				19–7			
Dec	31	Balance c/d	720	Jan	1	Balance b/d	600
				Dec	31	Profit & Loss	120
			720				720
				19–8			
				Jan	1	Balance b/d	720

The debit entry in the profit and loss account for the year ended 31 December 19–7 would be as follows:

Profit and Loss Account for the Year Ended 31 December 19–7

	£		£
Provision for Bad Debts	120	Gross Profit b/d	6,750

The debtors figure would appear on the Balance Sheet as follows:

Balance Sheet as at 31 December 19–7 (Extract)

Current Assets		£
Debtors	18,000	
Less Provision		
for Bad Debts	720	17,280

Decreasing the Provision

A provision for bad and doubtful debts is created in order that a 'true and fair' figure for debtors is shown on a balance sheet. Consider the following: at the end of the next financial year S. Ramsden's total debtors figure had fallen to £16,000, the provision estimate of 4 per cent of the total debtors is still considered sufficient (4 per cent of £16,000 = £640). The existing provision is £720, therefore a reduction is required. When the provision is to be decreased the provision for bad debts account must be debited with the amount of the reduction (£80) and the profit and loss account should be credited with the same amount – the amount of the *difference* between the existing provision and the new provision. The total of the provision which is now required is 4 per cent of £16,000, which is £640; this is deducted from the existing provision of £720, which leaves £80, the amount of the *decrease* in the provision.

The entries to decrease the amount of the provision for bad debts for the year ending 31 December 19–8 would appear as follows:

Provision for Bad Debts Account

19–8			£	19–8			£
Dec	31	Profit & Loss	80	Jan	1	Balance b/d	720
	31	Balance c/d	640				
			720				720
				19–9			
				Jan	1	Balance b/d	640

Profit and Loss Account for the Year Ending 31 December 19–8

	Gross Profit b/d	7,985
	Reduction in Provision	80

The credit entry in the profit and loss account will increase the net profit for the year 19–8.

The debtors figure would appear on the balance sheet as follows:

Balance Sheet as at 31 December 19–8 (Extract)

Current Assets	£	
Debtors	16,000	
Less Provision		
for Bad Debts	640	15,360

The following is an illustration of the entries in the provision for bad debts account for the three years 19–6, 19–7 and 19–8.

Provision for Bad Debts Account

19–6		£	19–6		£
Dec 31	Balance c/d	600	Dec 31	Profit & Loss	600
19–7			19–7		
Dec 31	Balance c/d	720	Jan 1	Balance b/d	600
			Dec 31	Profit & Loss	120
		720			720
19–8			19–8		
Dec 31	Profit & Loss	80	Jan 1	Balance b/d	720
31	Balance c/d	640			
		720			720
			19–9		
			Jan 1	Balance b/d	640

POINTS TO REMEMBER   When a debtor fails to pay his account and the amount owed becomes irrecoverable, the debt becomes a bad debt. When a bad debt occurs, the bad debts account is debited with the amount of the debt; the debtors account is credited with the same amount.

The bad debts account is a 'collecting together' account of all the bad debts incurred during the accounting period. At the end of the financial year the bad debts account is totalled, and the total transferred to the profit and loss account.

It is considered prudent to make provision for debts which are doubtful and may eventually prove to be bad debts. When it is decided to create a provision (this is an amount set aside from the profits) the amount decided upon is placed at the

197

credit side of the provision for bad debts account; the debit entry is in the profit and loss account.

The provision for bad debts account is totalled and balanced, and the balance brought down at the end of each accounting period. In subsequent years any new provision will be adjusted on this account; it is the amount of the *difference* between the existing provision and the new provision which will be transferred to the profit and loss account.

On the balance sheet the amount of the provision is shown as a deduction from the total debtors.

Assignment Exercises

23.1
On 1 March 19–7, D. Nelson, a debtor, owes your firm £76.50. He is declared bankrupt and it is reluctantly decided to write off the debt as a bad debt on 30 March 19–7. You are required to show the appropriate ledger account entries.

23.2
Alan Senior, a debtor, owes your firm £350. Because of serious personal and financial difficulties he is unable to pay and asks you to agree to a payment of 50 per cent in full settlement of the debt. After consideration, you agree and he pays by cheque on 30 November 19–7. Required: show the appropriate ledger account entries.

23.3
A. Baxter is declared bankrupt owing the firm £175. In due course the firm receives a full and final settlement of 45 pence in the £ in cash on 15 April 19–7. You are required to show the appropriate ledger account entries to deal with this matter.

23.4
John London's debt of £220 was written off some time ago. On 3 August 19–7 he sends a cheque for £231 representing the complete payment of the original debt plus 5 per cent interest. You are required to open the necessary ledger accounts to show how this matter would be dealt with.

23.5
Every business which sells goods on credit wishes to avoid bad debts. Describe the steps which may be taken before a new customer is allowed credit.
How may the customer be treated if his creditworthiness is a matter of doubt?

(The Royal Society of Arts)

23.6

(a) What are bad debts? Why is it necessary to write off bad debts?

(b) From the information below write up the bad debts account in the books of Jean Wilder for the year 19–7. Debts written off as irrecoverable:

		£
June 30	A. Noble	16
	P. Jones	120
Dec 31	R. Scott	25
	L. Skirrow	30

On 1 December 19–7 a first and final dividend of five pence in the £ was unexpectedly received in respect of the debt due formerly from P. Jones. Close off the bad debts account as on 31 December 19–7 and show the amount to be transferred to profit and loss account.

(Royal Society of Arts)

23.7

Nigel Barker has an exporting business and maintains a provision for bad debts equal in amount to 5 per cent of the total debtors outstanding at the end of each financial year.

	Total Debtors
31 December 19–5	£ 9,000
31 December 19–6	£10,500

From the above information:

(a) Prepare the provision for bad debts account for the year ended 31 December 19–5 and 19–6.

(b) Show the appropriate entries in the profit and loss account for the years 19–5 and 19–6

(c) Prepare the balance sheet entries (extracts) for the years 19–5 and 19–6.

23.8

H. Crawford had a business which adjusted its provision for bad debts at the end of the year, at a given percentage of the total debtors. The percentage varied each year, depending on the economic situation. Irrecoverable debts were written off during the year to a bad debts account, as and when they occurred.

	Bad debts written off during year to bad debts account	Total debtors at year end	Rate of percentage for provision of doubtful debts
	£	£	
31 December 19–1	750	14,000	5%
31 December 19–2	4,085	10,000	10%
31 December 19–3	2,900	15,000	5%

From the above information you are required to show:

(a) The bad debts account as affected by the closing entries at the end of the financial years 31 December 19–1, 19–2 and 19–3.
(b) The provision for doubtful debts account for the same years showing the provision brought forward for each year; the balance on this account on 1 January, 19–1 was £500.
(c) An extract from the balance sheets showing how the provision would affect the total debtors, as at 31 December 19–1, 19–2 and 19–3.

23.9
On 20 September 19–7 B. Fox's debtors totalled £12,000. He decided to write off the following as bad debts:

	£
G. Green	60
H. Wilson	80

He further decided to make a provision for doubtful debts of 10 per cent on the remaining debtors. Debtors on 30 September 19–8 totalled £10,000 when Fox decided to maintain the provision at 10 per cent. You are required to show for each of the years ended 30 September 19–7 and 19–8:

(a) provision for doubtful debts account:
(b) the appropriate entries in the profit and loss account; and
(c) the necessary balance sheet entries on each of the above dates.

(Royal Society of Arts)

23.10
(a) What are the differences between bad debts written off and provision for bad debts?
(b) Give two reasons for creating a provision for bad debts.
(c) What is meant by bad debts recovered? How are such items entered in the profit and loss account of a business?
(d) On 1 January 19–4 there was a balance of £500 in the provision for bad debts account, and it was decided to maintain the provision at 5 per cent of the debtors at each year end.

The debtors on 31 December each year were as follows:

	£
19–4	8,000
19–5	8,000
19–6	11,000

You are required to show the necessary entries for the years ended 31 December 19–4 to 31 December 19–6 inclusive in
 (i) the provision for bad debts account, and
(ii) the profit and loss account.

(Joint Matriculation Board)

24 Adjustments for Final Accounts: Prepayments and Accruals – Ledger Accounts

OBJECTIVES To examine and consider the necessity to calculate and include the *exact* amounts of all revenue received and all expenses incurred which relate to the accounting period, in the preparation of the trading and profit and loss account, and to show the amount of any prepayments or accruals on the balance sheet. This is essential in order to produce a 'true and fair view' of the state of the business.

Adjustments of certain ledger account balances are often necessary in order to calculate the true profit (or loss) for the accounting period under review. Expense accounts and revenue received accounts may be prepaid at the end of the financial period; that is to say, the business may have paid for something or received revenue in advance, of that item being 'used up'.

Expense accounts and revenue received accounts may also be outstanding – owing at the end of the accounting period. This would mean the business would have outstanding debts, either owed to the business or owed by the business at the end of the financial year. The purpose of making adjustments is to present a 'true and accurate' set of final accounts for the trading period.

Prepayments

Payments Made in Advance by the Firm

A prepayment or a payment made in advance means that the business has paid in advance for some item before fully 'using up' the benefit paid for. Certain expense payments made by a business are nearly always paid in advance; typical examples are rates, insurances and rent. These accounts often have a 'portion' of prepayment; this 'portion' refers to the part of the year unexpired at the end of the accounting period.

The 'accounting period' is the length of time from the preparation of one set of final accounts to the next. It is normally one year. It is essential that the length of the 'accounting period' should remain consistent, otherwise the business cannot properly compare one period's achievements and results with another.

All revenue received and all expenses incurred during the accounting period must be included in the trading and profit and loss account. This is necessary in order to calculate the 'true and accurate' figures; any benefit paid for but not fully used up will require an adjustment, as only the true cost for the accounting period should be transferred to the profit and loss account.

Many firms whose financial year ends on the 31 December will have already paid their annual rates up to 31 March of the following year. On 31 December there will be an unused 'portion' of the rates – the business will have paid in advance for something which it has not fully received. In this situation a year-end adjustment will be required in respect of the unexpired part of the year. This will create a balance equal to the amount of the prepayment. Similarly, insurance payments are always made in advance. An insurance company will not offer or provide any cover until the first premium is paid.

Consider the following example. A sole trader's financial year is 1 January to 31 December. Rates of £1,500 per annum are payable by instalments. The following payments were made for rates, by cheque, during the year ended 31 December 19–7:

31 January 19–7   £375 for the three months to 31 March 19–7.
 1 April   19–7   £750 for the six months to 30 September 19–7
1 October 19–7   £750 for the six months to 31 March 19–8.

Each time a payment is made the details are entered in the rates account. The rates account for the year 19–7 would appear in the general ledger as follows:

Rates Account

19–7			£	
Jan	31	Bank	375.00	
Apr	1	Bank	750.00	
Oct	1	Bank	750.00	

The payment on 1 October 19–7 of £750 was for the six months to the 31 March 19–8. Clearly only three months (half of the cost of £750) will be used up in the financial year ending 31 December 19–7, and three months (£375) will be prepaid. The transfer to the profit and loss account must be the 'true' cost of the rates for the financial year ending 31 December 19–7, which is £1,500. To adjust the rates account at the end of the financial year the amount of the prepayment is entered in the rates account, at the credit side. This will create a balance equal to the amount which is prepaid, and will be brought down to the debit side, showing the amount of the prepayment. The completed Rates Account would appear as follows:

Rates Account

19–7			£	19–7			£
Jan	31	Bank	375.00	Dec	31	Profit and Loss	1,500.00
Apr	1	Bank	750.00	Dec	31	Prepaid c/d	375.00
Oct	1	Bank	750.00				
			1,875.00				1,875.00
19–8							
Jan	1	Prepaid b/d	375.00				

On the balance sheet for the year ending 31 December 19–7 the amount of the prepayment is shown under the current assets – rates prepaid £375.

Consider another example: A business whose financial year is 1 January to 31 December 19–7 takes out a new insurance policy on 1 February 19–7. The yearly premium, paid by cheque on 1 February, is £360. The insurance account would appear as follows:

Insurance Account

19–7			£		
Mar	1	Bank	360.00		

At the end of the financial year on 31 December 19–7 the business still has one months' value of Insurance unexpired – it has been paid in advance. The transfer to the profit and loss account must be the 'true cost' of insurance for the current financial year, therefore a year-end adjustment will be required for the part of the year which is unexpired and prepaid.

This is calculated as follows: the cost for the year is £360; this figure is divided by 12 to give the cost of one month: £30. The business has 'used up' 11 months of the cover: that is, 11 months at £30 per month, which is £330. One month is prepaid (£30). This amount is entered at the credit side of the insurance account to create a balance equal to the amount which is prepaid. The completed insurance account for the year ending 31 December 19–7 would appear as follows:

Insurance Account

19–7			£	19–7			£
Mar	1	Bank	360.00	Dec	31	Profit and Loss	330.00
				Dec	31	Prepaid c/d	30.00
			360.00				360.00
19–8							
Jan	1	Prepaid b/d	30.00				

Payments Made in Advance to the Firm

Payments can be made to the firm in advance. This is income received by the firm in advance for services or benefit which have not yet been given. The final accounts should reflect the 'true and accurate' figures of the income actually 'earned' during the financial year under review. Therefore an adjustment should be made for any revenue which has been received in advance by the firm at the end of the financial year. Special attention is always required with regard to revenue received: any amounts received, for example, for rent received or commissions received will be a debit entry in the cash book and a credit entry in the revenue received account.

Consider the following example. A firm has larger premises than is required and on 1 March 19–7 a section of the premises was sub-let to another business for the sum of £1,200 per annum. During the year ended 31 December 19–7 the following amounts were received from the sub-tenant, by cheque:

19–7
Mar 1 £300 For the three months to 31 May 19–7.
June 2 £300 For the three months to 31 August 19–7.
Sept 1 £300 For the three months to 30 November 19–7.
Dec 2 £300 For the three months to 28 February 19–8.

Each time a payment is received the details are entered in the rent receivable account. The rent receivable account would appear as follows:

Rent Receivable Account

	19–7			£
	Mar	1	Bank	300.00
	Jun	2	Bank	300.00
	Sept	1	Bank	300.00
	Dec	2	Bank	300.00

During the current financial year £1,200 has been received from the sub-tenant. However, the tenancy commenced on 1 March 19–7, at an 'annual' rental of £1,200, therefore during the current financial year 10 months' benefit has already been received by the sub-tenant, two months having been paid in advance. The amount to be transferred to the profit and loss account must be the actual amount earned during the current year, namely 10 months, clearly showing that two months have been paid in advance. A calculation should be carried out to ascertain the rent receivable for one month, as follows: £1,200 divided by 12 is £100. Ten months' benefit has been received by the sub-tenant, that is, £1,000. This is the amount which should be transferred to the profit and loss account; £200 has been paid in advance.

To adjust the rent receivable account at the end of the year, the amount which has been paid in advance (£200) is entered at the debit side, to create a balance equal to the amount which has been paid in advance, and will be brought down to the credit side, clearly showing the amount of the prepayment. The completed rent receivable account would appear as follows:

Rent Receivable Account

19–7			£	19–7			£
Dec	31	Profit and Loss	1,000.00	Mar	1	Bank	300.00
Dec	31	Prepaid c/d	200.00	Jun	2	Bank	300.00
				Sept	1	Bank	300.00
				Dec	2	Bank	300.00
			1,200.00				1,200.00
				19–8			
				Jan	1	Prepaid b/d	200.00

On the balance sheet any revenue received in advance will appear under current liabilities; this is because at the end of the financial year the business has the liability, in this example, to provide accommodation for the sub-tenant, for which he has already paid.

Accruals

The accounting term used for expenses which are owing is 'accrued' or an 'accrual'.

Expenses Owed by the Firm

It is essential that all the expenses which are incurred during the financial year, and the amounts which are subsequently transferred to the trading and profit and loss account, contain a full year's expenses. Invariably at the end of the financial year there are certain expenses which are outstanding (owing by the firm). Typical examples of these are wages, electricity, rent and advertising. These are expenses which have been incurred during the financial year, but the full payment has not yet been made. These are called 'accrued expenses'.

The amount of any expenses which are still outstanding at the end of the financial year will require adjusting. The amount which is transferred to the trading and profit and loss account should be the 'true and accurate' cost for the current year. Consider the following example. A firm whose financial year is 1 January to 31 December occupies premises at an annual rental of £1,800. The tenancy commenced on 1 January, 19–7 and the rent is paid, by cheque, at the end of each quarter which has expired. Each time a payment is made the details are entered and recorded in the rent account. The rent account would appear as follows:

Rent Account

19–7			£		
Apr	1	Bank	450.00		
Jul	3	Bank	450.00		
Oct	2	Bank	450.00		

On 31 December 19–7, at the end of the financial year, three months' rent was still owing. This will not be paid until 3 January, 19–8. The 'actual cost' of rent for the year 19–7 is £1,800, therefore this is the amount which should be charged and transferred to the profit and loss account for the year 19–7. To adjust the rent account at the end of the financial year, the amount owing of £450 is entered at the debit side; to create a balance equal to the amount owing, this will be brought down to the credit side, clearly showing the amount which is outstanding at the end of the financial year.

The completed rent account for the year 19–7 will appear as follows:

Rent Account

19–7			£	19–7			£
Apr	1	Bank	450.00	Dec	31	Profit and Loss	1,800.00
Jul	3	Bank	450.00				
Oct	2	Bank	450.00				
Dec	31	Accrued c/d	450.00				
			1,800.00				1,800.00
				19–8			
				Jan	1	Accrued b/d	450.00

On the balance sheet for the year ending 31 December 19–7 the amount of £450 would appear under the current liabilities – rent accrued £450.

Expenses Owed to the Firm

It is also possible that, at the end of the financial year, there may be revenue outstanding (these are amounts owing to the firm). This is income which has been 'earned' during the current year, and should have been received, but at the end of the year is still outstanding. In order to calculate the true and accurate profit or loss, the amount transferred to the profit and loss account should be the 'actual amount earned' during the year, even if it has not yet been received. Typical examples of these are:

(a) Rent receivable – a sub-tenant may be behind with his payments for rent;
(b) Commission receivable – the firm may have earned commission which has not yet been received.

In these situations the amounts transferred to the profit and loss account should be the actual amount earned during the current year, even if a 'portion' has not yet been collected.

Consider the following example. Alison Jones is a business consultant. She receives her commission on a quarterly basis. Her accounting year is 1 January to 31 December. During the year 19–7 she had received the following amounts, for commission, by cheque: 2 April – £230; 4 July – £316; 3 October – £294.

On 31 December 19–7 there was £310 commission due, but not yet received. On each occasion the commission is received the details are entered in the commission receivable account. The account would appear as follows:

Commission Receivable Account

			£
19–7			
Apr	2	Bank	230.00
Jul	4	Bank	316.00
Oct	3	Bank	294.00

The amount transferred to the profit and loss account for the year ending 31 December 19–7 should be the actual amount of commission earned during the year 19–7, therefore a year-end adjustment will be required. To make the necessary adjustment at the end of the financial year, the amount of the commission due of £310 is entered at the credit side in the commission receivable account. This will create a balance equal to the amount due, and will be brought down to the debit side, clearing showing a balance of the amount owing at the end of the current year.

The completed commission receivable account on the 31 December 19–7 would appear as follows:

Commission Receivable Account

19–7			£	19–7			£
Dec	31	Profit and Loss	1,150.00	Apr	2	Bank	230.00
				Jul	4	Bank	316.00
				Oct	3	Bank	294.00
				Dec	31	Owing c/d	310.00
			1,150.00				1,150.00
19–8							
Jan	1	Owing b/d	310.00				

On the balance sheet for the year ending 31 December 19–7 the amount of £310 would appear under current assets – commission due £310.

Unused Stocks

At the end of the accounting period there are often some unused stocks remaining, such as fuel oil, packing materials and stationery. These items are not usually entirely used up in the accounting period in which they are bought. Frequently there will be a stock in hand at the end of the financial year. The value of these remaining stocks must be deducted from the amount spent during the year; it is only the cost of the actual amount used, during the financial year, which is transferred to the profit and loss account.

This can be illustrated in the following example. During the financial year ended 31 December 19–7 the following amounts were paid, by cheque, for packing materials: 10 March – £386; 3 September – £464.

On 31 December 19–7 there was an unused stock of packing materials, value £200. The amount to be transferred to the profit and loss account for the year ending 31 December 19–7 should be the 'true cost' of the packing materials used during the year. Therefore a year-end adjustment will be required to show the amount of the value of the stock remaining at the end of the year. The value of the unused stock is entered at the credit side of the packing materials account. This will create a balance equal to the value of the unused stock, and will be brought down to the debit side, clearly showing the value of the stock at the end of the financial year. The amount of the 'difference' between the two sides of the account is the 'true cost' of packing materials for the year 19–7, and this is the amount transferred to the profit and loss account.

The completed packing materials account for the year 19–7 would appear as follows:

Packing Materials Account

19–7			£	19–7			£
Mar	10	Bank	386.00	Dec	31	Profit and Loss	650.00
Sep	3	Bank	464.00		31	Stock c/d	200.00
			850.00				850.00
19–8							
Jan	1	Stock b/d	200.00				

On the balance sheet for the year ending 31 December 19–7 the value of the unused stock of packing materials of £200 is an asset of the business. It is shown under current assets, packing materials stock, £200.

In examinations, questions are frequently set which require adjustments for prepayments or accruals. Students are often a little apprehensive when they are asked to construct an account for the year, where there are amounts owing or prepaid at *both* the beginning and the end of the year. Here is a typical question. From the following information prepare the electricity account in the ledger of John Woodstock. The financial year ended on 31 December 19–7.

Owing at 1 January 19–7	£246
Payments made during the year by cheque:	
15 January	£246
19 April	£356
16 July	£242
18 October	£274

The bill for electricity supplied during the three months ended 31 December 19–7 was £382 and was not paid until 17 January 19–8.

Show the electricity account in John Woodstock's ledger, clearly showing the amount transferred to the profit and loss account, and the balance on the electricity account.

The following is a fully illustrated solution. The account should be constructed *strictly* in date order.

(1) Enter the details of the amount owing at the beginning of the year – 1 January 19–7   Accrued b/d   £246 (credit side)
(2) Enter the details of the amounts paid during the current year – in date order (debit side)
(3) Enter the details of the electricity bill owing at the end of the year – 31 December 19–7   Accrued c/d   £382 (debit side)

The electricity account would appear as follows:

Electricity Account

19–7			£	19–7			£
Jan	15	Bank	246.00	Jan	1	Accrued b/d	246.00
Apr	19	Bank	356.00				
Jul	16	Bank	242.00				
Oct	18	Bank	274.00				
Dec	31	Accrued c/d	382.00				

Once the dates and details of all the information given in the question are entered in the account, it is a simple procedure to calculate the correct amount to be transferred to the profit and loss account. The 'true cost' of electricity for the year 19–7, and the amount to be transferred to the profit and loss account, is the amount of the *difference* between the two sides of the account.

The completed Electricity Account is shown below:

Electricity Account

19–7			£	19–7			£
Jan	15	Bank	246.00	Jan	1	Accrued b/d	246.00
Apr	19	Bank	356.00	Dec	31	Profit and Loss	1,254.00
Jul	16	Bank	242.00				
Oct	18	Bank	274.00				
Dec	31	Accrued c/d	382.00				
			1,500.00				1,500.00
				19–8			
				Jan	1	Accrued b/d	382.00

The details and information given in these types of questions can require the construction of more than one account. In these situations it is extremely important

210

to enter the details of the information given, in *date* order, into the *separate* accounts.

The following is a typical example of a question which requires the construction of two accounts.

On 1 January 19–7 the rates account of Peter Davies showed a prepayment of £400. During the year ending 31 December 19–7 he paid £1,600 for Rates and £5,212 in respect of salaries.

At the end of the year Davies calculated that a further £434 was owing for salaries and that the rates were then prepaid to the extent of £485. The payments for rates and salaries were made by cheque.

You are required to write up separate accounts for rates and salaries, balance at the end of the financial year and bring down the balances, and show the transfers to the profit and loss account.

The completed accounts would appear as follows:

Rates Account

19–7			£	19–7			£
Jan	1	Prepaid b/d	400.00	Dec	31	Profit and Loss	1,515.00
Dec	31	Bank	1,600.00		31	Prepaid c/d	485.00
			2,000.00				2,000.00
19–8							
Jan	1	Prepaid b/d	485.00				

Salaries Account

19–7			£	19–7			£
Dec	31	Bank	5,212.00	Dec	31	Profit and Loss	5,646.00
	31	Accrued c/d	434.00				
			5,646.00				5,646.00
				19–8			
				Jan	1	Accrued b/d	434.00

POINTS TO REMEMBER A careful and methodical approach is always required with questions relating to the construction of ledger accounts which require adjusting for prepayments and accruals.

The 'accounting period' or 'trading period' is the length of time from the preparation of one set of final accounts to the next. It is normally one year. The *exact* amounts of all expenses incurred and of all revenue received during the accounting period are transferred to the profit and loss account.

A 'prepayment' is an amount paid in advance before fully using up the benefit paid for.

An 'accrual' is an expense which has been incurred during the financial year, and which has not yet been fully paid. 'Accrued' means owing, outstanding or in arrears.

The amounts transferred to the profit and loss account should represent the 'actual cost' of all the expenses incurred during the financial year, and the 'actual amount' of all revenue earned during the financial year.

A year-end adjustment for a prepayment or an accrual is necessary to ascertain the 'true and accurate' figure. It is essential that the amount of any prepayments or accruals should appear on the balance sheet in order to present a 'true and fair view' of the financial state of the business.

The details and information given in the question, should be entered and recorded in the ledger accounts in *date* order.

When an 'annual cost' is stated in the question, for example, 'a firm occupies premises at an annual rental of £2,000', the amount to be transferred to the profit and loss account is *always* the 'annual cost' (£2,000) and a calculation will usually be required to ascertain the 'part of the year' which is prepaid or accrued.

Assignment Exercises

24.1

From the following information you are required to write up James Grant's rent account for the year ended 31 December 19–7 and to show the amount transferred to the profit and loss account.

On 1 January 19–7 £500 was owing for rent in respect of the business premises. Payments for rent, made by cheque, during the year to 31 December 19–7 were as follows:

4 January – £500; 3 April – £500; 5 July – £500; 8 October – £500.

On 31 December 19–7 there was £500 owing for rent of the business premises.

24.2

From the following information you are required to write up the rates account in the ledger of K. Parker for the year ending 31 December 19–7.

On 1 January 19–7 the rates were prepaid £525. During the year the following payments were made by cheque:

30 April – £1,150 for 6 months ending 30 September 19–7.
5 October – £1,150 for 6 months ending 31 March 19–8.

Your rates account should clearly indicate the amount to be transferred to the profit and loss account for the year ended 31 December 19–7.

24.3
You are required to prepare the electricity account in the books of M. Summers for the financial year ending 30 June 19–7. The following information is available.

On 1 July 19–6 there was an unpaid bill for electricity of £287. During the year the following payments were made for electricity, by cheque:

15 July 19–6 – £287; 8 October 19–6 – £320; 10 January 19–7 – £543; 6 April 19–7 – £590.

On 30 June 19–7 there was an electricity account outstanding of £350.

Your electricity account should clearly show the amount to be transferred to the profit and loss account for the year ending 30 June 19–7 and the amount to be carried forward to the next financial year.

24.4
James Conway commenced trading on 1 January 19–7, on which date he acquired premises at an annual rental of £2,700. On 1 May 19–7 he sub-let a section of the premises at an annual rental of £900.

During the year ended 31 December 19–7 the following payments had been made in respect of rent, by cheque:

30 March – £675; 29 June – £675; 28 September – £675

and the following amounts had been received by cheque, from the sub-tenant:

3 May – £225; 1 August – £225; 4 November – £225.

Write up separate accounts for rent payable and rent receivable for the financial year ending 31 December 19–7. Balance the accounts and show the relevant transfers to the profit and loss account.

24.5
(a) On 31 May 19–2 J. Dougall's balance sheet showed that he had paid rates in advance of £600. On 17 November 19–2, J. Dougall paid his rates for the second half of the rating year to 31 March 19–3 (£900). On 13 May 19–3, J. Dougall paid an instalment of rates (£1,200) which covered the period 1 April to 30 September 19–3. J. Dougall's financial year ended on 31 May 19–3.
   Write up his rates account for the year, showing clearly the amount to be charged to the profit and loss account, and the amount to be carried forward to the next financial year.
(b) On 31 May 19–2, R. Sparrow held in stock packing materials to the value of £621. During the year his purchases of packing material totalled £1,890. On 31 May 19–3 his packing material in stock was valued at £480.

Write up the packing materials account for the year showing clearly the amount to be charged to the profit and loss account, and the amount to be carried forward to the next financial year.

(The Royal Society of Arts)

24.6

During the year ended 31 December 19–4 Nigel Giffard paid the following amounts for rent.

Jan 18   £86 for the half year ended 31 March 19–4.
Jul 10   £90 for the half year ended 30 September 19–4.
Dec 5   £90 for the half year ended 31 March 19–5.

(a) Enter the above information in the rent account of Nigel Giffard.
(b) Balance the rent account at 31 December 19–4, showing clearly the amount he should charge against his business profits for the year ended 31 December 19–4.

(Joint Matriculation Board)

24.7

You are required to write up the rent account, rates account and electricity account in the books of A. Trader for the year ending 30 April 19–3, using the following information. On 1 May 19–2 there was no balance on the rent account, the rates account had a debit balance of £90 and there was a credit balance on the electricity account of £40. During the year the following payments were made by cheque:

19–2
14 May   paid electricity bill £40.
31 July   paid rent £250 for 3 months ending 31 July 19–2.
 1 August   paid £180 rates for 6 months ending 31 January 19–3.
 8 August   paid electricity bill £60.
31 October   paid rent £250 for 3 months ending 31 October 19–2.
 5 November   paid electricity bill £80.
19–3
31 January   paid rent £250 for 3 months ending January 19–3.
 2 February   paid rates £180 for 6 months ending July 19–3.
 4 February   paid electricity bill £60.
30 April   paid rent £250 for 3 months ending April 19–3.

On 30 April 19–3 there was an amount of £50 owing for electricity.

Your accounts should clearly indicate the amounts to be charged to the profit and loss accounts for the year ended 30 April 19–3 and any relevant balance sheet entries at that date must be given.

(The Royal Society of Arts)

24.8

(i) L. George rents his premises at an annual rental of £1,200. On 1 June 19–3 George had paid his rent up to the end of July, and during the year ended 31 May 19–4 he made the following payments for rent, by cheque:

1 August	£300
5 November	£300
1 February	£300
1 June	£400

(ii) George sub-lets part of these premises to S. Broke at a rent of £480 per annum, and on 1 June 19–3 Broke's rent was one month in arrears. During the year ended 31 May 19–4 George received the following amounts in cash from Broke:

25 July	£ 40
18 August	£120
4 December	£150
9 April	£ 60

(iii) On 1 June 19–3 George owed the Electricity Board £74 for electricity supplies up to that date. During the year he made the following payments by cheque:

1 June	£ 74
10 September	£ 82
5 December	£104
7 April	£ 81

On 31 May 19–4 there was a balance outstanding on the electricity account of £96.

You are required:

(a) To write up George's rent payable account, rent receivable account, and electricity account for the year ended 31 May 19–4, showing clearly the amounts to be transferred to the profit and loss account in each case.

(b) To show how the balances brought down would appear in the balance sheet on 31 May 19–4.

(The Royal Society of Arts)

25 Adjustments for Final Accounts – including Prepayments and Accruals – Unused Stocks – and Other Types of Year-end Adjustments which must be taken into Consideration When Preparing the Trading and Profit and Loss Accounts and a Balance Sheet

OBJECTIVES   To apply the techniques required to carry out year-end adjustments, to show the twofold effect of such adjustments and to emphasise the importance of the fact that these are to be taken into consideration after the trial balance has been extracted.

At the end of the financial year a trial balance is extracted to test the arithmetical accuracy of the entries in the ledger accounts. It is important to recognise that a trial balance is not an account; it is a list of all the 'balances' remaining in the ledger accounts, including the cash and bank balances from the cash book. The 'balances' included in the trial balance have been passed through the double entry system.

It is normal accounting practice, as illustrated in Module 24, for any year-end adjustments which may be necessary to be carried out in the appropriate ledger accounts, *before* the trial balance is taken out. The information contained in the trial balance is the basis for the preparation of the trading and profit and loss account and a balance sheet.

In examination questions, where the construction of ledger accounts are not required, the question will often take the form of a trial balance accompanied by a series of instructions. These instructions will usually be presented as a list of year-end notes, to take specific information into consideration when preparing the final accounts. In these situations it will be necessary to consider and carry out the twofold effect of each individual adjustment. Both aspects must be taken into consideration when preparing the final accounts. One aspect of the adjustment may be shown in the trading account or the profit and loss account, and the other aspect be shown on the balance sheet.

These types of questions appear frequently on examination papers and the items requiring adjustment usually appear under one of the following headings:

'Notes'
'Taking the following into consideration'
'Take into account the following'
'The following information is also available'

The following is a typical example of this type of question, showing a trial balance extracted at the end of the financial year, followed by a series of year-end notes. Each item listed in the year-end notes will require adjusting on the basis of the information given.

The following trial balance was taken from the books of Michael Silverwood at 31 December 19–7

	Dr. £	Cr. £
Trade Debtors	5,480	
Trade Creditors		2,355
Stock (1 January 19–7)	4,340	
Motor Vehicle	6,550	
Rent	1,430	
Wages and Salaries	5,178	
Rates	565	
Purchases	25,282	
Sales		36,845
Bad Debts	142	
Cash at Bank	2,177	
Insurance	150	
Office Expenses	886	
Sundry Expenses	570	
Capital		16,800
Drawings	3,250	
	56,000	56,000

The following notes should be taken into consideration:

(a) Rates were prepaid £56 at 31 December 19–7.
(b) Included in 'office expenses' is the cost of stationery. There was a stock of stationery valued at £72 on 31 December 19–7.
(c) Wages and salaries accrued at 31 December 19–7 were £150.
(d) Stock at 31 December 19–7 was valued at £5,650.

You are required to prepare the trading and profit and loss account of Michael Silverwood for the year ended 31 December 19–7 and a balance sheet as at that date.

All items which appear outside the trial balance require careful consideration and must be dealt with before commencing the final accounts. These items have not been passed through the books and the double entry effect must be established.

In each of the above examples the twofold effect will involve the trading account or the profit and loss account and the balance sheet.

Consider (a) Rates were prepaid £56 at 31 December 19–7. The amount given in the trial balance for rates of £565 has not been adjusted in the rates account in the ledger, therefore it will be necessary to carry out the calculation of the year-end adjustment before commencing the final accounts. The amount shown for rates in the profit and loss account should be the 'true and accurate' cost of rates for the financial year, and the amount of the prepayment should be shown as a current asset on the balance sheet. The adjustment of (a) above must be dealt with twice. The 'workings' are as follows:

(a) Profit and Loss Account Entry		Balance Sheet entry
Rates	565	under Current Assets
Less prepaid	56	Rates prepaid £56
Rates adjusted	509	

It is the adjusted rates figure of £509 which is entered at the debit side in the profit and loss account, and the amount of the prepayment of £56 which is shown on the balance sheet.

Consider (b) Included in 'office expenses' is the cost of stationery. There was a stock of stationery valued at £72 on 31 December 19–7. The figure given in the trial balance for office expenses of £886 has not been adjusted in the ledger account to show the value of the unused stock of stationery at 31 December 19–7. It will be necessary to carry out a calculation to make the adjustment required for the stock remaining at the end of the financial year. The value of the stock remaining at the end of the financial year must be deducted from the cost of the office expenses for the current year. The amount shown for office expenses in the profit and loss account should be the 'actual cost' for the financial year. The amount of the value of the unused stock of stationery is an asset of the business, and is shown as a current asset on the balance sheet.

The adjustment required to show the value of the stock of stationery of £72, must be dealt with twice. The 'workings' are as follows:

(b) *Profit and Loss Account entry*   *Balance Sheet entry*
   Office Expenses   886 under Current Assets
   Less stock of Stationery   72   Stock of Stationery £72
                               ———
   Office Expenses adjusted: 814

It is the adjusted figure of £814 for office expenses which is entered at the debit side in the profit and loss account. On the balance sheet the value of the unused stock of stationery is shown under current assets.

Consider (c) Wages and salaries accrued at 31 December 19–7 were £150. The figure given in the trial balance for wages and salaries of £5,178 has not been adjusted in the wages and salaries account in the ledger. It will be necessary to carry out the calculation of the year-end adjustment before commencing the final accounts. It is essential that the amount shown in the profit and loss account for wages and salaries should be the 'actual cost' for the financial year. The amount owing for wages and salaries of £150 is shown as a current liability on the balance sheet.

The adjustment required for (c) must be dealt with twice. The 'workings' are as follows:

(c) *Profit and Loss Account entry*   *Balance Sheet entry*
   Wages and Salaries   5,178 under Current Liabilities
   Add accrued   150   Wages & Salaries accrued £150
                         ———
   Wages & Salaries adjusted   5,328

It is the adjusted figure of £5,328 for wages and salaries which is entered at the debit side in the profit and loss account, and on the balance sheet the amount owing of £150 is shown under current liabilities.

Consider (d) Stock at 31 December 19–7 was valued at £5,650. This is the value of the unsold stock of goods in which the business normally deals, at the end of financial year. The amount of £5,650 is the figure of 'closing stock'. It is entered in the trading account and is shown on the balance sheet as a current asset.

(d) *Trading Account entry*   *Balance Sheet entry*
   Closing Stock £5,650   under Current Assets
                          Stock £5,650

The completed trading and profit and loss accounts, and a balance sheet for the year ending 31 December 19–7, for the example question, would appear as follows:

Stock	4,340	Sales	36,845
Purchases	25,282		
	29,622		
Less closing stock	5,650		
Cost of goods sold	23,972		
Gross Profit c/d	12,873		
	£36,845		£36,845
Rent	1,430	Gross Profit b/d	12,873
Wages and Salaries	5,328		
Rates	509		
Bad Debts	142		
Insurance	150		
Office Expenses	814		
Sundry Expenses	570		
Net Profit	3,930		
	£12,873		£12,873

The 'workings' for all adjustments should be clearly shown (and is usually an examination requirement). This is best achieved by preparing a list of the items which require adjustment, displaying the details of any calculations necessary and showing the effect on the trading account or the profit and loss account and the balance sheet.

The 'workings' are also of considerable assistance if difficulties arise in making the balance sheet totals agree; this is often owing to the fact that an item requiring adjustment has been omitted.

Each 'balance' contained within the trial balance is used *once* only in preparing the trading and profit and loss account and the balance sheet. Any items which appear outside the trial balance, and which are given as additional information, will require careful consideration. The twofold effect should be ascertained, and the necessary year-end adjustment carried out, before preparing the trading and profit and loss accounts and the balance sheet.

	£	£		£	£
Fixed Assets			Capital	16,800	
Motor Vehicle		6,550	+ Net Profit	3,930	
				20,730	
Current Assets			Less Drawings	3,250	17,480
Stock	5,650				
Debtors	5,480		*Current Liabilities*		
Rates prepaid	56		Creditors	2,355	
Stock of Stationery	72		Wages accrued/	150	2,505
Bank	2,177	13,435			
		19,985			19.985

A balance sheet is a list of balances remaining on the trial balance after the trading and profit and loss accounts have been completed. The balance sheet should always present a 'true and fair view' of the financial position of the business.

Where there is more than one item of prepayment, the items are usually added together and shown as one figure on the balance sheet, as 'prepaid expenses'. Where there is more than one item owing for expenses, these are usually added together and shown as one figure on the balance sheet, as 'accrued expenses'. Other types of year-end adjustments are now covered in some detail.

Depreciation of Fixed Assets

Certain adjustments may have to be made regarding the decline in value of fixed assets. It has already been established that the amount of depreciation charged to the profit and loss account is an expense. On the balance sheet the value of the fixed asset is shown, in one of two ways:

Method 1 Direct Depreciation
   With this method the value of the fixed asset is shown at its original cost in the year of purchase, less the depreciation charges to date. In subsequent years, the value of the fixed asset appears at the reduced figure.
Method 2 Providing for Depreciation
   With this method the fixed asset is always shown at the original cost, less the total amount of all depreciation charges to date.

Any additional information given as a year-end adjustment for depreciation will require the consideration of the two-fold aspect, and a careful note should be made of the details before commencing the final accounts.

Consider the following example of a year-end adjustment note:

(i) Depreciate fixtures and fittings at 20 per cent per annum, on cost. (Assume the figure shown in the trial balance for fixtures and fittings at cost is £4,000.)

The following calculation is required: 20 per cent of £4,000 is £800. The amount charged for depreciation is an expense and is set against the profits of the business in the profit and loss account.

The fixed asset is reduced in value by the amount of the depreciation charged in each financial year. The adjustment required must be dealt with twice. For this example the 'workings' are as follows:

Profit and Loss Account	*Balance Sheet entry*		
Debit entry – Depreciation £800	under Fixed Assets		
	Fixtures & Fittings	4,000	
	Less depreciation	800	3,200

Bad Debts

Another type of year-end adjustment which frequently occurs is that concerned with bad debts. Consider the following example:

(ii) A debtor has been declared bankrupt and £250 is to be written off as a bad debt. (Assume the figure shown in the trial balance for debtors is £6,750.)

The twofold aspect must be considered to enable the necessary adjustment to be carried out. A debtor who cannot pay his debt is called a 'bad' debtor, and the debt owing is referred to as a 'bad debt'. A bad debt is a business loss, and must be treated in the same way as other losses and expenses, by charging the amount of the 'bad debt' against the profits of the business in the profit and loss account. On the balance sheet the figure given for debtors must be reduced by the amount of the bad debt.

Again the adjustment required must be dealt with twice. The 'workings' for this example are as follows:

Profit and Loss Account	*Balance Sheet entry*		
Debit entry – Bad Debts £250	under Current Assets		
	Debtors	6,750	
	Less Bad Debt	250	£6,500

Provision for Bad Debts

Increasing the Provision

Often year-end adjustments are required relating to the provision for bad debts. Consider the following example of a year-end adjustment where the Provision for Bad Debts is to be increased:

222

(iii) The provision for Bad Debts is to be increased to 10 per cent of Debtors. (Assume the following figures are given in the trial balance – provision for bad and doubtful debts, £250; Debtors, £4,500.)

Again the twofold aspect must be considered and any necessary calculations carried out.

Inevitably there will always be a proportion of the debtors who will be unable to pay their debts. Some businesses, therefore, consider it prudent to set aside a certain sum of money to create a reserve or provision to guard against the likelihood of some debtors failing to pay their accounts. The amount of the provision already existing is the figure given in the trial balance: provision for bad and doubtful debts £250. The adjustment requires this figure to be increased to 10 per cent of the debtors. (10 per cent of £4,500 is £450, therefore £450 less £250, which is £200 is the amount of the increase.) The profit and loss account should be debited with the amount of the *increase* only.

On the balance sheet the provision for bad and doubtful debts is shown as a deduction from the debtors. The adjustment required must be dealt with twice. The 'workings' for this example would appear as follows:

Profit and Loss Account	*Balance Sheet entry*		
Debit entry – Provision for Bad and	under Current Assets		
Doubtful Debts £200	Debtors	4,500	
	Less Provision	450	£4,050

Decreasing the Provision

Consider the following example of a year-end adjustment where the provision for bad debts is to be decreased.

(iv) The provision for bad debts is to be adjusted to 10 per cent of debtors. (Assume the following figures are given in the trial balance – provision for bad debts, £500; debtors, £4,000.)

The twofold aspect must be considered and any necessary calculations carried out.

When the provision for bad debts is to be decreased the profit and loss account should be credited with the amount of the *difference* between the existing provision and the new provision. The total of the provision which is now required is 10 per cent of £4,000, which is £400; this is deducted from the existing provision of £500, which equals £100, the amount of the reduction in the provision. The profit and loss account should be credited with the amount of the reduction.

On the balance sheet the amount of the provision for bad debts is shown as a deduction from the debtors. The adjustment required must be dealt with twice. The 'workings' for this example would appear as follows:

Profit and Loss Account	*Balance Sheet entry*		
Credit entry – Reduction in Provision	under Current Assets		
for Bad Debts £100	Debtors	4,000	
	Less Provision	400	£3,600

Drawings

Another variation of year-end adjustments is those concerned with the proprietor (the owner of the business). The additional information given as a year-end adjustment can be stated in various ways, but a careful study of the details given and of the twofold effect will enable any necessary calculations and adjustments to be carried out.

Consider the following typical example:

(v) One-third of motor expenses for the year is to be regarded as private use. (Assume the following figures were given in the trial balance – motor expenses, £1,050; drawings, £2,500.)

The following calculation is required: £1,050 divided by 3 equals £350 (one-third). The amount charged to the profit and loss account should be the 'true and accurate' cost of motor expenses for the financial year. The motor expenses will need to be reduced by the amount of the private use of the proprietor. The drawings (these are withdrawals from the business by the owner of the business) will need to be increased by the amount of the proprietor's private use.

The adjustment required must be dealt with twice. The 'workings' for this example would appear as follows:

Profit and Loss Account entry		*Balance Sheet entry*	
Motor Expenses	1,050	Drawings	2,500
Less Private Use	350	Add Motor Expenses	350
Motor Expenses adjusted	£700	Drawings adjusted	£2,850

Labour or Wages

Under normal circumstances wages and salaries will appear in the profit and loss account. However, a year-end adjustment may require the cost of wages to be apportioned, perhaps a quarter to the trading account and three-quarters to the profit and loss account. The procedure would be as follows: Calculate the amounts; the amount of one-quarter should then be debited in the trading account; the amount of the remaining three-quarters will be debited in the profit and loss account.

A *specific instruction will be given* if any element of labour, wages or any other item of expense is to be apportioned.

Final Accounts of Non-traders

If the final accounts being prepared are for people who are not trading in goods as such, for example, accountants, hairdressers, bookmakers, business consultants and similar, there *will not* be a trading account, because goods are not bought and sold. The final accounts for providers of services will consist of a profit and loss account and a balance sheet. The profit and loss account will contain all items of revenue received at the credit side and all items of revenue expense at the debit side. The balance sheet will be exactly the same as for traders.

It will now be apparent that there are numerous possibilities relating to year-end adjustments and sufficient practice is essential to gain competence. Most of the assignment exercises which follow are taken from past examination papers; they contain many variations of the different types of year-end adjustments, to enable the student to gain skill and confidence in these important techniques.

POINTS TO REMEMBER

Headings which are clear and concise are an essential requirement of final accounts.

Each 'balance' contained within the trial balance is used *once* only in preparing the trading and profit and loss account and the balance sheet.

The additional instructions which appear *outside* the trial balance will require careful consideration. It will be necessary to consider and carry out the twofold effect of each individual adjustment before commencing the final accounts.

The 'workings' for all adjustments should be clearly shown and is usually an examination requirement.

When there are several items of prepayment, these are usually added together and shown as one figure on the balance sheet, as 'prepaid' expenses.

Similarly when there are several items owing for expenses, these are usually added together and shown as one figure on the balance sheet, as 'accrued expenses'.

Special attention is always required with regard to a bank overdraft. If the bank account is overdrawn at the end of the accounting period, the amount of the overdraft would appear in the *credit* column of the trial balance. In this situation the amount of the overdraft would appear under the heading of *current liabilities* on the balance sheet.

The final accounts for non-traders will consist of a profit and loss account and a balance sheet; there will not be a trading account.

Assignment Exercises

25.1
The following trial balance was extracted from the books of B. Stanley, a sole trader, on 31 December 19–5

	£	£
Capital (as at 1 January 19–5)		31,660
Drawings	4,500	
Freehold Land and Buildings	28,000	
Motor Van	2,200	
Purchases	60,000	
Sales		82,000
Salaries	9,100	
Discount Allowed	820	
Discount Received		640
Debtors	2,400	
Creditors		1,800
Cash in Hand	600	
Cash at Bank	1,980	
Stock (as at 1 January 19–5)	3,800	
Rates	650	
Insurances	150	
Telephone	100	
Fixtures and Fittings	1,800	
	116,100	116,100

Notes

At 31 December 19–5 stock in trade was valued at £4,000.

A telephone bill for £30 was outstanding.

Insurances of £25 were prepaid.

Required: You are to prepare trading and profit and loss accounts for the year ended 31 December 19–5 and a balance sheet as at that date.

(Royal Society of Arts)

25.2

The following trial balance was taken from the books of Robert Witham at 31 December 19–6.

	£	£
Capital (1 January 19–6)		11,700
Drawings	2,100	
Rent and Rates	1,340	
Wages and Salaries	2,711	
Purchases	23,821	
Sales		32,484
Bad Debts	88	
Trade debtors	3,840	
Trade creditors		1,535
Stock (1 January 19–6)	3,112	
Cash at bank	247	
Carriage inwards	138	
Motor Vehicles	7,037	
Office expenses	488	
Sundry expenses	797	
	45,719	45,719

Notes: (i) Stock at 31 December 19–6 was valued at £2,477.
(ii) 'Office Expenses' includes the cost of stationery, of which there remained stock worth £56 at 31 December 19–6.
(iii) Wages in arrears at 31 December 19–6 were £42.

You are required to prepare the trading and profit and loss account of Robert Witham for the year ended 31 December 19–6, and a balance sheet as at that date.

(Royal Society of Arts)

25.3

Julie Bright is in business as a business consultant. The following trial balance was extracted from her books:

	£	£
Freehold Premises	27,000	
Office Equipment	3,500	
Cash in hand	390	
Fixtures and Fittings	1,100	
Advertising	6,680	
Cash at Bank	4,980	
Repairs to Equipment	410	
Rates	1,100	
Rent received from sub-letting		1,248
Telephone	602	
Stationery	180	
General Expenses	1,034	
Drawings	9,070	
Wages	3,980	
Insurances	970	
Loan from Loamshire Bank (over five years)		4,000
Loan Interest	300	
Commissions received for Professional services		28,847
Capital, 1 January 19–3		27,201
	61,296	61,296

The following should be taken into consideration:
 (i) Rates prepaid £325 at 30 June 19–3.
 (ii) A telephone bill of £415 has not been paid.
 (iii) There was a small stock of stationery in hand on 30 June 19–3, valued at £24.
 (iv) A bill for cleaning expenses, £35, was outstanding (these should be charged to General Expenses).
 (v) Wages due to staff at 30 June 19–3 were £120.
Required:
(a) A profit and loss account for the six months ending 30 June 19–3, and
(b) A balance sheet as at that date.

(Royal Society of Arts)

25.4

The following trial balance was extracted from the books of R. Colebrook on 31 May 19–6. You are required to prepare his trading and profit and loss account for the year ended 31 May 19–6 and his balance sheet as at that date. Your trading account should clearly show:

(a) The cost of goods/stock sold;

(b) The cost of sales.

Trial balance as at 31 May 19–6

	Dr. £	Cr. £
Capital		29,250
Drawings	4,600	
Bank & Cash	9,200	
Salaries & Wages	23,000	
Purchases & Sales	35,000	68,000
Debtors & Creditors	12,350	18,000
Office Expenses	2,500	
Light & Heat	1,700	
Rates	1,400	
Premises	15,000	
Fixtures & Fittings	2,300	
Vehicles	4,200	
Stock at 1 June 19–5	4,100	
Sales & Purchase Returns	400	500
	115,750	115,750

The following information as at 31 May 19–6 is also available:

(i) Stock on 31 May 19–6 was £3,900.

(ii) Wages owing but not yet paid £100.

(iii) Light, heat and rates are to be apportioned:
$\frac{1}{4}$ to trading account,
$\frac{3}{4}$ to profit and loss account.

(iv) Included in the office expenses is an insurance prepayment of £50.

(Royal Society of Arts)

25.5

The following trial balance was extracted from the books of Robert Owen on 30 April 19–5.

	£	£
Capital 1 May 19–4		30,640
Furniture & Equipment	10,500	
Sales		46,800
Postage & Stationery	1,750	
Returns inwards	1,320	
Rates & Insurance	1,200	
Wages & Salaries	8,440	
Purchases	27,560	
Drawings	6,000	
Trade creditors		2,830
Petty cash	80	
Bank balance		4,600
Sundry expenses	8,570	
Stock 1 May 19–4	6,500	
Loan from Mercantile Bank		5,000
Interest on loan	750	
Freehold premises	15,000	
Trade debtors	2,200	
	89,870	89,870

The following additional information is given:
(a) Stock on 30 April 19–5 was valued at £7,640.
(b) Provide for carriage on purchases owing at 30 April 19–5, £140.
(c) The annual fire insurance premium of £240 was paid on the due date, 1 February 19–5. Make the necessary adjustment for the unexpired portion at 30 April 19–5

You are required to prepare the trading and profit and loss account for the year ended 30 April 19–5, and a balance sheet as at that date.

(Royal Society of Arts)

25.6

W. Sims is self-employed as a painter and decorator. From the figures given below prepare his profit and loss account for the year ended 31 May 19–7 and a balance sheet as at that date.

	£	£
Income from decorating		29,000
Introductory commissions		
from builders		950
Cost of paint & wallpapers	4,750	
Equipment	1,675	
Vehicles	4,700	
Rent & Rates	2,250	
Wages	6,900	
Drawings	7,000	
Stationery	1,750	
Vehicle Expenses	2,700	
Insurance	650	
Sundry expenses	1,800	
Customer's unpaid account	790	
Trade Creditors		840
Telephone	190	
Cash at Bank and in Hand	126	
Capital 1 June 19–6		4,491
	35,281	35,281

Notes:
(a) There were no opening or closing stocks of paint and wallpapers.
(b) The vehicle expenses include £100 road tax for the year ending 31 May 19–8.
(c) There is an unpaid telephone bill of £36 on 31 May 19–7.
(d) Rates prepaid at 31 May 19–7 are £90.
(e) On 31 May 19–7 there was an unused stock of stationery amounting to £300.

(Royal Society of Arts)

25.7

E. Sweet is a confectionery wholesaler. The following trial balance was extracted from his books on 31 March 19–2

	Dr. £	Cr. £
Capital at 1 April 19–1		20,000
Fixtures and Fittings	5,000	
Debtors and Creditors	26,200	13,400
Discount allowed	1,300	
Discount received		1,700
Stock at 1 April 19–1	11,700	
Rent	1,100	
Rates	600	
Sales		54,500
Purchases	39,300	
Electricity	400	
Salaries	1,500	
Repairs and maintenance	300	
Purchase returns		600
Loan from Finance Co.		6,000
Bad Debts	300	
Drawings	2,400	
Hire of motor van	700	
Cash in hand	800	
Cash at bank	4,600	
	96,200	96,200

Notes
(1) Stock at 31 March 19–2 amounted to £13,300.
(2) Salaries due but not paid £200.
(3) Fixtures and Fittings should be depreciated by 10 per cent.
(4) A provision of £1,400 for doubtful debts should be created.
(5) Rates paid in advance amounted to £100.
(6) Interest due on loan amounts to £800.

Required

Prepare a trading and profit and loss account for the year ended 31 March 19–2 and a balance sheet as at that date.

(London Chamber of Commerce and Industry)

25.8

Elaine Mellor is a toy wholesaler. She extracted the following trial balance from her books at the close of business on 31 March 19–9.

	Dr. £	Cr. £
Purchases and Sales	17,620	38,330
Stock 1 April 19–8	6,740	
Capital 1 April 19–8		17,290
Bank overdraft		2,450
Cash	480	
Discounts	380	490
Returns inwards	670	
Returns outwards		890
Carriage outwards	1,050	
Rent	1,530	
Rates and Insurance	960	
Provision for Bad and Doubtful Debts		520
Fixtures and Fittings	5,200	
Delivery Van	7,000	
Debtors and Creditors	13,790	8,030
Drawings	3,960	
Wages and Salaries	7,980	
General Expenses	640	
	68,000	68,000

Notes

(a) Stock at 31 March 19–9, £5,430.
(b) Wages and salaries accrued at 31 March 19–9, £700.
(c) Rates prepaid at 31 March 19–9, £160.
(d) Increase the provision for bad and doubtful debts by £270 to £790.
(e) Provide for depreciation as follows: fixtures and fittings £200; delivery van £500.

You are required to prepare the trading and profit and loss accounts of Elaine Mellor for the year ended 31 March 19–9 together with a balance sheet as at that date.

26   The Journal

OBJECTIVES   To examine and consider the function and the various uses of the journal proper in book-keeping.

It has already been established that the use of subsidiary books is both desirable and of benefit to the business. The subsidiary books already covered in previous modules, namely, the sales day book, the purchases day book, the returns inwards and the returns outwards day books, are books of 'original entry' where the details of the original documents are first entered before being posted to the double entry accounts in the various ledgers. This procedure assists and improves efficiency in the various accounts departments. By the use of the subsidiary books already covered, it can be seen that each transaction is first entered in a book of 'original entry', sometimes referred to as a book of 'prime entry', before being posted to the ledgers.

The cash book, although it is part of the ledger, is a separate book, which contains entries of a particular nature concerning the amounts of money received and the payments made, either in cash or by cheque. The cash book, therefore, provides a record from which the details can be 'posted' to their respective ledger accounts. The cash book is regarded as a book of original entry, but is not referred to as a subsidiary book.

In businesses which use subsidiary books a rule is made that no entry should be made in the ledger unless the details have first been entered in the appropriate book of 'original entry'. This rule provides a foundation for the consideration and the main uses of the journal proper.

The journal proper is a day book in the form of diary. Originally, all the commercial transactions of a business were first entered in the journal proper before being recorded in the ledger but, as the volume of business expanded and the number of entries required increased, it became necessary to sub-divide certain classes of transactions into the various subsidiary books. The introduction of the 'grouping together' system of certain classes of transactions, with the use of the various subsidiary books, has now considerably reduced the number of entries required in the journal proper.

The journal proper is a book of 'original entry', in which the details are first entered of transactions which are of a special or unusual nature, and which cannot suitably be entered in any other book of original entry. In practice, the particular transactions which are entered in the journal are comparatively rare and require a specific explanation, and are not the regular day-to-day occurrences previously considered.

Some of the present main uses of the journal are set out below:

(1) The purchase and sale of fixed assets on credit.
(2) The correction of errors.
(3) Opening entries – required when opening a new set of books.
(4) Transfers between accounts.
(5) Bad debts – written off and recovered.

The Journal Proper has a standard design and layout, as illustrated below:

Date	Details	F	Debit	Credit

The debit and credit aspects of each transaction must first be determined. The entry made in the journal, is the setting down of this twofold aspect; each journal entry should contain the following:

(a) The date.
(b) The name of the account(s) to be debited in the details column, the amount involved placed in the debit column.
(c) The name of the account(s) to be credited, a little indented, in the details column, the amount involved placed in the credit column.
(d) A brief description explaining the reason for the entry. This is called 'the narration'.

It must be emphasised at this point, that, although the debit aspect and the credit aspect of a transaction are recorded in the journal, it is *not* part of the double entry system. They are entered in the journal as the book of original entry, *before* being posted to their respective double entry accounts.

1 The Purchase and Sale of Fixed Assets on Credit

Consider the following example of the purchase of a fixed asset on credit.
(a) On 1 March 19–7, Daniel Mason purchased office furniture for £680 on credit from Jenkins Supplies.

The twofold aspect of the transaction should be considered, and the double entry determined. The double entry required for the purchase of an asset on credit is debit the asset account; credit the supplier, in this example, Jenkins Supplies. The journal entry would appear as follows:

The Journal

19–7		F	Dr.	Cr.
Mar 1	Office Furniture Account		680.00	
	Jenkins Supplies Account			680.00
	Purchase on credit of Office Furniture			

The entries made in the journal cover many different types of transactions. It is, therefore, only necessary to draw a line underneath each entry. When posted to the ledger accounts they will appear as follows:

Office Furniture Account

Mar 1 Jenkins Supplies	680.00	

Jenkins Supplies Account

	Mar 1 Office furniture	680.00

Consider the following example of the sale of a fixed asset on credit.
(b) On 15 May 19–7 the delivery van was sold for £2,200 on credit to B. Robson.

The twofold aspect of the transaction should be considered, and the double entry determined. The double entry required for the sale of a fixed asset on credit is: debit the receiver, in this example, B. Robson; credit the asset account, in this case the delivery van account. The journal entry would appear as follows:

19–7	F	Dr.	Cr.
May 15			
B. Robson Account		2,200.00	
Delivery Van Account			2,200.00
Sale on credit of used Delivery Van			
Registration No. EUM 34			

The recording of reference numbers, such as the serial number or the registration number, as part of the narration is a good policy, as this additional information is very useful for reference purposes.

2 The Correction of Errors

Inevitably, from time to time errors will occur in the ledger. Alterations and erasures are not made in the ledger. When an error is discovered the correction should be made through the double entry accounts. It will be necessary to examine the error and to determine the action required to make the correction. The twofold aspect will need to be ascertained.

Consider the following example. On 1 June 19–7 a sale of goods (£236.00) to W. Jones had been entered in error in B. Jones' account.

The twofold aspect of the correction must be determined, and the details are first entered in the journal as the appropriate book of original entry. To correct the error, a debit entry will be required in W. Jones' account and a corresponding credit entry will be required in B. Jones' account. The journal entry necessary to correct the error, would appear as follows:

19–7		F	Dr.	Cr.
Jun 1	W. Jones Account		236.00	
	B. Jones Account			236.00
	Correction of error, posted to wrong personal account.			

Consider another example of an error in posting. On 15 June 19–7 an amount of £250 paid for rent had been entered in error in the rates account.

To correct the error, a debit entry will be required in the rent account and a corresponding credit entry will be required in the rates account. The journal entry required to correct the error, would appear as follows:

19–7		F	Dr.	Cr.
Jun 15	Rent Account		250.00	
	Rates Account			250.00
	Correction of error, posted to wrong expense account.			

3 Opening Entries

The entries which are made in the journal will cover many different types of events and transactions. An opening entry will be required when a business is first established or in the opening of a new set of books. An opening journal entry is usually made on the first day a new business begins, but one is also necessary in the case of an existing business which has not kept proper records. The opening of a new set of books using the double entry system will also require an opening journal entry.

The financial position of a business is summarised by listing all the assets and the liabilities in the journal. Consider the following example. On 1 March 19–7 John Clayton decides to open a new set of books on the double entry principles. He establishes that his assets and liabilities are as follows:

ASSETS: Cash in hand £325; cash at bank £3,862; office equipment £750; motor van £4,600; stock of goods £3,500; debtors: J. Lister, £763; K. Turner, £450.

LIABILITIES: Creditors: B. Freeman, £670; F. Brooks, £580.

In preparing the journal entry the calculation of the amount of the capital will be required. The amount by which the assets exceed the liabilities is the capital. This is calculated by the formula: ASSETS LESS LIABILITIES EQUALS CAPITAL.

	£
The Assets in total are	14,250
Less the total liabilities	1,250
Capital	13,000

The opening journal entry is made as follows:

The Journal

19–7		F	Dr.	Cr.
Mar 1	Cash in hand	CB	325.00	
	Cash at bank	CB	3,862.00	
	Office Equipment	GL	750.00	
	Motor Van	GL	4,600.00	
	Stock	GL	3,500.00	
	Debtors: J. Lister	SL	763.00	
	K. Turner	SL	450.00	
	Creditors: B. Freeman	PL		670.00
	F. Brooks	PL		580.00
	Capital	GL		13,000.00
			£14,250.00	£14,250.00
	Being the Assets and Liabilities at this date entered to open the books			

This summary of the financial position, made in the journal on 1 March 19–7, is a permanent record to which reference can be made at any time. In practice an opening journal entry will seldom occur more than once during the lifetime of a business. However, in examinations this type of question often occurs. The question will usually give details of the assets and the liabilities; the student will be required to draft the journal entry necessary to open the books and calculate the amount of the capital.

The opening journal entry is a preliminary record showing how the accounts will appear in the ledger. The assets accounts will be opened with debit balances, the liability and capital accounts will be opened with credit balances. The following is an illustration of the posting of the opening journal entry to the double entry accounts in the ledgers.

Cash Book

		F	Cash £	Bank £	19–7		F	Cash £	Bank £
19–7									
Mar 1	Balances	J	325.00	3,862.00					

General Ledger

Office Equipment Account

Mar	1	Balance	J	750.00	

238

Motor Van Account

Mar	1	Balance	J	4,600.00				

Stock Account

Mar	1	Balance	J	3,500.00				

Capital Account

					Mar	1 Balance	J	13,000.00

Sales Ledger

J. Lister Account

Mar	1	Balance	J	763.00				

K. Turner Account

Mar	1	Balance	J	450.00				

Purchase Ledger

D. Freeman Account

					Mar	1 Balance	J	670.00

F. Brooks Account

					Mar	1 Balance	J	580.00

As each item is entered in the ledger the folio column is completed. This will lesson the risk of mistakes and omissions in posting to the ledger. When the posting of the opening balances has been completed and the details entered in the ledgers, the accounts are then ready for the day-by-day transactions to be recorded, as and when they occur.

4   Transfer Between Accounts

There are numerous different types of transfers between accounts which may be required during the normal events of a business. Whenever a transfer is necessary, a formal preliminary record should first be made in the journal, with the narration clearly explaning the circumstances.

Consider the following example: On 17 June 19–7 a garage bill of £250 for stereo equipment fitted to the proprietor's private car had been entered in the motor expenses; this should have been charged to drawings.

The twofold aspect will need to be determined; in this example, a debit entry will be required in the drawings account and a corresponding credit entry in the motor expenses account. The details should first be entered in the journal as the appropriate book of original entry, as follows:

19–7		F	Dr.	Cr.
Jun 17	Drawings Account		250.00	
	Motor Expenses			250.00
	Proprietor's private motor expenses			
	transferred to Drawings Account.			

5 Bad Debts written off

A debtor who cannot pay his debt is called a 'bad debtor', and the debt owing is referred to as a 'bad debt'. Usually many attempts will have been made in an effort to recover the outstanding amount but, whatever the reason or circumstances, if a debtor cannot pay what is owed, and the amount becomes irrecoverable, there is no point or advantage in continuing to maintain the debtor's account in the ledger.

When it becomes necessary for a bad debt to be written off, the preliminary record of the details is first entered in the journal as the book of original entry. The following is an example of a debt which is entirely bad.

Charles Bentley is a debtor who owes the firm the sum of £290. He is declared bankrupt and it is decided to write the debt off on 31 July 19–7. The double entry effect of the transaction would be: a debit entry in the bad debts account and a corresponding credit entry in Charles Bentley's account. The journal entry would appear as follows:

19–7		F	Dr.	Cr.
Jul 31	Bad Debts Account		290.00	
	Charles Bentley Account			290.00
	Irrecoverable debt written off.			

A Debt Which is Partially Bad

In certain circumstances, if a debtor is declared bankrupt or goes into voluntary liquidation, the debtor may only be able to pay a 'composition' or dividend of so much in the pound of the outstanding debt. In these cases the amount received will be debited in the bank account or cash account, and the same amount credited to the debtor's account. The balance remaining on the debtor's account is a bad debt.

Consider the following example of a debt which is partially bad. On 1 August 19–7 Brian Forbes is a debtor for goods supplied for £268. He goes into voluntary liquidation, and after negotiation the firm agrees to accept a payment of 50 pence in the pound in full settlement of the debt. A cheque is received on 22 August 19–7. The preliminary record would be first entered in the journal as follows:

19–7		F	Dr.	Cr.
Aug 22	Bank		134.00	
	Bad Debts Account		134.00	
	Brian Forbes Account			268.00
	Being the agreed full settlement			
	of the outstanding debt.			

Bad Debts Recovered

Because of the bankruptcy laws and the limitations imposed, some bankrupts do their best to pay off their debts. This can often take a considerable time, but cases are recorded regularly of people paying their debts many years after their insolvencies. In such cases it is usual for interest to be charged on the amount of the original debt.

Consider the following example of a bad debt recovered. K. Stead, whose account of £68 was written off as a bad debt two years ago, pays £74.80 by cheque on 8 October, 19–7 in full settlement of the debt. K. Stead's account was closed two years ago in 19–5 and has been removed from the sales ledger. The amount of the original debt was £68, which with interest at five per cent per annum amounts to £74.80. The preliminary record of the details of the bad debt recovered are first entered in the journal as follows:

19–7		F	Dr.	Cr.
Oct 8	Bank		74.80	
	Bad Debts Recovered Account			68.00
	Interest Received Account			6.80
	Being K. Stead's original debt recovered			
	with interest.			

It is important to note that no entry will be made in the debtor's 'dead' account.

POINTS TO REMEMBER

The journal proper, which is generally referred to simply as 'the journal' is the book of original entry for events and transactions of a more unusual nature whose entry requires a specific explanation.

The debit and credit aspects of each entry must first be determined. The entry made in the journal is the preliminary setting-down of the twofold aspect.

Each journal entry should be recorded, stating the date; the name of the account to be debited, always shown first; the name of the account to be credited, a little indented; the narration, which is an explanation of the entry and should be restricted to a few words which clearly indicate the reason for the entry.

Examiners frequently set questions which require the drafting of an opening journal entry showing the amount of the proprietor's capital. This is calculated by the formula: total assets less total liabilities equals capital.

It must be emphasised that although both aspects, debit and credit, are recorded in the journal it is *not* part of the double entry system; they are entered in the journal as the book of original entry.

Examiners sometimes make the request that all transactions should be 'journalised'; this simply means drafting the journal entry.

The assignment exercises which follow are all taken from past examination papers, and will enable the student to gain sufficient practice in the drafting of journal entries.

Assignment Exercises

26.1

A. Teagle owns a hardware shop. The following transactions and adjustments occurred during February, 19–3.

Feb 4 Teagle purchased some new shop fittings from Arthur Blake (Shopfitters) on credit for £8,600.
15 Peter Payne bought some old shop fittings from A. Teagle at an agreed price of £400, payable on 1 April 19–3.
18 Simon Bates owed A. Teagle £51. The debt had been outstanding for over a year. Teagle decided to treat this as a bad debt.
29 Goods purchased on credit from Henry Jones (£210) had been incorrectly posted to the account of Harry Albert Jones.

You are required to draft journal entries including brief narrations to record the above items.

(Royal Society of Arts)

26.2

Draft the journal entries required to record the following in the books of a grocer.

19–3		£

June 3 Purchased on credit, office furniture from
          Crescent Furniture Manufacturers Ltd.   4,500
    7 Wrote off Philip Richards' account as a bad debt.   470
    9 Corrected an error in posting: John Bell had been debited in
       error, instead of John Belling.   150
  10 Sold on credit to Car Trader old motor van at book value.   70

Marks will be given for narrations which explain and clarify the entry.

(Royal Society of Arts)

26.3

P. Green had been in business for several years and had not kept proper records. His new financial year began on 1 May 19–7 and he decides to convert his accounts to a full double entry system and ascertains the following balances from his personal records:

Freehold Premises £32,000; Motor Van £2,600; Fixtures £1,800; Stock £6,400; Bank and Cash £2,965; Debtors – T. Ross £90; A. Baker £64; T. Bone £128; Long-Term Loan at 10 per cent p.a. £10,000; Trade Creditors – T. Black £271; D. Bacon £194; Rates Prepaid £42; Interest on loan outstanding £1,100.

You are required to:

(a) To draft the journal entry necessary to open the books showing therein the proprietor's capital.
(b) To prepare journal entries in respect of the following:
    (NB Suitable narrations must be given in all cases.)

		£

May 6 Purchased on credit fixtures from Micawber & Sons.   950
    8 Returned some of the fittings as unsuitable to Micawber & Sons.   60
  12 Green was notified that Baker had been declared bankrupt. The
      account was written off as a bad debt.   64
  22 Some of the fixtures which had been purchased from
      Micawber, cost price £90, were found to be surplus to
      requirements and were sold to Gatt & Co on credit.   90
  29 Correct an error in posting. T. Davis had been debited
      in error instead of T. Davies.   130

(Royal Society of Arts)

26.4

(a) Draft the journal entries to record the following items in the books of George Jones:

19–6

May 1 Received an account from British Rail (£25) for carriage of goods to customer. It is Jones's policy to sell all goods on carriage paid terms.

    8 Motor expenses of £100 were for Jones's private use and are to be charged to drawings account.

(b) Give journal entries to correct the following errors:

19–6

May 7 An amount of £40 paid for rent had been entered in error in the rates account.

  16 A motor van costing £2,400 bought for use in the business had been entered into the purchases account.

  18 An amount of £250 received from John Boon had been credited to Tom Boon's Account.

Marks will be given for narrations which explain and clarify the entries.

(Royal Society of Arts)

26.5

On 1 June 19–4, T. Jones had the following assets and liabilities:

Freehold Premises, £25,000; Mortgage on Premises £12,500; Motor Vehicle £2,700; Amount owing on motor vehicle £1,400; Fixtures and Fittings £2,000; Stock £2,750; Debtors £1,580; Bank overdraft £920; Unpaid electricity bill £72.

On 1 April 19–4, Jones had paid rates £180 for the half-year ending 30 September 19–4 and on 1 February 19–4 had paid one year's insurance premium £60.

You are required to prepare an opening journal entry as 1 June 19–4 showing clearly the capital of Jones at that date.

(Royal Society of Arts)

26.6

(a) On 1 May 19–5 J. Drake had the following assets and liabilities:

ASSETS: Freehold land and buildings £25,000, Fixtures and Fittings £1,250, Vehicle £2,000, Stock £2,600, Cash at Bank and in hand £1,580, Debtors £1,500.
LIABILITIES: Long-term loan £1,200, Trade Creditors £1,300, Electricity account outstanding £30.

You are required to prepare an opening journal entry for Drake showing his capital as at that date.

(b) During the month of May, the following transactions took place:

May 7 Drake purchased a new van costing £4,750 from Better Motors, paying £1,000 cash and being given credit for the remainder.

14 Drake sold on credit to A. Baker fixtures and fittings which the business no longer required, at their book value of £250.

18 Notification was received by Drake that J. Smith, a debtor for £100, had been declared bankrupt. It was decided to write off this account as a bad debt.

21 It was discovered that a purchase of goods on credit from T. Murphy, value £25, had been debited to Murphy's account and credited to sales.

You are required to show the necessary journal entries.

(Royal Society of Arts)

27 Errors Not Affecting Trial Balance Agreement

OBJECTIVES To examine and consider the six classes of errors which can occur but are not revealed by the construction of a trial blance.

A trial balance is usually drawn up periodically to ascertain the arithmetical accuracy of the book-keeping. All the items recorded in the accounts at the debit side should equal, in total, all the items recorded on the credit side. When the two columns of the trial balance agree, they are said to 'strike a balance', and this is recognised to be a good indication that the book-keeping has been methodically carried out.

However, the 'balance' or agreement of the trial balance does not positively prove that no errors have been made. It has certain limitations, and for this reason it is only considered to be a 'prima facie' proof of accuracy. 'Prima facie' means at first sight, on the face of it. The trial balance agreement is a proof only of the arithmetical accuracy of the postings. There are six classes of errors which can occur and not be disclosed by the construction of a trial balance.

(1) Original errors.
(2) Errors of omission.
(3) Errors of commission.
(4) Errors of principle.
(5) Compensating errors.
(6) Complete reversal of entries.

1 Original Errors

These are errors which have been made in the original documents, or errors made when the details of the original documents are being entered into the subsidiary books. The original documents are: the copies of the sales invoices, the purchase invoices received from the suppliers, and the credit notes and debit notes.

Consider the following examples of an 'original error'. If an error is made in the calculation of a sales invoice, the amount entered in the sales day book will be incorrect. The incorrect amount would then be posted to the double entry accounts, that is, to the debit side of the customer's personal account and to the credit side of the sales account. The trial balance would still 'balance'; it would not reveal that the original amount posted was incorrect.

Another example of an 'original error' could occur when the details of the purchase invoices were being entered in the purchases day book. When copying the figures from the document into the purchases day book an error could be made for example, a purchase invoice for £412 received from the supplier James Cartwright might be entered as £421. The incorrect amount is then posted to the debit side of the purchases account and the credit side of the supplier's account. The trial balance would still agree; it would not disclose the error of the transposition of the figures.

An original error occurs, therefore, when the original figure is incorrect and double entry is carried out, using the incorrect figure. When errors are discovered they will need to be corrected, and the twofold aspect of the correction will need to be determined.

Example: A purchase invoice for £412 received from James Cartwright was entered in the books as £421.

Solution: In this example the amount posted to the double entry accounts was greater than the correct amount. The correction needed will be the amount of the difference, namely, £9. A debit entry in the supplier's account will record the necessary reduction, with a corresponding credit entry in the purchases account.

The details of the correction would first be entered in the journal, as follows:

The Journal

19–8		Dr.	Cr.
Mar 8	James Cartwright Account	9.00	
	Purchases Account		9.00
	Correction of error, purchase		
	invoice entered as £421 for £412.		

2 Errors of Omission

As the name suggests, errors of omission occur when a transaction is completely overlooked and omitted from the books; neither debit entry nor credit entry has been made in the ledger. The trial balance would still agree; it would be unaffected by the omission of a transaction.

Consider the following example of an error of omission:

Example: An invoice for a new typewriter received from R. Ramsden for £365 had been mislaid. Entries for this transaction had not been made in the ledger.

Solution: A transaction which has been completely overlooked will require the twofold aspect to be determined and the correct double entry to be recorded in the accounts. In this example the double entry would be: a debit entry in the office equipment account and a credit entry in R. Ramsden's account.

The details would first be entered in the journal as follows:

19–8		Dr.	Cr.
Apr 4	Office Equipment Account	365.00	
	R. Ramsden Account		365.00
	Correction of omission of invoice for new		
	typewriter.		

3 Errors of Commission

The word 'commission' in this context means 'instruction to perform certain duties'. An error of commission occurs when a mistake is made in the operation of these duties, and the posting has not been accurately carried out.

Errors of commission happen when both the debit entry and the credit entry are made, on the correct side of each account in the ledger, but with a wrong account being used. These types of errors occur most often when the amount is correctly recorded, in the correct type of account, but entered in the wrong personal account.

Consider the following example of an error of commission:

Example: On 7 May 19–8 a cheque for £280 received from C. Green had been credited to C. Gray's account.

Solution: In order to correct this error the twofold aspect will need to be determined; a debit entry will be required in C. Gray's Account to cancel out the error, and a corresponding credit entry made in C. Green's account, to post the amount to the correct debtor's account.

The details of the correction would first be entered in the journal as follows:

19–8		Dr.	Cr.
May 7	C. Gray Account	280.00	
	C. Green Account		280.00
	Correction of error posted to		
	wrong personal account.		

4 Errors of Principle

An error of principle is caused through a mistake being made in the principles of book-keeping, and most frequently occurs when a transaction is entered in the wrong class of account. The double entry system has an account for every asset, liability and capital. If for example, the purchase on credit of a new office desk from Office Supplies was entered at the debit side of the office expenses account, instead of the debit side of the asset account, and the credit side of the supplier's account, this would result in no entry being made in the asset account. One of the entries is wrong in principle, but the trial balance would still agree; it would not reveal this type of error.

Example: On 17 June 19–8 the purchase of a new office desk for £250 from Office Supplies was entered in the office expenses account.

Solution: The correction necessary will be: a debit entry in the office furniture account; this will enter the amount where it should be; and a credit entry in the office expenses account to cancel the amount incorrectly entered.

The details would first be entered in the journal as follows:

19–8		Dr.	Cr.
Jun 17	Office Furniture Account	250.00	
	Office Expenses Account		250.00
	Correction of error, purchase of an office desk		
	debited to Office Expenses		

5 Compensating Errors

Compensating errors, as the name implies, are errors which cancel out or compensate for each other. These are usually caused by two separate errors, of the same amount, being made in the ledger, one error affecting an account on the debit side, and one error affecting an account on the credit side.

The trial balance totals would still agree; the total of the debit column and the credit column of the trial balance would be incorrect by the same amount, but the errors would cancel out each other.

There are many possible combinations of compensating errors and they will need to be corrected when they are discovered.

Example   In the addition of the sales account an error is made, and it is overcast by £100; the general expenses were also incorrectly calculated and overcast by £100.

Solution: A debit entry will be required in the sales account; this will record a reduction and cancel the amount of the overcast; a corresponding credit entry will be necessary in the general expenses account which will record the reduction of the amount of the overcast.

The details of the correction would first be entered in the journal as follows:

19–8		Dr.	Cr.
Jul 2	Sales Account	100.00	
	General Expenses Account		100.00
	Correction of overcasts, £100 in each, the sales		
	account and the general expenses account which		
	compensated for each other		

6 Complete Reversal of Entries

These errors happen when the amounts are entered in the correct ledger accounts, but the amount involved is recorded on the wrong side of the account. For example, a cheque paid to a supplier for £450, was entered at the debit side of the bank account and the credit side of the supplier's account. The amount entered in the bank account was correct, but it was entered at the wrong side: a payment by cheque should be recorded at the credit side of the bank account. Similarly, the amount entered in the supplier's account was correct, but it was entered at the wrong side; the corresponding entry in the supplier's account should have been recorded at the debit side.

The trial balance totals would still agree; they would be unaffected by this type of error. These errors can be more difficult to correct, as it is not always a simple matter of reversing the original incorrect entries.

Consider the example:

On 3 August 19–7 a cheque for £450 paid to D. Mason was entered at the debit side of the bank account and the credit side of D. Mason's account.

The correction necessary in this situation will be *double* the original amount: that is £900. Entering the original amount only would merely cancel the error, leaving no entry of the transaction: an entry of £450 at the credit side of the bank account would only cancel out the £450 entered at the debit side. Similarly, an entry of £450 at the debit side of D. Mason's account would only cancel out the original error, and this would result in the actual transaction not being recorded. The correction required, therefore, will be double the original amount. The details would be entered in the Journal as follows:

19–8		Dr.	Cr.
Aug 3	D. Mason Account	900.00	
	Bank Account		900.00
	Correction of error, payment of £450 by cheque was entered at the debit side of the Bank Account and the credit side of D. Mason A/c		

This Module has illustrated the fact that errors can occur which are not disclosed by the construction of a trial balance. Questions which involve the correction of errors require a fundamental understanding of the double entry system and will invariably require careful consideration, as follows:

(a) Examine the error, and consider what has actually taken place.
(b) Determine what should have taken place.
(c) Decide the action necessary in order to make the correction.

POINTS TO REMEMBER 'Prima facie' means: at first sight, on the fact of it.

The Trial Balance agreement is a proof only of the arithmetical accuracy of the postings.

Certain information will need to be committed to memory and this applies particularly to the six classes of errors which are *NOT* revealed by the construction of a Trial Balance.

The two-fold aspect of the correction must first be determined, and when the Journal entry is requested the 'narration' should clearly explain and clarify the entry.

Assignment Exercises

27.1
(a) Explain why a trial balance which agrees is not conclusive proof of the complete accuracy of the books of account.
(b) Give examples of three types of errors which can occur but will not be revealed by the construction of a trial balance.

27.2
(a) To what extent is the agreement of the trial balance proof of accuracy of the books? How would the omission of
  (i) the opening stock, and
  (ii) the closing stock affect the trial balance?
(b) State the initial steps you would take to locate the error if the trial balance disagreed.

(Royal Society of Arts)

27.3
'If the trial balance totals agree, it proves that the accounts of the business are correct.'
By the use of FIVE examples, show whether you agree or disagree with this statement.

(Joint Matriculation Board)

27.4

The following balances appeared in the ledger of Terry Dennis on 31 March 19–4.

	£
Drawings	1,600
Rent and Rates	350
Stock 1 April 19–3	5,500
Bank current account (overdrawn)	750
Wages	8,000
Petty Cash	60
Creditor for Office Equipment	1,600
Selling expenses	3,100
Purchases	11,206
Trade Creditors	2,746
Carriage outwards	410
Sales	26,532
Office expenses	4,730
Trade debtors	2,650
Commission received	520
Furniture and Equipment	19,600
Discount allowed	428
Capital 1 April 19–3	?

Required:
(a) From the list of balances given above prepare a trial balance as on 31 March 19–4. Calculate and include your own figure for the capital account balance at 1 April 19–3.
(b) What procedures would you adopt if the trial balance does not agree?
(c) Certain types of error can occur even though the trial balance agrees. Described THREE types of such errors, with examples.

(Royal Society of Arts)

27.5

Philip Miller hurriedly extracted his trial balance on 31 October 19–5 as follows:

	Dr. £	Cr. £
Capital		7,000
Sales		4,620
Purchases	2,966	
Sundry Expenses	848	
Leasehold property	4,000	
Fixtures & Fittings	2,870	
Debtors	819	
Creditors		403
Stock		363
Cash at bank	243	
	11,746	12,386

He then re-examined his accounts and the trial balance, and found the following errors:

(i) The correct balance of fixtures and fittings was £2,780.
(ii) The sales day book for October had been overcast by £100.
(iii) When a debtor paid him £78 the amount was properly entered in the bank account, but not entered on the personal account.
(iv) Bank charges of £18 had been properly entered in the sundry expenses account, but omitted from the bank account.
(v) One of the balances in the trial balance was entered in the wrong column.

You are required to:
(a) Re-write the trial balance, correcting it where necessary, and
(b) Explain briefly any TWO kinds of mistakes which would NOT have caused the trial balance to disagree.

(Royal Society of Arts)

27.6

The following balances appeared in the ledger of Roger Thomas on 28 February 19–7

	£
Trade creditors	3,740
Carriage outwards	152
Stock 1 March 19–6	4,500
Purchases	10,604
General expenses	7,286
Rates and insurance	1,534
Bank overdraft	8,578
Wages and salaries	9,800
Discount allowed	142
Carriage inwards	186
Premises and equipment	38,500
Sales	19,354
Trade debtors	2,550
Returns outwards	312
Petty Cash	150
Rent receivable	560
Capital 1 March 19–6	?

Further examination of the books revealed the following:

(i) Drawings by the proprietor of £48 per week over 50 weeks had been included in general expenses.

(ii) The total of the discount received column in the cash book, £121 had not been posted to the general ledger.

(iii) A cheque for £250 received from L. Smith had been posted to the credit of I. Smith's account.

(iv) A sales invoice for £132 had not been put through the books.

Required:

(a) From the list of balances and additional information given above, prepare a trial balance as on 28 February 19–7. Calculate and include your own figure for the capital account at 1 March 19–6.

(b) What is the main reason for compiling a trial balance?

(c) Describe and give examples of THREE errors which will not affect the trial balance agreement.

(Royal Society of Arts)

27.7

The following trial balance was extracted from the books of Andrew Scott, a retailer selling newspapers and confectionery, on 29 February 19–8.

	£ Dr.	£ Cr.
Capital		40,100
Drawings	5,000	
Rent and rates	2,500	
Lighting and heating	2,400	
Advertising	220	
Motor expenses	1,200	
Wages and salaries	8,500	
Insurance	500	
Purchases	26,100	
Sales		55,320
Creditors		2,500
Motor vehicles	15,000	
Equipment	20,000	
Stock of goods 1 March 19–7	12,000	
Cash in hand	100	
Cash at bank	4,400	
	97,920	97,920

After preparation of the trial balance the following errors were found:

(a) 15 June 19–7: A payment of £200 by cheque to D. Smith, a creditor, had been debited to the account of D. Smithson.
(b) 13 August 19–7: An invoice for the purchase of sweets and confectionery for £340 from R. Wallis and Co. had not been entered in the books.
(c) 24 September 19–7: A payment for repairs to the motor vehicles of £500 had been entered in the motor vehicles account.
(d) 30 October 19–7: Andrew Scott had bought petrol for his own use costing £200. This had been entered in the motor expenses account.

You are required:
(i) To show the journal entries necessary to correct these errors.
(ii) To rewrite the trial balance *after* the errors have been corrected.

(Royal Society of Arts)

28   Control Accounts

OBJECTIVES   To enable students to gain an understanding of control accounts and the preparation and presentation of a sales ledger control account and a purchase ledger control account.

Errors are made in the day-to-day running of a business, and these errors must be found. The larger the business, the more difficult the location of errors becomes. In most firms there are far more personal accounts than real accounts or nominal accounts, therefore it is more likely that errors will occur in the sales ledger and the purchase ledger than in the general ledger. To help locate errors accountants have applied a simple idea; they divide the ledger into smaller parts and check each one.

Even in a small firm there are usually a number of ledgers in use, and the larger the organisation the greater the number of ledgers. In large organisations the ledgers are usually sub-divided (the ledger is divided and separated into smaller parts). This sub-division could be, for example, A to F, G to L, M to S, T to Z.

Any errors or mistakes made could be difficult to find and extremely time-consuming and expensive, therefore a type of trial balance for each ledger or sub-division of a ledger is required. A control account for each ledger, or sub-division of a ledger, will meet this requirement, and it is only the ledgers whose control accounts do not balance that will require systematic detailed checking to discover the errors.

It must be emphasised at this point that control accounts are not necessarily part of the double entry system. They are in actual fact mathematical proofs performing the same function as a trial balance to a particular ledger, or sub-division of a ledger, and when *not* part of the double entry system, they are simply a means of checking the accuracy of the entries.

Control accounts are usually presented in the same form as an account, with the totals of all the debit entries in the ledger on the left-hand side of the control account, and the totals of each of the various credit entries in the ledger on the right-hand side.

Because totals are used, the control accounts are also known as *total accounts*. A control account for a sales ledger could be known as either a sales ledger control account or a total debtors account. In the same way a control account for a purchase ledger could be known as either a purchase ledger control account or a total creditors account.

The control accounts may be treated as being an integral part of the double entry system, the balances of the control accounts being taken for the purpose of extracting a trial balance. In this case, the personal accounts are being used as subsidiary records, and must be regarded as outside the double entry system, otherwise some entries could appear twice.

Because ledgers which have a control account system are proved to be correct, as far as the double entry is concerned, they are sometimes called self-balancing ledgers.

The preparation of control accounts is an excellent test of the ability of students, and these types of questions are popular with examiners. The student is given information referring to either a sales ledger or a purchase ledger, or both, and is asked to draw up the control accounts. A knowledge of the sources of information for a control account may also be required.

Sales Ledger Control Account

Hundreds of entries are made every day in the sales ledger, recording the sales made to customers, the cheques and cash received from customers, the discounts allowed, the returns inwards and any bad debts. All accounts in the sales ledger will have the same kind of entries, because they record the selling and the receiving of payment for the sales.

All accounts in the sales ledger will normally have debit balances. Therefore the sales ledger control account is constructed in *total* of all the individual items which have been entered in the debtors' accounts in any particular sales ledger or sub-division of a ledger.

Study the following sales ledger control account and the explanations following, showing how the account is compiled.

Sales Ledger Control Account

19–8			£	19–8			£
Jan	1	Balance b/d	23,524	Jan	31	Bank	17,450
	31	Sales	9,870		31	Discount Allowed	341
					31	Cash	560
					31	Returns Inwards	670
					31	Bad Debts	300
					31	Balance c/d	14,073
			33,394				33,394
Feb	1	Balances b/d	14,073				

Figure	Explanation	Source of information
	At the debit side:	
23,524	This is the total of all the debit balances on the customers' accounts.	Sales ledger
9,870	Total sales for the month.	Sales journal for the month or sales account if subsidiary books are not used.
	At the credit side:	
17,450	Total of all payments received form debtors by cheque.	Bank column of the cash book.
341	Total of discounts allowed to customers	The discount allowed column of the cash book.
560	Total of all payments received from debtors in cash.	Cash column of the cash book.
670	Total of returns inwards from customers	Returns inwards journal for the month or returns inwards account if subsidiary books are not used.
300	Total of bad debts written off as irrecoverable.	Bad debts account
14,073	The balance of the control account, which should equal the schedule of debtors on the date the account is prepared.	By balancing the control account.

In the same way, study the following purchase ledger control account and the explanations which follow, showing how the account is compiled.

Purchase Ledger Control Account

19–8			£	19–8			£
Jan	31	Bank & Cash	9,765	Jan	1	Balance b/d	20,900
	31	Discount Rec'd	540		31	Purchases	8,985
	31	Returns Outwards	490				
	31	Balances c/d	19,090				
			29,885				29,885
				Feb	1	Balances b/d	19,090

Figure	Explanation	Source of information
	At the credit side:	
20,900	This is the total of all the credit balances on the suppliers' accounts in the purchase ledger.	Purchase ledger.
8,985	Total purchases for the month.	Purchases journal for the month or purchases account if subsidiary books are not used.
	At the debit side:	
9,765	Total of all payments made to suppliers in cash and by cheque.	Cash book
540	Total of discounts received from suppliers.	Discount received column of the cash book.
490	Total of returns outwards to suppliers.	Returns outwards journal or returns outwards account if subsidiary books are not used.
19,090	The balance of the control account, which should equal the schedule of creditors.	By balancing the control account.

POINTS TO REMEMBER

The balance on the sales ledger control account should equal the schedule of debtors – if it does not, the errors must be investigated.

Likewise, the balance on the purchase ledger control account should equal the schedule of creditors – if it does not, again the errors must be found.

Occasionally an account in the sales ledger may have a credit balance. In this case, it will usually mean the firm is both a purchaser and a supplier to another business. At the end of the month, or accounting period, the balances can be 'set off' against each other.

Another contingency which can occur is a dishonoured cheque; this is a cheque returned by a debtor's banker unpaid. This would need to be entered at the debit side of the sales ledger control account. Control accounts are total accounts, therefore the entries appear on the same side of the control accounts as they appear in accounts in the sales ledger and purchase ledger.

Assignment Exercises

28.1

From the following particulars relating to a particular sales ledger, construct a sales ledger control account for the month of May, 19–7.

	£
Total debtors' balances in Sales Ledger at 1 May, agreeing with balance of Sales Ledger Control Account at 30 April.	4,760
Sales for the month.	5,912
Returns and allowances for month.	423
Cash and cheques received from debtors during the month.	3,969
Discounts allowed to debtors during the month	179
Bad Debts during the month	57

28.2

From the following particulars relating to a particular purchase ledger construct a purchase ledger control account for the month of May, 19–7

	£
Total of creditors' balances in Purchase Ledger at 1 May, agreeing with balance of Purchase Ledger Control Account at 30 April	8,904
Purchases for the month	7,038
Returns and allowances for the month	324
Cash and cheques paid to creditors during month	6,604
Discounts received during the month	272

28.3

Prepare a sales ledger control account for the month of June, 19–7 from the information given below:

	£
Sales Ledger Control Account balance at 1 June 19–6	6,869
Cash received during June	187
Cheques received during June	11,230
Sales for month of June	12,762
Cash refunded to customer in June	67
Bad Debts written off during June	552
Discount allowed during the month of June	536
Returns inwards during the month of June	295
Dishonoured cheques in June	52

28.4

Prepare a purchase ledger control account for the month of June, 19–6 from the information given below:

	£
Purchase Ledger Control Account balance at 1 June 19–6	13,561
Cheques paid to suppliers in June	12,760
Goods purchased during June	17,614
Goods returned to suppliers in June	232
Discount received during June	101

28.5

Prepare a sales ledger control account for the month of March, 19–8 from the following information.

	£
Sales Ledger balances at 1 March 19–8	6,780
Totals for March, 19–8	
Discounts allowed	298
Cash and cheques received from debtors	8,989
Sales Journal	11,555
Bad Debts written off	119
Returns Inwards Journal	221

28.6

Draw up a purchase ledger control account for the month of November, 19–8 from the information given below:

	£
Purchase Ledger balances at 1 November 19–8	7,565
Totals for November, 19–8	
Discounts received	244
Returns Outwards Journal	365
Cash and cheques paid to creditors	9,855
Purchases Journal	11,111

28.7

Prepare a sales ledger control account and a purchase ledger control account for the month of January, 19–7 from the information given below:

	£
Purchase Ledger Balances at 1 January 19–7	14,641
Sales Ledger Balances at 1 January 19–7	17,542
Totals for January, 19–7	
Purchases Journal	135,652
Sales Journal	197,961

Returns Outwards Journal	2,864
Returns Inwards Journal	4,231
Cheques and Cash paid to Suppliers	142,876
Cheques and Cash received from customers	197,580
Discounts allowed	5,180
Discounts received	2,708
Bad debts written off	342
Customers' cheques dishonoured	54

28.8
The following balances have been extracted from the books of R. Stevenson at 31 December 19–2

	£
January 1 19–2:	
Sales Ledger Balances	6,840
Further Balances	
Sales	46,801
Discounts Allowed	420
Bad Debts written off	494
Receipts from Customers	43,780
Returns inwards	296

Required:
(a) Prepare the sales ledger control account for R. Stevenson, showing clearly the balance carried forward at 31 December 19–2
(b) An explanation of the meaning and use of the final balance.

(Royal Society of Arts)

28.9
The following information relates to the sales ledger control account for ledger number 2, K to R.

	£
Debit balances on 1 May 19–4	3,788
Receipts on account of credit sales in the month:	
Cash	2,300
Cheques	14,568
Returns inwards	292
Bad debts (written off)	172
Discounts allowed	300
Total credit sales for the month	20,580
Debit balances on 31 May 19–4 as extracted from the sales ledger	6,781

Required:
(a) Write up the sales ledger control account from the information given above, and
(b) Comment on the significance of the closing figure as revealed by the control account with the figure for debtors as extracted from the sales ledger.

(Royal Society of Arts)

29 Capital and Revenue Expenditure and Receipts

OBJECTIVES To examine, determine and distinguish between capital and revenue expenditure and capital and revenue receipts, and to recognise the importance of this information.

It is important to understand the distinction between the two types of expenditure and the two types of receipts as this is one of the fundamental principles of accounting.

Capital Expenditure

Whenever a business spends money it receives some form of value representing goods or services, but the items which are purchased will be of benefit to the business for varying lengths of time. The fixed assets purchased by a firm are primarily intended for long-term use in the business, and will usually be retained by the business for some considerable time. Fixed assets consist of land, buildings, plant and machinery, furniture and fittings, office equipment, motor vehicles and all other assets which are purchased for use in the business. The assets possessed by a firm will generally be used in the business over long periods of time, and will permanently increase the profit-making capacity of the business.

Capital expenditure, therefore, can be defined as: expenditure on the purchase of fixed assets, or expenditure to increase the value of an existing fixed asset. Capital expenditure will increase the assets possessed by a firm and will appear on the balance sheet.

Revenue Expenditure

Revenue expenditure is the costs incurred during the day-to-day running of a business. They include all such items as salaries, wages, telephone, lighting and heating, rent, rates, insurance, discounts allowed, carriage costs and so on. These are costs for the services received, and the payments made for expenses incurred by the business, and form part of the expenditure involved in the daily routine operation of running a business; they will only be of benefit for a short period of time. The costs involved are 'used up', usually in less than a year, and they will only be of a temporary nature.

The difference, therefore, between these two types of expenditure is the *length of time* the expenditure is of useful benefit to the business. The general guideline is: longer than one year – capital expenditure; one year or less – revenue expenditure.

Difficulty is sometimes experienced in what is generally referred to as 'capitalisation' of revenue expenditure. This happens when a business incurs revenue expenditure on an item which is a fixed asset. This is best illustrated in the following example; of wages paid to workmen engaged in building a new office extension. Normally, the costs of wages are revenue expenditure, but in this example the wages are paid to workmen engaged in building a new office extension. The new building would be capital expenditure, and as the cost of these wages are directly involved with 'increasing the value of an existing fixed asset' these wages costs would be 'capitalised' and classified as capital expenditure.

Legal expenses are normally an item of revenue expenditure, but the legal charges incurred for conveyancing in the purchase of land or buildings would be costs directly involved with 'the purchase of a fixed asset', and these costs would be capital expenditure.

Another problem area is where an item of expenditure is part capital and part revenue expenditure, as in the example of the purchase of a soft drinks vending machine for the canteen with a stock of soft drinks. The expenditure incurred by the business in the purchase of the soft drinks vending machine would be the purchase of an asset, probably useful for a number of years, therefore this would be capital expenditure. However, the purchase of the stock of soft drinks would be revenue expenditure, as these would be 'used up' in a much shorter time.

The goods in which the firm normally deals and which are purchased with the intention of resale, or which are purchased for manufacture before being sold, are all regarded as revenue expenditure. Revenue expenditure consists of the costs incurred in the day-to-day running of the business, and at the end of the financial year these costs will be transferred to the profit and loss account.

Capital Receipts

When a firm receives money it is important to recognise the distinction between capital receipts and revenue receipts. Capital receipts consist of the sale of fixed assets. For example, if a fixed asset such as a piece of land was sold, the money received would be a 'capital receipt'. Similarly, if the proprietor of a business invested a further sum of money for use in the business, this would increase the capital, and would be a capital receipt.

When the capital is increased by someone other than the proprietor, by an outside investor, for example, with a loan or a mortgage, this is regarded as a capital receipt. However, the interest charged on the loan would be a revenue expense.

Revenue Receipts

Revenue receipts cover all money received from customers for goods supplied, discounts received, commissions received for services rendered and would also include rent received from sub-letting of premises.

At the end of the financial year, all items of revenue received are transferred to the profit and loss account to be set against the revenue expenses in order to ascertain the profitability of the business.

Examiners frequently set questions providing a list consisting of various items of receipts and expenditure, and will require the student to identify and classify each item as capital expenditure or revenue expenditure, capital receipt or revenue receipt. The following is a typical example of this type of question: In the case of a business selling and repairing motor vehicles classify the following items under:

Capital expenditure   Revenue expenditure
Revenue receipts   Capital receipts

(a) Income from repairs to customers' vehicles.
(b) Purchase of new motor van.
(c) Sale of old motor van.
(d) Commission received on sales of new vehicles.
(e) Showroom expenses.
(f) Purchase of vehicles for resale.
(g) Cost of extension to workshop.
(h) Cost of printing and stationery.

Solution
(a) Revenue receipt.
(b) Capital expenditure.
(c) Capital receipt.
(d) Revenue receipt.
(e) Revenue expenditure.
(f) Revenue expenditure.
(g) Capital expenditure.
(h) Revenue expenditure.

POINTS TO REMEMBER   Some information regarding certain fundamental principles will need to be committed to memory by the student, and often a shortened version of an important topic can be of great assistance. A sentence is very much easier to remember than a paragraph. With this purpose in mind the following one-sentence definitions may prove to be of assistance.

Capital expenditure is money spent on the purchase of fixed assets or on improvements to fixed assets.

Revenue expenditure is the day-to-day running costs of a business.

The main difference between these two types of expenditure is the length of time the expenditure is of benefit to the business.

By using the information and definitions given in this Module, the student should now gain practice in the identification and classification of capital and revenue expenditure, and capital and revenue receipts.

Assignment Exercises

29.1
State which of the following items should be treated as capital expenditure and which as revenue.
(a) The purchase of a new machine for use in the business.
(b) A quarterly account for electricity.
(c) The purchase of a new motor van.
(d) Cost of motor taxation for new van.
(e) Cost of repairs to accounting machine.
(f) Fire insurance premium.

29.2
John Conway has a retail food business. Classify the following items under the headings:

(i) capital expenditure.
(ii) revenue expenditure.
(a) Purchase of a refrigerated display counter.
(b) Repainting of shop door.
(c) Repairs to meat slicer.
(d) Purchase of a new cash register.
(e) Replacement of a broken window.
(f) New tyres for the delivery van.
(g) Installation of burglar alarm system.
(h) Insurance premium for delivery van.
(i) Wages of shop assistant.

29.3
(a) Explain the meaning of the following accounting terms:
   Capital expenditure   Revenue expenditure
   Capital receipts   Revenue receipts
(b) Angus Scott is in business as an estate agent and given below are some of his transactions. You are required to rule up four columns headed: Capital Expenditure, Revenue Expenditure, Capital Receipt and Revenue Receipt and list the items in the appropriate columns:
   Office rent.
   Purchase of photocopying machine.
   Commission received from builder.
   Fees charged to clients for professional services.

Wages of secretary.
Cost of new display equipment.
Cost of installing new display equipment.
Redecoration of shop front.
Proceeds from the sale of old typewriter.

29.4

(a) Briefly explain the term 'revenue expenditure'.
(b) The Pier View Garage last month paid for the items given below.
List them as appropriate under the headings
  (i) capital expenditure,
  (ii) revenue expenditure.
Breakdown truck.
Typewriter carbon paper.
Sweets for sale in forecourt kiosk.
Insurance for breakdown truck.
New petrol pumps.
Repairs to forecourt lighting.
A second-hand car for resale.
Wages of forecourt cashier.

(Royal Society of Arts)

29.5

A. Rogers opened his own business as a newsagent and paid the following:
(a) Wages of shop assistant.
(b) The purchase of a new cash register.
(c) Repairs to a leaking shop window.
(d) Payment of a fire insurance premium.
(e) The building of an extension to the rear of the premises to provide more storage space.
(f) Purchase of floor cleaning materials for use in the shop.
(g) Legal fees paid in connection with the building of the extension.
(h) The purchase of stock for resale.

Required
 (i) For each item state whether it is capital or revenue expenditure.
(ii) Explain clearly and concisely the difference between these two forms of expenditure.

(Royal Society of Arts)

29.6

Mr Brown has recently started in business on his own account and is puzzled by the terms 'capital expenditure' and 'revenue expenditure'.

(a) Explain to him what capital expenditure is.

(b) Mr Brown has purchased a new van; the details of the account were as follows:

	£
Van	3,000
Seat Belts	24
Delivery Charges	42
Number Plates	15
Road Tax	90
Insurance	220
	3,391

He has also received an account from his local builder, details of which are as follows:

	£
Redecorate shop front	400
Erect shelves in stock room	90
	490

You are required to list the items from both invoices under their respective headings of Capital and Revenue Expenditure.

(Royal Society of Arts)

29.7

State whether the following transactions of Salford Engineering Co. Ltd. are *capital* or *revenue* expenditure.

(a) Purchase of motor van.

(b) Yearly premium to insure motor van.

(c) Cost of rebuilding factory wall damaged by frost.

(d) Purchase of freehold land.

(e) Cost of building extension to factory.

(f) Cost of painting new extension.

(g) Legal costs on acquiring land for the extension.

(h) Repainting extension four years after completion.

(i) Cost of repairs to motor van.

(j) Repairing roof of extension.

(Joint Matriculation Board)

29.8

(a) Briefly explain the difference between capital and revenue expenditure.

(b) Identify each of the following items of expenditure as capital or revenue and state whether you would expect to find each item in the trading account, profit and loss account or balance sheet:

   (i) £200 paid to hauliers for carriage inwards.

  (ii) £25 paid to Better Garages for fitting seat belts to new van.

 (iii) £300 to A. Decorator for replacement of broken window.

 (iv) £450 to Unicold for supply and installation of refrigerated shop counter.

(Royal Society of Arts)

30   Bank Reconciliation Statements

OBJECTIVES   To establish the necessity and purpose of a bank reconciliation statement and the detailed preparation of such statements.

Banks are not in business for the buying and selling of goods. A bank's business is concerned with receiving, paying and the transfer of money. A bank has personal ledgers, and each customer has a separate account. When a customer pays money into the bank, that sum of money is placed at the credit side of the customer's account. When a customer withdraws money the account in the books of the bank is debited.

In business, as has already been seen, the bank account is kept in the cash book. When money is paid into the bank the details are recorded at the debit side of the bank account, and whenever money is drawn out of the bank the details are recorded at the credit side of the bank account.

Bank Statement

The bank sends the customer a copy of his account periodically. This copy is called a statement of account or a bank statement. The bank statement records all the customer's transactions through the bank. It is necessary for the business to check and verify that the balance shown in the bank column of the cash book agrees with the balance at the bank as shown on the bank statement.

The purpose of a bank reconciliation statement is to discover and explain any difference, at a given date, between the balance as shown in the firm's bank account in the cash book, and the balance as shown on the bank statement. The transactions are usually numerous and it is unlikely that the balance at the bank, as shown on the bank statement, will agree precisely, on any specific date, with the bank balance as shown in the firm's cash book. This is not usually the result of an error, but more often of a difference in timing.

There are several reasons to explain why these two balances may not agree at a particular date:

(1) Cheques drawn by the firm are entered in the cash book on the date the cheques are written. However, nearly all cheques suffer a delay through what is known as the Bankers' Clearing System, therefore it is likely that there will be some cheques which have not yet been presented for payment at the firm's bank.

(2) Cheques and/or cash paid into the bank by the firm and entered in the firm's cash book may not yet have been recorded on the bank statement.

(3) Banks receive money on behalf of their customers. These include interest from investments and money received by credit transfer. The money received in this way will appear on the bank statement on the day it is received by the bank, but the details cannot be recorded in the cash book until the firm receives their statement of account from the bank.

(4) Banks also make payments on behalf of their customers on direct debits and standing orders. The payments made in this way cannot be entered in the firm's cash book until the firm receives the details which will appear on their bank statement.

(5) Banks make charges for their services, and charge interest on overdrafts. They do not send a bill; they simply take the money out of the account by debiting it, and reducing the amount of the balance. The customer cannot enter the details in the cash book until the bank statement is received.

(6) Dishonoured cheques – when a cheque is paid into the bank, the bank will credit the customer's account immediately. It is usually some days before the customer is notified that the drawer of the cheque has insufficient funds in the account or that, for some other reason, the bank will not honour the cheque. The bank will then debit the account with the amount of the dishonoured cheque.
The amount of any dishonoured cheque must be recorded (at the credit side) of the cash book in order to reduce the balance.

(7) Errors, either by the bank or by the firm's cashier. Errors of this nature are unlikely to occur frequently. Banks make careful checks on their figures and the cashier of a firm is usually a responsible person. However, from time to time mistakes are inevitable.

Bank Reconciliation Statement

This is a statement drawn up at a particular date in order to match and agree (reconcile) the bank balance, as shown by the bank statement, with the bank balance as shown by the bank column of the cash book.

The bank reconciliation statement is not part of the double entry system as such. Its purpose and function is to prove that, although there may be differences between the balance at bank, as shown on the bank statement, and the bank balance in the cash book, these are due to logical, explicable reasons.

A neat copy of the bank reconciliation statement will be placed in the cash book or filed for reference purposes.

In examinations it is usual for questions to be presented as illustrated below:

The following is an extract from the bank columns of the cash book of Charles Gregory:

Cash Book (Bank columns only)

Dr.		£	Cr.		£
19–8			19–8		
Mar	1 Balance b/d	210.00	Mar	8 H. Ryder	38.00
	6 Cash	86.00		16 A. Jason	19.00
	13 C. Fox	24.00		28 E. Tyler	43.00
	31 B. Smith	47.00		31 Balance c/d	267.00
		367.00			367.00

On 31 March 19–8, he received the following bank statement from his bank:

19–8		£	£	Balance
Mar	1 Balance (Credit)			210.00
	6 Cash		86.00	296.00
	10 H. Ryder	38.00		258.00
	13 C. Fox		24.00	282.00
	15 Credit Transfer: J. Tyson		26.00	308.00
	18 A. Jason	19.00		289.00
	31 Bank Charges	12.00		277.00

You are required to:
(a) **Bring the cash book up to date, and show the new balance at 31 March 19–8.**
(b) **Prepare a statement to reconcile the difference between the new updated cash book balance and the balance as shown on the bank statement at 31 March 19–8.**

It is first necessary to check the items in the cash book against the items on the bank statement. The items on the debit side of the cash book are checked against the items on the credit side of the bank statement; the items on the credit side of the cash book against those on the debit side of the bank statement. This is carried out by placing a small tick against the items which agree, and appear on both, illustrated as follows:

The following is an extract from the bank columns of the cash book of Charles Gregory:

Dr.			£	Cr.			£
19–8				19–8			
Mar	1 Balance b/d	✓	210.00	Mar	8 H. Ryder	✓	38.00
	6 Cash	✓	86.00		16 A. Jason	✓	19.00
	13 C. Fox	✓	24.00		28 E. Tyler		43.00
	31 B. Smith		47.00		31 Balance c/d		267.00
			367.00				367.00

On 31 March, he received the following bank statement from his bank:

19–8			£	£	Balance
Mar	1	Balance (Credit)			✓ 210.00
	6	Cash		✓ 86.00	296.00
	10	H. Ryder	✓ 38.00		258.00
	13	C. Fox		✓ 24.00	282.00
	15	Credit Transfer: J. Tyson		26.00	308.00
	18	A. Jason	✓ 19.00		289.00
	31	Bank Charges		12.00	277.00

Any remaining unticked items on the bank statement should normally represent amounts of money received or payments made by the bank and not yet recorded in the cash book. The cash book should, therefore, be brought up-to-date to include these items.

The first unticked item on the bank statement is 'Credit Transfer: J. Tyson – £26'. (Credit transfer is a method of payment which makes it possible for any person to pay money into a clearing bank for the credit of the account of any customer of the bank's operating system). It is likely that J. Tyson is a customer who has paid his account by instructing his bank to pay direct through the banking system instead of paying by cheque. This item will have to be entered at the debit side of the cash book.

The second item unticked on the bank statement (Bank Charges – £12) means that the bank has made a charge for its services. This amount has been taken out of the account by debiting it, and reducing the amount of the balance. The bank charges need to be entered in the cash book, since the amount of any charges is not known until the customer receives their bank statement. This item will have to be entered at the credit side of the cash book.

The unticked item at the debit side of the cash book (B. Smith £47) is a 'bank lodgement'; this represents money paid into the bank but not yet entered on the bank statement. This will be adjusted on the bank reconciliation statement.

The unticked item at the credit side of the Cash Book (E. Tyler £43) represents a cheque sent, very recently, to E. Tyler which has not yet been presented to the bank for payment. This item is an 'unpresented cheque'. This item will be adjusted on the bank Reconciliation statement. The following is an illustration, showing the items which should be entered in the cash book, to give the amended and correct balance:

Dr.				Cash Book (Bank columns)				Cr.
19–8			£	19–8				£
Mar	31	Balance b/d	267.00	Mar	31	Bank Charges		12.00
	31	J. Tyson	26.00		31	Balance c/d		281.00
			293.00					293.00
Apr	1	Balance b/d	281.00					

The items unticked in the cash book appear on the bank reconciliation statement, as follows:

Bank Reconciliation Statement as at 31 March 19–8

Balance as per Cash Book	281.00
Add Unpresented Cheque (E. Tyler)	43.00
	324.00
Less Bank Lodgement not yet entered on Bank Statement	47.00
Balance as per Bank Statement:	£277.00

In some examination questions an extract of the cash book and the bank statement is not always provided. Occasionally the question will give details of the appropriate balances and of items not entered in the cash book, will indicate the total amount of cheques not presented, and any bank lodgements not yet entered on the bank statement. The comparison and 'ticking' of entries in the cash book against those shown on the bank statement are not required in such circumstances, but the cash book should be amended, if necessary, *before* the preparation of the bank reconciliation statement is begun. The following is an example of this type of question:

On 30 June 19–7, Brian Green's cash book showed a bank balance of £1,440.18, but at the same date the monthly statement from his bank showed a balance of £1,473.08.
The difference between the two balances was found to be due to the following:
(a) On 12 June 19–7 a charge of £15.40 for foreign exchange commission had been made by the bank. This had not been entered in Brian Green's cash book.
(b) A standing order for a trade subscription of £25 had been paid by the bank on 26 June 19–7 but no entry had been made in the cash book.
(c) Bank charges amounting to £32 had been charged on the bank statement but not yet entered in the cash book.
(d) A payment from D. Kaye to Brian Green of £265.50 by credit transfer had not been recorded in the cash book.
(e) Two cheques drawn by Brian Green during June 19–7 had not been presented for payment by the close of business on 30 June 19–7. These were for £76.20 and £49.60.
(f) On 30 June 19–7 Brian Green had paid cheques amounting to £286 into the bank but this item had not yet appeared on the bank statement.

You are required to open Brian Green's bank account in his cash book with the opening balance given above, £1,440.18; to enter such items as have been omitted; to find the new balance that results, and to prepare a bank reconciliation statement, reconciling the corrected cash book balance with the bank statement at 30 June 19–7.
The following is a worked example solution:

(a) This is a charge made by the bank for a service and not yet entered in the cash book. This item will have to be entered at the credit side of the cash book.

275

(b) This is a standing order, a payment made through the bank and not yet entered in the cash book. This item will have to be entered at the credit side of the cash book.

(c) These are charges made by the bank for their services and not yet entered in the cash book. This item will have to be entered at the credit side of the cash book.

(d) This is a customer who has paid his account of £265.50 by credit transfer. The money was received by the bank but no entry has been made in the cash book. This item will have to be entered at the debit side of the cash book.

(e) These two cheques, sent to creditors, were entered in the cash book on the day the cheques were written, but have not yet been presented to the bank for payment. These are 'unpresented cheques' and will be adjusted on the bank reconciliation statement.

(f) These are cheques entered in the cash book and paid into the bank on 30 June 19–7 but not yet entered on the bank statement. This item will be adjusted on the bank reconciliation statement.

The following is an illustration of this example with the cash book written up-to-date, followed by the bank reconciliation statement as at 30 June 19–7.

Cash Book (Bank columns)

19–7			£	19–7			£
Jun	30	Balance b/d	1,440.18	Jun	30	Foreign Ex. Comm.	15.40
	30	D. Kaye C/T	265.50		30	Trade Subscription	25.00
					30	Bank Charges	32.00
					30	Balance c/d	1,633.28
			1,705.68				1,705.68
Jul	1	Balance b/d	1,633.28				

Bank Reconciliation Statement as at 30 June 19–7

Balance as per Cash Book				1,633.28
Add	Unpresented Cheques:		76.20	
			49.60	125.80
				1,759.08
Less	Bank Lodgement not yet entered on Bank Statement:			286.00
Balance as per Bank Statement				£1,473.08

Bank Overdrafts

Great care is required if there is a bank overdraft (a credit balance in the cash book, a debit balance on the bank statement). When a bank account is overdrawn any amounts drawn out of the bank will cause the overdraft to *rise*, while amounts paid in will cause the overdraft to *decrease*.

The adjustments required to reconcile the bank overdraft with the firm's cash book are the complete opposite of those needed when the account is not overdrawn.

When a bank account has been overdrawn this is usually indicated by the placing of the abbreviation DR or O/D after the amount of the balance on the bank statement.

POINTS TO REMEMBER

In comparing the cash book with the bank statement it must be remembered that the cash at bank is an asset to the business and, as such, it will be recorded at the debit side of the cash book. Payments made by cheque are recorded at the credit side of the cash book. The bank statement represents the firm's personal account in the books of the bank and, therefore, the entries will be the opposite to the firm's cash book.

In a question where an extract of the cash book and the bank statement is provided, it is first necessary to place a 'tick' at the side of the items which appear, both in the cash book and on the bank statement. It is only the remaining unticked items which will require attention.

Unticked items which appear on the bank statement will usually need to be entered in the cash book.

Unticked items which appear at the debit side of the cash book will usually be amounts paid into the bank but not yet entered on the bank statement, which are called 'bank lodgements'. Unticked items which appear at the credit side of the cash book will usually be cheques drawn but not yet presented for payment; these are called 'unpresented cheques'.

The bank reconciliation statement is not part of the double entry system as such; its purpose is to prove that, although there may be a difference between the balance at bank as shown by the cash book, and the balance as per the bank statement, it is due to genuine logical reasons.

All the following exercises are taken from past examination papers to enable the student to gain essential practice in the preparation of bank reconciliation statements.

Assignment Exercises

30.1

The bank columns of your cash book for the month of February 19–2 are shown below:

19–2			£	19–2				Cheque Number	£
Feb	1	Balance	480.00	Feb	4	Wages	335		180.00
	22	A. Ball	250.00		5	F. Lowe	336		60.00
	22	C. Lamb	136.00		11	G. Dow	337		110.00
	22	E. Mann	208.00		12	J. Ives	338		244.00
	26	L. Day	85.00		23	K. Peel	339		401.00
					28	Balance			164.00
			1,159.00						1,159.00
Mar	1	Balance	164.00						

The following bank statement was received for the month of February:

				Dr.	Cr.	Balance	
Feb	1	Balance				600.00	
	3	Cheque Number	334	120.00		480.00	
	8		335	180.00		300.00	
	16		338	244.00		56.00	
	17		336	60.00		4.00	O/D
	23	Sundries			594.00	590.00	
	26	D. May credit transfer			65.00	655.00	
		Ace Insurance standing order		26.00			
		Charges		18.00		611.00	

(a) Make the necessary entries in the cash book and ascertain the correct balance as on 28 February 19–2
(b) Reconcile your revised cash book balance with the balance shown in the bank statement.

(The Royal Society of Arts)

30.2

On 28 February 19–1 the bank column of W. Payne's cash book showed a debit balance of £600.
A bank statement written up to 28 February 19–1 disclosed that the following items had not been entered in the cash book:
items had not been entered in the cash book:

278

(i) the sum of £1,500 received from P. Jones by credit transfer;
(ii) the transfer of £1,000 from Payne's private bank deposit account into his business bank account;
(iii) bank charges £180.

When the bank statement was further checked against the cash book the following items were discovered:

(i) cheques drawn in favour of creditors totalling £8,300 had not yet been presented;
(ii) cash and cheques £4,100 had been entered in the cash book but not yet credited by the bank;
(iii) a cheque for £50 drawn by W. Payne in respect of drawings had been correctly entered in the cash book but debited twice in the bank statement.

You are required to prepare as at 28 February 19–1:

(a) The cash book showing the adjusted cash book balance.
(b) A bank reconciliation statement showing the balance appearing in the bank statement.

(The Royal Society of Arts)

30.3
J. C. Ash received the following bank statement on 30 June 19–0:

J C Ash
Nonsuch Bank Ltd
Muswell Hill
London

	£ Debit	£ Credit	£ Balance
Balance			800.00
N. Charles	80.00		720.00
Sundry		50.00	770.00
D. Wood	90.00		680.00
Interest Savings Bonds		30.00	710.00
Charges	40.00		670.00

His cash book at that date is given below:

Cash Book

	£		£
Balance (1/6/19–0)	800.00	N. Charles	80.00
Bank	50.00	D. Wood	90.00
Bank	100.00	F. Frank	150.00
		W. Watson	95.00
		Balance 30/6/19–0	

You are required to:
(a) Write the cash book up to date and ascertain the correct cash book balance at 30 June 19–0; and
(b) reconcile the bank statement to the corrected cash book balance.

(The Royal Society of Arts)

30.4

William Tanner received the following bank statement on 31 May 19–3:

			Debit	Credit	Balance
19–3			£	£	£
May	1	Balance			332
	7	110119	102		230
	11	Cash		518	748
	18	Credit transfer investment dividends		600	1348
	19	110121	340		1008
	26	Direct debit insurance	78		930

William Tanner checked the statement against his cheque counterfoils and found that cheques numbered 110118 for £235 and 110120 for £136 had not been presented.

The names of the payees of the cheques are:
110118   S. Lyle
110119   N. Faldo
110120   C. O'Connor
110121   K. Brown

As William Tanner has not written up his cash book for the month of May 19–3 you are required to:

(i) write up the bank columns for that month;
(ii) balance the bank columns, and reconcile that balance with the amount shown on the bank statement at the end of the month.

(The Royal Society of Arts)

30.5

On 31 October 19–5 the cash book of N. Orange showed a balance at bank of £570. An examination of his records located the following errors:

(a) Orange paid to R. Jones £175 by cheque on 15 October. This cheque was entered in the cash book as £195.
(b) Bank charges not recorded in the cash book amounted to £25.
(c) A cheque dated 19 October, value £150, payable to T. Jack was not paid by the bank until 5 November.
(d) Orange on 23 October received from W. Green a cheque, value £125. This cheque was dishonoured on 29 October. No entry for the dishonour has been made in the cash book.

(e) On 31 October a cheque, value £200, received from F. Brown was banked; however, the bank statement was not credited until 1 November.

You are required to:
(a) Make the necessary entries in the cash book in order to show the revised cash book balance at 31 October 19–5.
(b) Prepare a statement reconciling the corrected cash book balance with the bank statement at 31 October 19–5.
(c) State the balance at bank at 31 October 19–5 as shown by the bank statement.

(The Royal Society of Arts)

30.6
The bank columns of your cash book for the month of May 19–8 are shown below:

19–8			£	19–8			£
May	1	Balance	320	May	3	Rates	150
	9	G. Brown	300		9	D. Lynch	75
	12	R. Williams	175		16	R. Button	130
	17	R. Termatrie	54		31	J. Cottam	210
	31	K. Jones	13		31	P. Black	150
					31	Balance	147
			862				862
Jun	1	Balance	147				

The rates were paid with cheque number 110, subsequent payments being made strictly in numerical order.
The bank statement for the month of May is below:

			£	£	£
May	1				370
	2	Cheque No. 109	50		320
	5	110	150		170
	19	112	130		40
	20	Sundries		529	569
	31	Charges	10		559
	31	Credit transfer:			
		J. Rickman		40	599

281

(a) Make the necessary entries in the bank columns of the cash book, and find the correct balance.
(b) Reconcile the cash book bank columns with the bank statement.

(The Royal Society of Arts)

30.7

(a) On 31 May 19–5 the bank columns of R. Barker's cash book showed a balance at bank of £850.

A bank statement written up to the same date disclosed the following items had not been entered in the cash book:

  (i) The sum of £42 paid to White Rose Insurance Company by standing order on 28 May.

  (ii) Commissions received, £120, from N. Newall had been paid directly into Barker's account by credit transfer on 25 May.

  (iii) Bank charges of £90 had been charged directly to Barker's account on 29 May.

A further check revealed the following:

  (i) Cheques drawn in favour of creditors totalling £642 had not yet been presented.

  (ii) Cash and cheques £210 deposited at the bank on 30 May had been entered in the cash book but did not appear on the bank statement.

You are required to write up Barker's cash book on 31 May 19–5 after taking into account the above matters and to prepare a bank reconciliation statement showing the balance appearing in the bank statement.

(The Royal Society of Arts)

30.8

C. Dickens reconciled his cash book with the bank statement every month. His bank reconciliation statement for the month of November 19–1 was as follows:

Balance as per statement 30.11.–1		4,500.00 Overdrawn
Add unpresented cheques:		
J. Soap	54.00	
A. Smith	110.00	
M. Pym	26.00	190.00
Balance as per cash book (CR)		£4,690.00

The following is the extract of the bank column in the cash book for the month of December 19–1, and a copy of the bank statement for the same month:

19–1	Receipts	£	19–1	Payments	£
Dec 1	L. Cleary & Sons	4,180.00	Dec 1	Balance B/D	4,690.00
4	Lewis & Stanley Ltd.	750.00	5	Perkins Ltd	46.00
5	Ralfs Computers	3,420.00	8	Haynes & Co.	92.00
19	Mullin Printers	221.00	16	Pyper Finance	110.00
23	Higson Ltd.	540.00	23	Hodgson Building Co.	249.00
29	Moore & Co.	399.00	29	Pennington Printers	75.00
			31	Balance C/D	4,248.00
		£9,510.00			£9,510.00

19–1		Dr. £	Cr. £	Balance £
Dec 1	Balance B/F			4,500.00 O/D
	J. Soap	54.00		4,554.00 O/D
2	L. Cleary & Sons		4,180.00	374.00 O/D
4	Lewis & Stanley Ltd		750.00	376.00 CR
	A. Smith	110.00		266.00 CR
5	Regal Insurance – Standing order	65.00		201.00 CR
	Ralfs Computers		3,420.00	3,621.00 CR
8	Perkins Ltd	46.00		3,575.00 CR
19	Pyper Finance	110.00		3,465.00 CR
	Bank charges	66.00		3,399.00 CR
22	Mullen Printers		221.00	3,620.00 CR
23	Carus Ltd – Credit transfer		365.00	3,985.00 CR
29	Higson Ltd.		540.00	4,525.00 CR
	Bank commission	45.00		4,480.00 CR
	L. Cleary & Sons – refer to drawer	4,180.00		300.00 CR

From the above information you are required to prepare:
(a) the corrected cash book balance as at 31 December 19–1;
(b) a bank reconciliation statement as at 31 December 19–1, using the amended cash book balance.

(Joint Matriculation Board)

30.9
Write short notes explaining one difference between the two items of each of the following pairs:
(a) capital and revenue expenditure:

....
....
....

(b) bank statement and bank reconciliation statement;

....
....
....

(c) bad debts written off and provision for doubtful debts.

....

....

....

(Joint Matriculation Board)

31 Reconciling Ledger Accounts

OBJECTIVES To enable the student to understand the need, function and purpose of reconciling ledger accounts with a supplier's statement or remittance advice, and the detailed layout and preparation of these summarised statements.

In any business the checking of statements and remittance advices with the relevant ledger account is an essential procedure. In some respects these are very similar to the bank reconciliation statements covered in Module 30 in that it is important and necessary to match and agree the balance as shown on a ledger account with the amount outstanding as shown on a statement of account or a remittance advice.

The main function and purpose of a reconciliation is to prove that, although there may be differences, on a particular date, between the two balances these are not usually or necessarily because of errors, but more often result from a difference in timing.

Consider the following reasons:

(1) On 4 November 19–8, Harry Foxworth sold goods on credit (£170) to David Alexander. The goods are despatched and the sales invoice is prepared and posted on 4 November 19–8. It will be several days before the goods and the invoice are received by David Alexander. Only when the goods and the invoice have been received and thoroughly checked will the invoice be entered in the purchase ledger. Clearly there is a difference in timing.

(2) Goods returned: Goods previously purchased which are subsequently returned to the supplier. The person returning the goods would enter and record the details on the date the goods were despatched. It would be some days before the goods reached the supplier, when he would make the necessary entries in his records, and issue a credit note. This is another case of a difference in timing.

(3) Payment by cheque to a creditor. The details of any payment made by cheque to a creditor would be entered and recorded in the cash book and posted to the ledger, on the date the cheque was written and mailed. However, it would be some days before the cheque was received by the creditor, the details recorded and the cheque presented to the bank. This is clearly yet another difference in timing.

This situation would, in effect, involve an 'unpresented cheque' and would require an adjustment on the reconciliation statement in order to reconcile the two balances.

(4) Errors and omissions.

Errors: unfortunately it is inevitable that mistakes will occur, and very often these errors are the 'transposition of figures' (for example, a purchase invoice for goods amounting to £124, but written in the Ledger Account as £142; or a sales invoice for £267 entered on the statement as £276). In either of these situations, an adjustment for the difference would be required when attempting to reconcile the two balances.

Omissions: an example of an omission could be when an amount of £15 cash discount received from a supplier for prompt payment which had been entered in the ledger account had been omitted on the statement. An adjustment of the amount omitted would be necessary in order to complete a reconciliation of the balance.

(5) Contra accounts: with this type of account, the same firm is both a supplier and a customer; the indebtedness is set off. Example: Keith Ramsden is a debtor in the sales ledger of our firm. Our firm also on occasions buys electrical components from Keith Ramsden, therefore he has an account in our purchase ledger. This means our firm has dealing with Keith Ramsden in both capacities; selling to him and buying from him. Keeping two separate accounts is the most efficient procedure. At the end of the month the smaller account will be transferred and set off against the larger account. The word 'contra' is written to explain that an 'opposite' account is being cancelled out by this entry.

Consider the following. David Alexander has a small wholesale business. One of his main suppliers is Harry Foxworth. His account is set out below:

PURCHASE LEDGER

Harry Foxworth Account

19–8			£	19–8			£
Nov	10	Returns outwards	28.00	Nov	1	Balance b/d	325.00
	20	Bank	852.00		7	Purchases	170.00
	26	Returns outwards	35.00		14	Purchases	220.00
	30	Balance c/d	245.00		18	Purchases	165.00
					26	Purchases	280.00
			1,160.00				1,160.00
				Dec	1	Balance b/d	245.00

On 1 December the following statement of account is received from Harry Foxworth.

Statement of Account

19–8			Dr.	Cr.	Balance
Nov	1	Balance b/d			325.00
	4	Sales	170.00		495.00
	10	Sales	220.00		715.00
	14	Returns		28.00	687.00
	15	Sales	165.00		852.00
	21	Sales	280.00		1,132.00
	25	Bank		852.00	280.00
	27	Sales	305.00		585.00

You are to prepare a statement reconciling the balance as due by Harry Foxworth with the amount shown in David Alexander's ledger.

The best method and procedure is to compare the two documents and place a small tick against each item which can be identified on both. Any entries which appear in the ledger account but *not* on the statement or remittance advice are known as 'outstanding items' and will require adjusting. Any items shown on the statement or remittance advice that do *not* appear in the ledger account will be 'outstanding' and will require adjusting.

In examination questions it is always important to study carefully the transactions which have taken place, to decide the effect of any outstanding items, and make any necessary adjustments. Unless an instruction is given to the contrary, commence with either the balance as shown in the ledger account, or the balance as per the statement or remittance advice, and prepare a reconciliation statement by drawing up a summary of the outstanding items, to prove that the ledger account and the statement or remittance advice will agree, when allowing for the oustanding items.

The solution to the example is now illustrated:

David Alexander's PURCHASE LEDGER

Harry Foxworth Account

19–8				£	19–8				£
Nov	10	Returns outwards	√	28.00	Nov	1	Balance b/d	√	325.00
	20	Bank	√	852.00		7	Purchases	√	170.00
	26	Returns outwards		35.00		14	Purchases	√	220.00
	30	Balance c/d		245.00		18	Purchases	√	165.00
						26	Purchases	√	280.00
				1,160.00					1,160.00
					Dec	1	Balance b/d		245.00

On 1 December the following Statement of Account is received from Harry Foxworth.

Statement of Account

19–8			Dr.	Cr.	Balance
Nov	1	Balance b/d			✓ 325.00
	4	Sales	✓ 170.00		495.00
	10	Sales	✓ 220.00		715.00
	14	Returns		✓ 28.00	687.00
	15	Sales	✓ 165.00		852.00
	21	Sales	✓ 280.00		1,132.00
	25	Bank		✓ 852.00	280.00
	27	Sales	305.00		585.00

A tick has been placed against each item which appears both in the ledger account and on the statement of account.

It is only the outstanding items of 26 November (Returns outwards £35) in the ledger account and 27 November (Sales of £305) on the statement of account which will require to be summarised on the reconciliation statement, as follows:

Reconciliation Statement as at 30 November 19–8

Balance as per Statement				585.00
Less:	Item 1	26 November, Sales not yet received by David Alexander and not entered in his Purchases Ledger	305.00	
	Item 2	26 November, Returns outwards not yet received by Harry Foxworth	35.00	340.00
Balance as per Ledger Account:				£245.00

Explanation:

Commencing with the balance (as instructed) according to the statement of account of £585:

Item 1   The goods sold on 26 November for £305 are recorded on the statement, but these goods have not yet been received by David Alexander and, therefore, are not entered in his purchase ledger. As the amount of these goods, £305, had increased the balance as shown on the statement, this amount must now be deducted from this balance on the reconciliation statement.

Item 2   The returns outwards of £35 were despatched to Harry Foxworth on 26 November and the details entered in the ledger. On 30 November, the date of the statement of account, the goods returned had not been received by Harry Foxworth and, therefore, were not entered on his statement of account. In effect the ledger account had been decreased by the amount of £35 in respect of the goods returned. This amount must now be deducted from the balance as shown on the statement, in order to reconcile (match) the two balances.

On examination papers these types of questions are very often
fully displayed showing the details on the ledger account and
the statement or remittance advice. It is extremely important to
check carefully and mark with a small tick all the amounts
appearing on both which match and agree – it is only any
'outstanding items' which will require consideration and adjustment on a reconciliation statement.

Ensure the opening balances at the start of the month or
period agree, both in the ledger account and on the statement
or remittance advice. If they do not agree, make a note of the
difference; usually the amount of any difference will become
evident before the matching procedure is completed.

Occasionally questions are presented in the form of a summary of events. In this situation, unless a specific instruction is
given, the reconciliation statement could begin with either the
balance as shown on the ledger account, or the balance as
shown on the statement. Having commenced with one of the
balances, it is then necessary to consider and decide the effect,
on the commencing balance, of each of the summarised transactions – and the need either to add or deduct in order to
reach a reconciliation.

Assignment Exercises

31.1

J. S. Kingsley is one of your suppliers. Their account in your ledger is set out
below:

J. S. Kingsley Account

19–6			£	19–6			£
Jan	29	Bank	350.00	Jan	1	Balance b/d	150.00
	31	Balance c/d	350.00		7	Purchases	200.00
					17	Purchases	350.00
			700.00				700.00
				Feb	1	Balance b/d	350.00

Statement of Account (Received from Supplier)

			£	£	£
Jan	1	Balance b/d			350.00
	3	Invoice	200.00		550.00
	4	Cheque		200.00	350.00
	11	Invoice	350.00		700.00
	27	Invoice	250.00		950.00
	29	Invoice	190.00		1,140.00

You are required to draw up a statement reconciling the balance shown as due by J. S. Kingsley with the amount shown as owing in your ledger account.

31.2

Nigel Hunt, who purchases building materials from Morgan & Co, sent the following remittance advice.

Remittance Advice

19–7			£	£	£
Mar	1	Balance b/d			700.00
	10	Invoice No. 672		675.00	1,375.00
	12	Credit Note No. 394	85.00		1,290.00
	18	Invoice No. 702		474.00	1,764.00
	20	Cheque	800.00		964.00
	24	Credit Note No. 399	60.00		904.00
	30	Cheque	430.00		474.00

Nigel Hunt's account in the ledger of Morgan & Co is set out below:

Nigel Hunt Account

19–7			£	19–7			£
Mar	1	Balance b/d	700.00	Mar	10	Returns Inwards	85.00
	6	Sales 672	675.00		24	Bank	800.00
	12	Sales 702	474.00		20	Returns Inwards	60.00
	27	Sales 739	386.00		31	Balance c/d	1,585.00
	30	Sales 751	295.00				
			2,530.00				2,530.00
Apr	1	Balance b/d	1,585.00				

Prepare a reconciliation statement as at 31 March 19–7, reconciling the balance as shown on the remittance advice with the amount shown outstanding on Morgan & Co's ledger.

31.3

In the purchase ledger of Graham Green the account of Simon Temple showed a balance owing of £547 on 31 August 19–7. On 1 September 19–7 a statement was received from Simon Temple showing a balance outstanding of £885.

Upon further examination the following differences were discovered:

(a) A cheque for £255 sent by Graham Green on 28 August had not yet been received by Simon Temple.

(b) Simon Temple had despatched goods to Graham Green, value £126, on 29 August; the invoice had not yet been received by Graham Green.

(c) A credit note for the amount of £58 issued by Simon Temple, in respect of goods returned, had not yet been received by Graham Green.

(d) Cash discount of £15 deducted by Graham Green in respect of prompt payment had not been entered on the statement from Simon Temple.

You are required to prepare a reconciliation statement in order to reconcile the balance as shown on the statement received from Simon Temple with the account in Graham Green's purchase ledger.

31.4

M. Dixon is a customer of James Peterson.

M. Dixon Account

19–7			£	19–7			£
Mar	1	Balance b/d	800.00	Mar	16	Returns inwards	85.00
	6	Sales	895.00		24	Bank	800.00
	18	Sales	990.00		31	Balance c/d	3,500.00
	30	Sales	1,700.00				
			4,385.00				4,385.00
Apr	1	Balance b/d	3,500.00				

Remittance Advice From M. Dixon

19–7			Debit £	Credit £	Balance £
Mar	1				800.00
	6	Invoice		895.00	1.695.00
	16	Credit Note	85.00		1,610.00
	18	Invoice		990.00	2,600.00
	24	Cheque	800.00		1,800.00
	30	Cheque	750.00		1,050.00

Prepare a reconciliation statement to explain the difference between the amount shown due by M. Dixon and the amount shown as owing in the ledger.

31.5

J. M. Newton is one of your suppliers. Their account is your ledger is set out below:

19–7			£	19–7			£
May	29	Bank	550.00	May	1	Balance b/d	150.00
	31	Balance c/d	550.00		6	Purchases	400.00
					16	Purchases	550.00
			1,100.00				1,100.00
				Jun	1	Balance b/d	550.00

On 1 June 19–7 the following statement is received by J. M. Newton.

19–7			Statement Debit £	Credit £	Balance £
May	1				350.00
	3	Invoice	400.00		750.00
	4	Cheque		200.00	550.00
	12	Invoice	550.00		1,100.00
	28	Invoice	250.00		1,350.00
	29	Invoice	180.00		1,530.00

Prepare a statement reconciling the balance as shown due by J. M. Newton with the amount shown as owing in your ledger.

31.6

J. Brown & Co. Ltd is one of your suppliers. Their account in your bought ledger is set out below:

19–0			£	19–0			£
May	4	Bank	4,056	May	1	Balance b/d	4,160
	4	Discount	104		9	Purchases	3,120
	9	Returns	193		16	Purchases	1,313
	28	Bank	4,134		31	Purchases	1,310
	28	Discount	106				
	31	Balance c/d	1,310				
			9,903				9,903
				Jun	1	Balance b/d	1,310

During the first week of June 19–0 the following statement of account is received from J. Brown & Co Ltd.

		Dr. £	Cr. £	Balance £
May	1			4,160
	4 Bank		4,056	104
	9 Sales	3,120		3,224
	14 Returns		193	3,031
	15 Sales	1,313		4,344
	28 Sales	1,310		5,654

(a) Explain why the entries which you have credited in your ledger account appear as debit entries in the statement received from J. Brown & Co Ltd.
(b) Prepare a reconciliation statement to explain the difference between the amount shown due by J. Brown & Co. Ltd and the amount shown as owing in your ledger.

(The Royal Society of Arts)

31.7
The personal account of C. Street in the purchase ledger of E. Farm showed there was an amount of £273.36 owing to Street on 31 May 19–4. However, the statement received from Street by Farm on 1 June 19–4 showed a balance outstanding of £312.54.

On comparing the two documents the following differences were found:

(a) Credit note CN22 for £28 in respect of an overcharge had not been received by Farm.
(b) A cheque for £78.28 despatched by Farm on 28 May had not yet been received by Street.
(c) Street had despatched goods as per Farm's order number ON 276, value £27.64, on 30 May; these had not yet been received by Farm.
(d) Street had offset a contra invoice of £38.74 from Farm against the account. Farm had recorded this separately in the sales ledger.

You are required to reconcile Street's statement with his ledger account in Farm's books.

(The Royal Society of Arts)

31.8
J. Meredith who supply Thomson & Company with most of their raw materials for manufacture of their main biscuit products sent the following statement of account to Thomson & Co. on 31 August 19–8.

J. Meredith

Thomson & Co.   31 August 19–8
Grey-friar Works
Bolton

Statement of Account

19–8			£	£	£
1	Aug	Balance			200
10		Goods	300		500
		Returns		40	460
21		Cash		150	
		Discount		5	305
31		Goods	600		905

Thomson & Co's book-keeper examines the ledger account of J. Meredith which is given hereunder.

J. Meredith (Purchase Ledger)

			£
1 August		Balance	45
21		Goods	300
		Returns	40
31		Returns	100

You are required to prepare:
(i) A statement reconciling J. Meredith's ledger account in Thomson & Co's books at 31 August 19–8.
(ii) Briefly explain the reasons for any discrepancies between the ledger account and the statement of account.

(The Royal Society of Arts)

31.9
J. Thomas is one of your suppliers. Their account in your ledger is set out below.

			£				£
May	4	Bank	980	May	1	Bal b/d	1,000
		Discount	20		18	Purchases	980
	24	Returns	180		24	Purchases	450
	26	Bank	784		26	Purchases	520
		Discount	16				
	28	Bank	441				
		Discount	9				
		Bal c/d	520				
			2,950				2,950
				June	1	Bal b/d	520

On 7 June 19–5 the following statement of account is received from Thomas.

			Dr.	Cr.	Bal.
			£	£	£
May	1				1,000
	8	Bank		980	20
	16	Sales	980		1,000
	22	Sales	450		1,450
	26	Sales	520		1,970
	26	Returns		180	1,790
	27	Adjustment		10	1,780
	28	Bank		874	906
	28	Discount		16	890
	29	Sales	600		1,490

You are required to:
 (i) Prepare a statement reconciling the balance shown as due by Thomas with the amount shown as owing in your ledger.
(ii) Explain briefly why the entries which you have debited in your ledger account appear as credit entries in the statement received from Thomas.

(The Royal Society of Arts)

32   Wages and Salaries

OBJECTIVES   To consider the preparation and calculation of wages to employees, on a time basis and a piece-work basis. To examine deductions from pay – statutory deductions, voluntary deductions and the preparation of summarised notes/coin analysis.

The distinction between salaries and wages is not clearly defined, but generally salaries are income from employment which is paid on a monthly basis. Salaries are usually expressed as an amount for a whole year. For example, an employee is paid an annual salary of £10,500; the amount of each month's pay is calculated by dividing the annual amount by twelve, so that the gross pay for each month would be £875. In most cases salaries are paid directly into the employee's bank account.

It is extremely rare for salaried employees to be paid on a weekly basis. Wages are usually considered to be earnings which are calculated on a weekly basis and paid in cash. Wages can be earned and calculated on a 'time rate' or a 'piece rate' basis.

Rates of Pay – Time Rate

With this system the employee is paid an agreed amount for each hour worked up to a given number of hours. This is the basic rate or standard rate of pay, with extra payment for any hours worked in excess of this number of hours. Any additional time worked is calculated at a higher rate of pay, referred to as 'overtime'. Overtime rates of pay are generally quoted as 'time and a quarter', 'time and a half' and 'double time'. If the standard rate of pay is £6 per hour, then:

time and a quarter would be £6 + a quarter = £7.50 per hour
time and a half would be £6 + half   = £9.00 per hour
Double time would be £6 + £6   = £12.00 per hour

Example: an employee is paid a basic wage of £6.00 per hour for a 40-hour week; any hours worked in excess of this are paid at time and a half. During the week ending 17 June 19–8 the employee worked a total of 46 hours. The calculation of the gross pay would be as follows:

	£
40 hours at £6.00 per hour	240.00
6 hours at £9.00	54.00
Gross pay	294.00

The 'gross pay' is the total amount earned by the employee before any deductions have been taken off.

A 'bonus' is a sum of money paid to an employee as an additional payment. This is usually offered as an incentive to increase the effort or efficiency of the employee.

Rates of Pay – Piece Rate

This method of payment relates the earnings to the results of the work. The payment made to the employee is calculated on the quantity of good work produced. A figure is agreed between the management and the workers, and payment is made according to the number of items produced.

For example, if the agreed 'piece rate' is £3.00 per 100 items produced, and the employee completes 5,000 items in the week, the gross pay would be £150.

Deductions From Pay

Statutory deductions are compulsory deductions from pay. It is the responsibility of the employer to deduct Income Tax and National Insurance contributions from the individual wages and salaries of the employees.

Income Tax – Pay As You Earn

Income Tax in the United Kingdom is a tax on personal incomes which is the main means of obtaining money by the government for use in running the public services. It is reimposed annually by the Finance Act and is assessed and collected by the Board of Inland Revenue.

The system of Income Tax in the United Kingdom is 'Pay As You Earn' which is usually abbreviated to PAYE. The amount of Income Tax which is payable will depend on the personal circumstances of each individual person. Each employee is given a notice of coding by the Inland Revenue. This is a code number based upon the personal allowances and circumstances of the employee. The actual amount of Income Tax which is payable by the employee is subject to, and will depend upon, the code number. The amount of PAYE due to be paid by the employee must be calculated and deducted each week by the employer. At the end of the month, the total amounts of PAYE deducted from the pay of all the employees is paid by the employer to the Inland Revenue.

National Insurance Contributions

These are payments to the state insurance scheme which is administered by the Department of Health and Social Security (DHSS) and made by every employer, employee and self-employed person. As each employee is required to pay National Insurance Contributions, these are also calculated and deducted by the employer from each wage payment. The payment of National Insurance contributions ensures that the employee has the benefit of the extensive services provided by the state:

health services, sickness benefit, unemployment benefit, retirement pension and so on.

Superannuation Contributions

These are private pension schemes whereby employers, and very often employees as well, contribute to the financing of a retirement pension fund for the special purpose of providing additional retirement pensions and widows' pensions for their employees. These are in addition to the state retirement pension.

This type of scheme is referred to as either a 'contributory' or 'non-contributory' pension scheme.

Contributory Pension Scheme

With this type of scheme both the employer and the employee make regular contributions. The amount paid by the employee is usually calculated as a percentage of the earnings, and is a deduction from the pay.

Non-Contributory Pension Scheme

When a pension scheme is stated to be 'non-contributory', this means that the employer bears the entire cost of financing the scheme and the employee does not contribute.

Other Deductions

Many employees also make voluntary contributions to specific organisations. These include: contributions to local or national charities, union membership fees, private medical schemes, social and welfare clubs and savings schemes. Many employers will agree to deduct these types of voluntary contributions from the wages of the employees.

The net pay is the actual amount received by the employee after the statutory and voluntary deductions have been made. The pay-roll is a complete list of all the employees, containing details of the amounts paid, or due to be paid, and how these amounts are calculated. It may be divided into a weekly pay-roll and a monthly pay-roll, according to whether the employees are paid a weekly wage or a monthly salary.

It is the responsibility of the wages clerk to deal with the work of paying the employees their wages or salaries and of keeping detailed records of all such payments. It is normal procedure for each employee to be given a reference number for identification purposes.

Each employee receives a pay advice slip giving details of the gross pay, Income Tax, National Insurance, any other deductions and clearly showing the amount of net pay. The pay advice slip should contain the following information:

Name of employee and reference number
Date
Tax Code Number

National Insurance Number
Gross pay and how it is calculated
Overtime pay
Bonus
Statutory deductions
Voluntary deductions
Net Pay

The preparation and calculation of gross pay, and the calculation as appropriate of statutory and voluntary deductions resulting in the net pay, are the usual requirements of this type of question. The following is an example of a typical question:

James Miller is paid a standard rate of £4 per hour for a 40-hour week; any hours worked in excess of this are paid at time and a half, except for hours worked on a Sunday which are paid at double time. During the week ending 17 June 19–8 he worked a total of 52 hours, 4 of which were on Sunday.
His deductions for the week were:

Company pension fund	5 per cent of his basic wage, excluding all overtime payments.
Income Tax	30 per cent of all earnings in excess of £50 per week.
National Insurance	10 per cent of his gross wage.
Union membership fee	£1.00 per week.

You are required to:
(a) Calculate his gross pay for the week ending 17 June 19–8.
(b) Show the amount of each deduction and calculate his net wages.

The calculation of wages should always be carried out carefully to ensure the correct amounts are ascertained. The following is an example solution of the above question:

James Miller
Week ending 17 June 19–8

40 hours at £4 per hour		160.00
8 hours at £6 per hour		48.00
4 hours at £8 per hour		32.00
	Gross pay:	240.00

Deductions

Company Pension Fund	8.00	
Income Tax	57.00	
National Insurance	24.00	
Union membership fee	1.00	90.00
	Net pay:	£150.00

Notes/Coin Analysis

In order to calculate the number of notes and coins which will be required to make up the wage packets, it will be necessary to prepare a detailed summary showing the number of notes and coins required for each individual employee.

Occasionally an arrangement is negotiated between the firm and the employees regarding the denomination of notes to be used when making up the wage packets. For example, it may be: '£10 is the highest denomination of note to be used and each employee must receives at least one £1 coin'. The student should, of course, comply with any requirement imposed by such circumstances. Each individual employee should always receive the *least* number of notes and coins possible.

To carry out the calculations, a classified summary should be made of the note and coin values as follows:

£20	£10	£5	£1	50p	20p	10p	5p	2p	1p

A list is then made of employees down the left-hand side. The calculations for each individual employee is then carried out. When these are completed, all the columns are totalled, thus indicating the number of notes and coins required in order to make up all the wage packets. The following is an example. The net wages to be paid to six employees are as follows:

	£
G. Collins	120.39
M. Sandford	103.94
H. Williams	97.45
K. Douglas	118.72
L. Stephenson	125.68
R. Ford	109.87

Calculate the number of each denomination of note and coin required. £10 is the highest denomination of note to be used and each employee must receive the lowest number of notes and coins possible.

The calculations would be carried out as follows:

		£10	£5	£1	50p	20p	10p	5p	2p	1p
G. Collins	120.39	12				1	1	1	2	
M. Sandford	103.94	10		3	1	2			2	
H. Williams	97.45	9	1	2		2		1		
K. Douglas	118.72	11	1	3	1	1			1	
L. Stephenson	125.68	12	1		1		1	1	1	1
R. Ford	109.87	10	1	4	1	1	1	1	1	
	£676.05	64	4	12	4	7	3	4	7	1

The quantity calculations can be verified as follows:

		£
64 × £10	=	640.00
4 × £5	=	20.00
12 × £1	=	12.00
4 × 50p	=	2.00
7 × 20p	=	1.40
3 × 10p	=	30
4 × 5p	=	20
7 × 2p	=	14
1 × 1p	=	01
		676.05

POINTS TO REMEMBER

Salaries are usually paid monthly and expressed as an amount for a whole year; the monthly pay is calculated by dividing the annual amount by twelve.

Wages are usually defined as earnings which are calculated on a weekly basis and paid in cash.

In the preparation of wages *accuracy* in carrying out the calculations is essential.

Certain deductions are required to be made by law; these are known as *statutory deductions*.

Other deductions which are agreed by the employee are known as *voluntary deductions*.

In questions relating to the construction of a note/coin analysis candidates often fail to read the question properly and completely ignore the stated restraints. An example could be: '£20 notes are not to be used, and each employee will have a minimum of five £1 coins in his wage packet.'

Assignment Exercises

32.1
Paul Davies is paid at a basic rate of £3.50 per hour for a 38-hour week; all overtime is paid at time and a half. During the week ended 30 July 19–8 Davies worked a total of 50 hours.

Income Tax is paid at 30 per cent of all earnings in excess of £55 per week. National Insurance contributions are calculated at 5 per cent of the gross wage.

Davies makes a voluntary contribution towards the Social and Athletic Club of £1.50 a week.

You are required to calculate the net pay and set out the pay slip for the week ending 30 July 19–8.

32.2

The following information relates to two employees for the week ending 8 August 19–8.

Name	Number of items produced.
G. Forbes	4800
B. Carr	5200

The firm operates a piece work system at a rate of £3 per 100 items produced and a productivity bonus of £10 is paid to each employee who completes in excess of 5000 units in a working week.

G. Forbes pays Income Tax at 30 per cent on all earnings in excess of £60 per week and National Insurance contributions are 10 per cent of his gross wage.

B. Carr pays Income Tax at 30 per cent on all earnings in excess of £50 per week and National Insurance contributions are 10 per cent of his gross wage.

You are required to calculate the net pay of each employee and set out their pay slips for the week ended 8 August 19–8.

32.3

Peter Price is paid a basic wage of £2.40 per hour for a basic 35-hour week: the first five hours in excess of this are paid at time and a quarter and any further hours are paid at time and a half.

During the week ending 15 June 19–5, he worked a total of $42\frac{1}{2}$ hours and received in addition to his basic pay and overtime a productivity bonus of £10. His deductions for the week were:

Company pension fund	5 per cent of his gross wage.
National Insurance	10 per cent of his gross wage.
Income Tax	30 per cent of all earnings in excess of £40 per week.
Holiday and Welfare Fund	£2.00 per week.

You are required to:
(a) Calculate his gross pay for the week ending 15 June 19–5.
(b) Show the amount of each deduction and calculate his take home pay for the same period.

(Royal Society of Arts)

32.4

Ace Garden Services employs John Brooke and Philip Daly to lay turves on new housing estates. Each is paid £5 for every 100 turves laid and if in any week a worker lays more than 2,000 turves he receives a bonus of 50 per cent for laying the extra turves, in addition to the normal rate for all turves laid.

In the week ended 15 March 19–5 Brooke laid 2,200 turves and Daly laid 2,600 turves.

Income Tax of £18 is due from Brooke, and £32 from Daly. Five per cent of the gross earnings of each must be deducted for Social Security contributions. Each makes a voluntary contribution of £2 weekly to the Lawn Layers' Union. You are required to calculate the net pay of each employee and set out their pay slips for the week ended 15 March 19–5.

(Royal Society of Arts)

32.5

Robert Smith is paid a basic wage of £2.50 per hour for a 36-hour week. Any hours worked in excess of this are paid at time and a half, except for hours worked on a Sunday, which are paid at double time. During the week ending 13 June 19 –6 he worked a total of 46 hours, 4 of which were on Sunday.

His deductions for the week were:

Company pension fund	5 per cent of his basic wage, excluding all overtime payments.
National Insurance	10 per cent of his gross wage.
Income Tax	30 per cent of all earnings in excess of £40 per week.
Sports and Social Club	£1.50 per week.

You are required to:
(a) Calculate his gross pay for the week ending 13 June 19–6.
(b) Show the amount of each deduction and calculate his take-home pay for the same period.

(Royal Society of Arts)

32.6

(a) The following table refers to a typical week for a small factory employing four workers:

	Hours worked		
Name	Basic	Overtime	Number of items produced
J. Outridge	36		3,600
K. Bullard	40	10	5,400
H. Downing	40	7	5,000
L. Beech	40	8	4,900

The firm pays a basic rate of £3 per hour with an overtime rate of time and a third. The firm is offering to pay piece rates of £3 per 100 items produced.

Calculate the gross wage for each employee at time rates and at piece rates. Indicate which would be most favourable to each one.

(b) When calculating net pay, statutory and voluntary deductions may be made from the gross pay. State which of the following deductions are statutory deductions and which are voluntary deductions:

Income Tax,

Contributions to a firm's social club,

Trade Union contributions,

National Insurance contributions.

(Royal Society of Arts)

32.7

The following is an extract from the pay-roll of a retail store employing six shop assistants.

Pay-roll for week ending 3 August 19–8.

Name	Net Pay
	£
W. Greenwood	74.85
P. Summers	98.67
D. Connors	83.96
F. Marshall	79.33
A. Harrison	91.90
K. Caldwell	89.74

You are required to calculate the number and denomination of notes and coins required for the making up of each employee's pay packet.

Note: £20 is the highest denomination note to be used and each employee must receive the lowest number of notes and coins possible.

32.8

The following are the net wages of the employees:

	£
F. Gibson	94.11
T. Simpson	133.99
M. Jackson	87.81
G. Smith	91.19
W. Mellor	124.62
A. Fell	111.75
E. Jones	103.33
S. Moore	98.96
C. Wood	82.57
V. Benn	123.49
H. West	131.36
T. Camp	74.67
B. Dixon	80.80

You are required to prepare a summarised notes/coin analysis for the above employees, bearing in mind that £20 notes are not to be used, and that each employee will have a minimum of five £1 coins in his wage packet. Each employee must receive the lowest number of notes and coins possible.

Total and verify your analysis to prove your figures.

32.9

The wages to be paid to five employees are:

	£
G. Billison	74.63
P. Farraday	91.17
H. Oliver	82.53
R. Watt	78.76
T. Yoeman	87.80

Calculate the number of each denomination of note and coin required. £10 is the highest denomination of note used and each employee must receive the lowest number of coins or notes possible.

(Royal Society of Arts)

32.10

The following are the net wages of the four employees within your company:

	£
A	84.86
B	79.54
C	102.13
D	91.17

Assuming that your company does not use notes of a greater denomination than £20 and that each employee receives at least 5 £1 coins, from your calculations, prepare a summarised notes/coin analysis for the employees.

NB   The company always uses the highest denominations possible: for example, one 20p coin would be used in preference to two 10p coins.

(Royal Society of Arts)

32.11

You are employed as an assistant in the wages department. Five employees are working on a site in a nearby town, and the net pay of each is due today as follows:

Mr A	£31.80
Mr B	£43.65
Mr C	£79.20
Mr D	£83.45
Mr E	£87.45

You are required to calculate how many of each of the various denominations of notes and coins given below will be needed to pay them, using the least number of notes and coins possible.

Notes: £10 and £5
Coins: £1, 50p, 20p, 10p and 5p

Set out your answer in a table which will enable your colleague to check your results.

(Royal Society of Arts)

33　Stock Records

OBJECTIVES　To consider the function of advice notes and works requisitions in controlling and recording internal stock movements and the preparation of stock record cards for updating on a quantitative basis.

The keeping of methodical and accurate records is an essential part of any business. It is equally important in the internal movement of stock items purchased for manufacture or purchased to be used in the pursuance of the firm's normal business activities. The profitability of a business could be seriously affected if adequate stock levels are not maintained in order to meet the usual anticipated demand.

Accurate information should always be available regarding the number of items in stock of small parts, components or materials for manufacture. A stock record card is often used as a manual method of providing the necessary information regarding a particular commodity. With this system the details of a particular item are recorded, in date order, commencing with the existing quantity in stock, (if any) adding the number of items received (this may also include information regarding the supplier), subtracting the number of items issued, and recording an up-to-date 'running balance' of the remaining stock in hand.

An advice note (sometimes referred to as a delivery note) is a written notice from the sender of the goods containing details of the quantity and description of the goods supplied. The advice note is the document used by the stores ledger clerk to enter the details regarding the number of items received on the appropriate stock record card, increasing the 'running balance' of the stock in hand. When supplies of the particular item are required by the employees, a document known as a works requisition is issued. The requisition is then given to the stores department as authorisation to obtain the quantities required. Each works requisition is numbered, and will be signed as an acknowledgement of the receipt of the specified quantity. The stores ledger clerk then enters the date, the requisition number and the details of the quantity issued on the stock record card.

Any items returned by an employee would be acknowledged and recorded by the issue of a returns note, giving details of the number of items returned.

From time to time, in order to verify that the stock records are correct a careful check is carried out. This is done by counting the actual quantity in stock at a certain date, and is called a physical stocktaking.

Occasionally a 'stock loss' may occur. This would be discovered when the theoretical figures reached by the calculations on the stock record card, for a particular item, do not agree with the actual number of items in the stores. This would become evident when a physical stock count has taken place.

The information contained on the relevant stock record card would be available and of assistance to the firm when investigating the reason for any discrepancy. In many types of business the use of stock record cards is valuable. A typical example could be a firm repairing and servicing motor vehicles. The internal stock control of the various items of small components used in this type of business would be an essential requirement, to ensure the continuous availability of the numerous small parts which are necessary for the purpose of repairing and servicing vehicles.

Very often the small parts or components would be known by an individual reference code, for example, stock of a particular gasket could be classified as item CHG. The information required for the completion of a stock record card should be presented as follows:

Complete the stock record card for item CHG for the month of January 19–8 from the following information, commencing with an opening balance of 250 units.

January	2	Received (Invoice 7719)	20
	4	Issue W370	14
	8	Issue W385	37
	12	Issue W401	12
	14	Returns R18	4
	18	Received (Invoice 8081)	50
	21	Issue W414	34
	23	Issue W422	46
	24	Returns R24	8
	26	Issue W436	28
	28	Received (Invoice 9122)	60
	31	Issue W453	27

The Stock Record Card would be completed as follows:

Item CHG

Date		Reference	Receipts	Issues	Balance
Jan	1	Balance b/forward			250
	2	Invoice 7719	20		270
	4	Issue W370		14	256
	8	Issue W385		37	219
	12	Issue W401		12	207
	14	Returns R18	4		211
	18	Invoice 8081	50		261
	21	Issue W414		34	227
	23	Issue W422		46	181
	24	Returns R24	8		189
	26	Issue W436		28	161
	28	Invoice 9122	60		221
	31	Issue W453		27	194

In questions requesting the preparation of a stock record card, the information supplied relating to a particular item may include details of both quantity and value. It is normal procedure for stock items to be valued at the cost price. The following is an example where both quantity and value are recorded on the stock record card. Complete the stock record card for the month of February 19–8 from the following information. The item has a reference number of MN/34. The cost price per item is £5. There was an opening balance of 100 units on 1 February 19–8.

	Receipts	Units		Issues	Units
Feb 4	Invoice No 915	50	Feb 6	Requisition No 55	60
Feb 8	Invoice No 930	20	Feb 10	Requisition No 63	70
Feb 17	Invoice No 946	45	Feb 15	Requisition No 69	25
Feb 27	Invoice No 976	60	Feb 24	Requisition No 78	55

In such situations, it will first be necessary to calculate the value of the opening balance – 100 units at £5 per unit equals £500 – and to enter these figures under their respective column headings. The details of each receipt and issue is then calculated and entered in *date order* on the stock record card. The following is an example solution:

Item Number MN/34		STOCK CARD						
Date	Details	Receipts		Issues		Balance	
		Units	£	Units	£	Units	£
Feb 1	Balance b/f					100	500
4	Invoice No 915	50	250			150	750
6	Requisition No 55			60	300	90	450
8	Invoice No 930	20	100			110	550
10	Requisition No 63			70	350	40	200
15	Requisition No 69			25	125	15	75
17	Invoice No 946	45	225			60	300
24	Requisition No 78			55	275	5	25
27	Invoice No 976	60	300			65	325

POINTS TO REMEMBER

A stock record card is kept for each separate item and these should always be constructed carefully and *in date order*.

A 'running balance' is maintained of the quantity in stock.

Stock which is received is added to the balance in hand, and the value calculated if this is indicated in the question.

Items which are issued are deducted from the balance in hand.

To check and verify the closing balance is correct a physical stocktaking should be carried out.

Assignment Exercises

33.1

From the following information rule up a suitable stock record card for item DWT/8 for the month of March 19–8. There was an opening balance on 1 March 19–8 of 225 items.

19–8			Number of Items
March	2	Received Invoice 767	60
	4	Issue W/454	20
	6	Issue W/467	28
	10	Issue W/476	35
	15	Received Invoice 786	50
	18	Issue W/482	42
	19	Returns R.26	8
	22	Issue W/491	26
	24	Issue W/498	32
	25	Returns R.28	4
	28	Received Invoice 797	50
	31	Issue W/502	38

33.2

Rule up a stock record card with suitable columns headings. The Item has a Reference Number DN/X. You are required to complete the stock record card for the month of April 19–8 from the following information, commencing with an opening balance of 200 items, having a total cost price of £1,200. It is the firm's policy to maintain stock records at cost. During the month of April 19–8 the cost price per item of all items purchased was £6.

		Receipts	Items			Issues	Items
Apr	2	Invoice No 6120	60	Apr	3	Requisition No 122	50
	9	Invoice No 6220	40		7	Requisition No 131	25
	18	Invoice No 6317	50		11	Requisition No 139	35
	30	Invoice No 6424	70		22	Requisition No 150	44

33.3

(a) Rule up a stock card with heading as under:
Item 261

Date	Reference	In	Out	Balance

Complete the stock card for January 19–0 from the following information, commencing with an opening balance of 200 units.

Date		Reference	Issues	Receipts
19–0				
Jan	1	R.20	80	
	4	R.21	80	
	5	Invoice 4891		200
	8	R.22	40	
	11	Returns Note 342		4
	19	R.23	190	
	21	Invoice 5001		200
	22	R.24	136	
	31	Due to deterioration 3 units had to be scrapped.		

(b) State what procedure should be followed to verify that the closing balance of units on 31 January 19–0 was correct.

(Royal Society of Arts)

33.4
The Bestly Bottle Company supplies various sizes of bottles to the retail trade. Deliveries of bottles are made to the warehouse and orders are sent to customers from the despatch department.

There was an opening balance of 530 bottles on 1 October 19–6. The following amounts of half-litre clear glass bottles were received and issued by the warehouse manager during October.

Received

6 October 19–6	Delivery Note No 684	120 bottles
9 October 19–6	Delivery Note No 732	50 bottles
22 October 19–6	Delivery Note No 786	135 bottles
24 October 19–6	Delivery Note No 789	50 bottles

Issued

7 October 19–6	Requisition Note No 54	35 bottles
8 October 19–6	Requisition Note No 55	70 bottles
15 October 19–6	Requisition Note No 56	40 bottles
28 October 19–6	Requisition Note No 57	80 bottles

There was a stock check on 10 October and 3 bottles were found to be broken.

You are required to:
(1) Rule up a stock record card with suitable columns including a column for a running balance.
(2) Make the necessary entries for October 19–6

(Royal Society of Arts)

33.5

The following information relates to component number PC 241. At 31 December 19–4 the opening stock was 210.

Jan	2	Received (Invoice 6608)	20
	4	Issue V601	16
	7	Issue V628	41
	10	Issue V701	10
	21	Received (Invoice 6691)	80
	21	Issue V780	27
	25	Issue V808	24
	28	Returns R14	6
	30	Issue V831	14

On 31 January it was discovered that there was a stock loss of five units .

Required
(a) From the information given above write up the stock card for component PC 241.
(b) How would you have discovered the stock loss on 31 January?

(Royal Society of Arts)

33.6

Use the information given below to complete a stock ledger card. All items are recorded in the ledger at cost, and throughout February, 19–6 the unit price was £12.

Date		Item C 486	Units
19–6			
1 February		Opening Stock	150
5	"	Materials Requisition Note No. 181	30
13	"	Goods Received Note No. 717	200
18	"	Materials Requisition Note No. 197	90
20	"	Materials Requisition Note No. 211	120
25	"	Materials Requisition Note No. 243	70
27	"	Goods Received Note No. 801	300
28	"	Closing Stock (per physical check)	335

(Royal Society of Arts)

33.7

The receipts and issues for the various items in the stores managed by M. Kuhler are recorded manually on stock record cards.

You are required to:
(i) Rule up a stock record card with the following headings:

Item	STOCK CARD					
Date	Details	Receipts		Issues		Balance
		Units	£	Units	£	Units	£

(ii) Complete the stock record card for October 19–7 from the following information. The item has a reference of 621/AB. The cost price per item is £8. There was an opening balance of 200 units.

	Receipts	Units	Issues		Units
October 6	Invoice No 65	60	October 5	Requisition No 22	100
October 9	Invoice No 80	25	October 17	Requisition No 28	75
October 22	Invoice No 81	30			

On 31 October 19–7 M. Kuhler did a physical check of the stock and found there was a closing stock of 136 units.

(Royal Society of Arts)

34   The Accounts of Non-Trading Concerns

OBJECTIVES   To establish a clear understanding of non-trading organisations and to study in detail the accounting principles and procedures regarding non-profit making concerns.

The main purpose and function of social clubs, societies and other voluntary organisations is the pursuit of some interest for the benefit of its members. These types of organisations are not primarily concerned in trading as such or in profit making. Clubs, societies and associations are established by people who have joined together to pursue a common interest, and are maintained by subscriptions and donations from the members. In many cases, the affairs of a club or similar organisation are managed by a committee which is elected by the members. The committee consists of elected officers, such as a chairman, secretary and treasurer. At the end of each year, the committee is usually required to hold an Annual General Meeting. This is normal procedure for this type of organisation, and at the Annual General Meeting, the treasurer will be required to produce the accounts of the club or organisation to the members. It is the treasurer's responsibility to collect the subscriptions from the members and to make any payments which may arise.

The treasurer will be required to prepare suitable final accounts to be approved by the committee. In the case of a small club these final accounts are called receipts and payments accounts. The larger organisations, in particular those with substantial assets, present their final accounts in the form of income and expenditure accounts, which are followed by a balance sheet.

The Cash Book of a Club or Organisation

Many clubs use the analytical cash book. This type of cash book, has the advantage of analysis columns, which will enable the treasurer to allocate the income and the expenses under the appropriate headings. The treasurer enters, in date order, the details of all sums of money received and paid out and, as each entry is made, analyses each item, under the various headings. In this way the treasurer is able to find the totals of each of the various receipts and payments.

A treasurer who does not keep an analysed cash book, but merely keeps an ordinary cash book (without the advantage of the extra columns) would have to analyse the cash book at the end of the year. This type of analysis is time-consuming and laborious, and necessitates the 'collecting together' of each of the various items, in order to find the total amount of each item which has been received and paid out.

The Receipts and Payments Account

The receipts and payments account is the simplest way a treasurer can present the accounts of a club or organisation. It is drawn up from a summary of the analysed cash book. It is a record of all monies received and all monies paid out during the period. It does not, however, classify these receipts and payments within the 'period of time' to which they refer, nor is any distinction made between capital and revenue expenditure. Any adjustments which may be required for prepayments or accruals are carried out in the preparation of the income and expenditure accounts.

The closing balance on the receipts and payments account represents the amount of bank and cash at the end of the year, or the period, of the club or organisation and is required for the completion of the balance sheet. The receipts and payments account is a summary of the cash book, therefore the details of all money received is entered at the debit side. All payments made are entered at the credit side.

In the case of a small organisation, where a full set of accounts are not kept, the information contained in the receipts and payments account is often the basis for the preparation of the income and expenditure account. Consider the following example. For the year ended 31 December 19–6 the following summarised information is available of the Queensway Cricket Club:

	£
Balance in Bank at 1 January 19–6	852
Cleaners' wages	220
Ground maintenance	356
Members' subscriptions	920
New Equipment	384
Insurance Premium for year 19–6	95
Competition proceeds	175
Repairs to Equipment	162
Net proceeds of Jumble Sale	138
Rates	130

You are required to prepare a receipts and payments account, clearing showing the balance in hand at 1 January 19–7. The following is an illustration of the solution and the presentation of the receipts and payments account:

Receipts and Payments Account for the Year Ending 31 December 19–6

19–6		£	19–6		£
Jan 1	Balance b/d	852.00		Cleaners' Wages	220.00
	Members' Subscriptions	920.00		Ground Maintenance	356.00
	Competition proceeds	175.00		New Equipment	384.00
	Jumble Sale proceeds	138.00		Insurance premium	95.00
				Repairs to Equipment	162.00
				Rates	130.00
			Dec 31	Balance c/d	738.00
		2,085.00			2,085.00

19–7			
Jan 1	Balance b/d	738.00	

It should be noted that *all items of income* and *all* items of expenditure are entered in the receipts and payments account, no distinction being made between capital or revenue expenditure.

The student should now gain practice in the preparation of receipts and payments accounts by completing the following assignment exercises.

Assignment Exercises

34.1

Prepare a receipts and payments account for the year ending 31 May 19–7 from the following information of the Greenside Social Club.

	£
Cash in hand at 1 June 19–6	484
Purchases of refreshments	365
Postage and stationery	72
Members' subscriptions	850
Purchase of new equipment	276
Sales of Refreshments	564
Rent and Rates	290
Net proceeds of Raffle	86
General Expenses	65
Competition entry fees	112

34.2

The following information is available of the Brookside Badminton Club for the year ending 31 December 19–7. You are required to prepare a receipts and payments account.

Balance in Bank at 1 January 19–7 £582; Competition expenses £86.50; Sales of refreshments £445.60; Rent and Rates £285; Subscriptions received £750; Repairs to equipment £122; Net proceeds of Jumble Sale £98; Purchases of refreshments £296.30; Sundry expenses £86.70; Christmas Dance expenses £96.

34.3

From the following information you are required to prepare a receipts and payments account for the year ending 31 October 19–7 for the Heathfield Music Society.

Cash in hand at 1 November 19–6 £985.50; Transport to concerts £395.20; Members' subscriptions £688; Contribution to local orchestra £100; Printing and Stationery £124.20; Cost of refreshments £344.60; Sales of refreshments £492; Sales of blazer badges £264.50; Secretary's honorarium £150; Charges for hire of hall £250.

Only very small organisations would produce their year ending accounts in the form of a receipts and payments account, for the following reasons:

(a) The receipts and payments account gives no details of any existing assets purchased in previous years and already owned by the club, other than the cash and bank balance and any assets purchased during the current year. (Some clubs have considerable assets, including premises and equipment.)
(b) There is no mention of liabilities outstanding. (There may be an electricity account unpaid at the end of the year.)
(c) The members cannot see whether a profit or loss was made on any particular activity.

For these important reasons, it is usual for a club or organisation to present their final accounts in much greater detail, using business-like techniques. These are income and expenditure accounts, followed by a balance sheet.

The main function of a non-trading organisation is to pursue a common interest. However, many clubs will carry out some activity in order to make a profit and have an additional source of income, for example, running a licensed bar, holding a dance or having a coffee bar. In these situations, a separate trading account may be constructed for the particular activity, and any profit or loss is then transferred to the income and expenditure account.

Bar Trading Accounts

The main function of clubs and similar organisations is not trading as such or profit making. However, many of these organisations will run a bar for the benefit of its members, or carry out some other activity primarily to make a profit to help finance the main activities.

These types of activities are intended to be profit-making and, in order to ascertain if a profit has been made, the treasurer may construct a separate trading account for each particular activity. In this way, the profit or loss can be established for each particular activity.

A trading account for any particular profit-aimed activity is constructed in the same way as the trading accounts for trading organisations. There may be additional expenses incurred with a profit-aimed activity, for example, the running of a bar; the wages of any bar staff would need to be charged to the bar trading account, as these costs apply directly to this activity.

In examinations, the question may not specifically state the need for a separate trading account, but this will often be required. This requirement will be evidenced in the question by the inclusion of, for example, an opening stock of drinks, or a closing stock of drinks, or both. Where there is no indication of opening and/or closing stocks any amounts stated for bar purchases would be entered at the debit side of the income and expenditure account. Similarly, any figure given for bar sales would be entered at the credit side of the income and expenditure account.

The Income and Expenditure Account

The purpose of constructing an income and expenditure account is to ascertain whether a surplus or deficit has been made during the period under review. The income and expenditure account is very similar to a profit and loss account of an ordinary trading concern, and follows all the basic rules of a profit and loss account. Clubs, associations and other non-trading organisations depend almost entirely for their income on subscriptions and donations from their members, and from any profit-aimed activity. The items of income are entered at the credit side, the items of revenue expenditure are entered at the debit side.

Where the income exceeds the expenditure the difference is called a 'surplus' (the profit of a business). If, however, the expenditure is greater than the income, this would result in a deficit (a loss in the case of a business). The income and expenditure account, like the profit and loss account, is a revenue account and follows the rule: *capital expenditure nevers enters a revenue account*. Any capital expenditure, such as the purchase of new equipment, would not be entered in the income and expenditure account. The amount of any new equipment purchased would be added to any existing equipment. This would then correctly increase the figure for equipment under fixed assets on the balance sheet. In a situation where no previous equipment had been purchased, the new equipment would be entered on the balance sheet, under fixed assets.

Any adjustments which may be required for prepayments or accruals should be carried out, making a detailed list, *before* the preparation of the income and expenditure account. It is the adjusted figure which is used in the income and expenditure account, and the amount of the prepayment or the accrual which will appear on the balance sheet.

Subscriptions

A subscription is the annual payment made by a member of a club or similar organisation. In some cases an additional fee is payable on application for membership.Such fees are called 'entrance fees' and are paid once only and are completely separate from the monthly or annual subscriptions.

The income and expenditure account should show the actual amount of subscriptions for the current period. Therefore adjustments may be required for subscriptions paid in advance (subscriptions paid for next year), and for subscriptions in arrears (members who have not yet paid their subscriptions for the current year).

Subscriptions in Advance

Any subscriptions which have been paid in advance for next year should be deducted from the subscriptions received for the current year. Subscriptions paid in advance are a *liability*, as the club or organisation will owe the members the value of the facilities or entertainment in return for their subscriptions.

In the income and expenditure account, any subscriptions paid in advance for next year should be *deducted* from the subscriptions total. On the balance sheet, the amount of any subscriptions paid in advance are shown under current liabilities.

Subscriptions in Arrears (Owing)

These are members who have not paid their subscriptions for the current year. These are members who have probably left the club or organisation and in fact never pay the amounts owing. In practice, most clubs do not include any subscriptions owing at the end of the current year in the income and expenditure account. It would be prudent to assume that these would not be received. If they are eventually paid, the amount received will be brought into the calculation of the subscriptions in the year of receipt. However, in examination questions, unless an instruction is given to the contrary, the student will be expected to include any amounts due for subscriptions outstanding (owing at the end of the period) in the calculation of the subscriptions.

In the income and expenditure account any amount for subscriptions owing for the current year is *added* to the subscriptions total for the current year. On the balance sheet, the amount of any subscriptions owing is shown under current assets.

The Accumulated Fund

Where a sole trader would have a capital account, a non-trading organisation has an 'accumulated fund'. The accumulated fund is calculated in the same way as the capital of a sole trader. At the beginning of the period it is found by listing and adding together the existing assets of the organisation and deducting any liabilities; the difference is the accumulated fund.

Consider the following example. The assets and liabilities of the Fairgate Social Club as at 1 January 19–7 were as follows:

Assets: Balance at bank £685; Equipment £460; Stock of stationery £75.
Liabilities: Rent of hall owing £70
Required: A calculation of the accumulated fund as at 1 January 19–7.

The procedure is as follows:

Fairgate Social Club – Calculation of the Accumulated Fund

Assets	£
Balance at bank	685
Equipment	460
Stock of stationery	75
	1,220
Less Liabilities	
Rent of hall owing	70
Accumulated Fund at 1 January 19–7	1,150

The accumulated fund of a club or organisation appears on the balance sheet and is entered in the same position as the capital.

Balance Sheet

The balance sheets drawn up for non-trading organisations follow the same principles of construction and layout as those prepared for sole traders. A 'surplus' (profit) will increase the accumulated fund; a deficit will decrease it.

If the final accounts are being prepared at the end of the first year a club or organisation has been in existence (this would be stated in the question) there will be no existing accumulated fund. However, if there is a surplus at the end of the first year, the amount of the surplus would be entered on the balance sheet as the accumulated fund.

In the following illustration of an example question a trial balance is the basis for the preparation of a bar trading account, an income and expenditure account and a balance sheet.

The treasurer of the Deansgate Sports Club kept the accounts by double entry and extracted the following trial balance on 31 December 19–7.

	£	£
Equipment	950	
Cash in hand	74	
Cash at bank	694	
Bar takings		2,972
Lighting and heating	246	
Sundry expenses	98	
Bar supplies purchased	1,850	
Rates	250	
Rent	300	
Wages of bar staff	650	
Members' subscriptions		1,250
Bar stock at 1 January 19–7	475	
Cleaning expenses	138	
Printing and stationery	120	
Accumulated Fund at 1 January 19–7		1,623
	5,845	5,845

Notes:
(1) Rates prepaid £32 at 31 December 19–7.
(2) £25 was outstanding for rent at 31 December 19–7.
(3) There was a stock of drinks valued at £520 at 31 December 19–7.
   You are required to prepare for the year ending 31 December 19–7:
(a) an account showing the profit or loss on the bar;
(b) an income and expenditure account;
(c) a balance sheet.
   The following is a fully worked and illustrated solution:

Deansgate Sports Club
Bar Trading Account for the Year Ending 31 December 19–7

Opening stock	475.00	Bar takings (Sales)	2,972.00
Purchases	1,850.00		
	2,325.00		
Less closing stock	520.00		
Cost of drinks sold	1,805.00		
+ Bar staff wages	650.00		
	2,455.00		
Profit c/d	517.00		
	£2,972.00		£2,972.00

Income and Expenditure Account for the Year Ending 31 December 19–7

Lighting and heating	246.00	Profit from Bar b/d	517.00
Sundry expenses	98.00	Members' subscriptions	1,250.00
Rates (£250 − £32)	218.00		
Rent (£300 + £25)	325.00		
Cleaning expenses	138.00		
Printing and stationery	120.00		
Surplus:-	622.00		
	£1,767.00		£1,767.00

The calculation of the 'surplus' is carried out as follows:

Total Income	1,767.00
Less total expenses	1,145.00
Surplus	£622.00

Balance Sheet as at 31 December 19–7

Fixed Assets			Accumulated Fund		
Equipment		950.00	at 1 January		
			19–7	1,623.00	
			Add Surplus	622.00	2,245.00
Current Assets					
Bar stock	520.00				
Rates prepaid	32.00		Current Liabilities		
Bank	694.00		Rent accrued		25.00
Cash	74.00	1,320.00			
		£2,270.00			£2,270.00

POINTS TO REMEMBER The receipts and payment account is drawn up from a summary of the cash book of a club or similar organisation. It is a record of *all* monies received and *all* monies paid out during the year, or the period under review. No distinction is made between capital and revenue expenditure. The closing balance on the receipts and payments account is important, as it represents the amount of bank and cash of the club or organisation at the end of the year, or the accounting period.

The income and expenditure account is a revenue account; it is very similar to a profit and loss account of a trading concern and follows all the basic rules of a profit and loss account.

Capital expenditure, that is, the purchase of any new equipment is *not* entered in the income and expenditure account. The amount of any new equipment would be added to any existing equipment and entered on the balance sheet under fixed assets.

Any notes for consideration and adjustment should be detailed, and the necessary calculations carried out before the preparation of the income and expenditure account. It is the adjusted figure which is used in the income and expenditure account and the amount of the prepayment and/or the accrual which will appear on the balance sheet.

Any subscriptions paid in advance are deducted from the subscriptions total for the current year; any subscriptions owing at the end of the year are added to the subscriptions total for the current year.

The accumulated fund appears on the balance sheet in the same position as the capital – a 'surplus' will increase the accumulated fund, a 'deficit' will decrease it.

In examination questions relating to income and expenditure accounts several variations are possible. For example, a question may require the construction of any of the following or a combination of them:

(a) A receipts and payments account.
(b) A bar trading account, or a trading account for some other profit-aimed activity (such as a dance or a raffle).
(c) The calculation of the accumulated fund.
(d) An income and expenditure account.
(e) A balance sheet.

The following assignment exercises are all taken from past examination papers to enable the student to gain the necessary practice in the construction of the accounts of non-trading organisations.

Assignment Exercises

34.4

Shown below is the balance sheet of the Deepdale Church Youth Centre at 31 December 19–3.

Balance Sheet for the Deepdale Church Youth Centre at 31 December 19–3

Fixed Assets	£		£
Furniture and Fittings	1,500	Accumulated Fund at	
Games Equipment	640	31 December 19–3	3,600
Motor Van	1,000		
	3,140		
Current Assets		Current Liabilities	
Cash at Bank and in Hand	460	Nil	
	3,600		3,600

The following summarised transactions took place during the period 1 January 19–4 to 31 December 19–4

Receipts	£
Subscriptions (160 members at £5 per annum)	800
Donation (treated as a revenue receipt)	80
Sale of Tickets from Annual Fete	540
Payments	
Light and Heat	205
Expenses of Annual Fete	310
New Games Equipment	160
Cleaner's Wages	104
Repairs and Renewals	83
Motor Van repairs	126

Note: An electricity bill of £45 was owing at 31 December 19–4 (analysed under Light and Heat).

Required

Prepare:

(a) A receipts and payments account showing clearly the balance in hand at 1 January 19–5.
(b) An income and expenditure account for the year ended 31 December 19–4.
(c) A balance sheet as at 31 December 19–4.

(Royal Society of Arts)

34.5

The assets and liabilities of the Scotgate Social Club on 1 April 19–2 were:

	£
Freehold Premises	30,000
Furniture, Fittings & Fixtures	12,000
Bar Stock	150
Balance at Bank	600

The following is a summary of the receipts and payments for the club for the year ended 31 March 19–3.

Receipts	£	Payments	£
Balance at Bank	600	Bar Supplies	4,300
Subscriptions	480	Raffle Prizes	60
Bar Sales	4,750	Expenses of Annual Dance	130
Sale of Raffle Tickets	150	Cost of Refreshments for	
Annual Dance	200	sale on Club nights	80
Sales of Refreshments	160	Rates	250
		Electricity	500
		Repairs to equipment	200
		New tables for use in bar	200
		Balance at 31.3.19–3	620
	6,340		6,340

On 31 March 19–3 bar stocks were £200; £80 was owing for electricity and rates were prepaid by £45.
You are required to:
(a) Calculate the accumulated fund as at 1 April 19–2.
(b) Prepare an income and expenditure account for the year ended 31 March 19–3 and a balance sheet as at that date.

(Royal Society of Arts)

34.6

The following were the assets and liabilities of the Fitorama Sports Club on 1 July 19–3.

Assets	£
Premises at cost	28,000
Fittings and Equipment	4,200
Deposit in Building Society	2,700
Cash and Bank Balance	2,027
Liabilities	
Electricity bill outstanding	168

The club's cash book for the year to 30 June 19–4 showed the following:

Receipts	£	Payments	£
Balance b/fwd	2,027	Rates	1,250
Subscriptions for year	4,870	Groundsman	2,200
Competition entry fees	2,700	Purchase of sports	
Sale of dance tickets	450	equipment	1,650
		League entry fee	20
		Dance expenses	300
		Prizes for competitions	3,050
		Electricity	740
		Bal. c/fwd	837
	10,047		10,047

You are required to:
(a) Calculate the accumulated fund at 1 July 19–3.
(b) Prepare the club's income and expenditure account for the year ended 30 June 19–4, and a balance sheet on that date after taking into account the following points:
 (1) An electricity account of £194 was outstanding at the end of the year.
 (2) The amount paid for rates included £200 paid in advance.
 (3) During the year interest of £107 had been received from the building society. This interest has been re-invested in the society.

(The Royal Society of Arts)

34.7
Prepare, from the information below, a bar account showing the profit or loss made on the bar activities extracted from the books of the Greenacres Social Club for the year ended 31 May 19–6.

(a)	1 June 19–5	31 May 19–6
	£	£
Creditors for bar-supplies	1,328	1,436
Debtors for bar sales	23	50
Stock of bar supplies	1,523	2,090
Bar wages outstanding	32	34

(b) An extract from the receipts and payments account for the year ended 31 May 19–6 showed the following:

Receipts	£	Payments	£
Bar takings	16,403	Bar supplies	14,572
		Bar wages	1,476

All calculations must be clearly shown.

(Joint Matriculation Board)

34.8

On 1 November 19–5, The Kingsley Sports and Social Club had the following assets and liabilities.

Assets	£
Club premises	15,000
Fixtures and Fittings	1,250
Sports equipment	150
Bar stock	130
S. Batten (Sundry Debtor)	25
Bank and cash	1,100

Liabilities	£
M. Blackall (Sundry Creditor)	55
Accumulated Fund	17,600

During the year ended 31 October 19–6 the following amounts were received and paid.

Receipts	£	Payments	£
Subscriptions	1,500	M. Blackall	55
Bar Sales	2,950	Purchases of bar stock	1,760
Competition fees	380	Printing, postage and	
S. Batten	25	stationery	425
		Competition expenses	300
		Sports equipment	150
		Cleaning expenses	200
		Rates	400

You are required to:
(i) Prepare the Club's bar trading account and income and expenditure account for the year ended 31 October 19–6.

(ii) Prepare a balance sheet as at 31 October 19–6.
The following points are to be taken into consideration:

1. There was a closing bar stock valued at £165.
2. There was an unpaid invoice for printing for £10 and a stock of stationery of £30.

(The Royal Society of Arts)

34.9
At 1 January 19–5 the assets of the Potters Snooker Club were as follows. There were no liabilities.

	£
Freehold premises	15,000
Equipment and furniture	8,500
Bar stock	380
Balance at bank	120

The following is a summary of the club's receipts and payments for the year ended 31 December 19–5.

Receipts	£	Payments	£
Balance 1 January 19–5	120	Bar stock purchased	4,140
Members' subscriptions	2,200	Repairs to equipment	480
Bar takings	6,470	Purchase of new equipment	2,400
Visitors' fees	810	Stationery and postage	170
		Rates	690
		Steward's wages	480
		Insurance	250
		Competition entry fees	130
		Travelling expenses	770
		Balance 31 December 19–5	90
	9,600		9,600

At 31 December 19–5 bar stock was valued at £520, rates prepaid amounted to £110, and wages accrued due were £40. You are required to:
(a) Calculate the accumulated fund on 1 January 19–5.
(b) Prepare the club's income and expenditure account for the year ended 31 December 19–5.
(c) Prepare the balance sheet as at that date.

(The Royal Society of Arts)

35　Accounting with Computers – Continuous Balance Ledger Accounts

OBJECTIVES　To consider the development of three-column style ledger accounts with running balance.

The preceding modules have emphasised the importance of the fundamental principles of book-keeping and accounting, and these will always remain constant but, as a result of the ever-increasing volume of business, alternative methods have been introduced of recording and storing the essential information. The first machine accounting systems were introduced many years ago and these significantly reduced many of the time-consuming operations of recording information, which had previously been hand-written in bound ledgers.

The first accounting machines were a combination of a typewriter and an adding machine and were considered, at the time, to be a great improvement, as they were able to carry out postings and calculations.

The further development of mechanised accounting machines led to the various 'punched card systems' being introduced. These systems used cards in which small holes were punched, in various combinations, as a method of recording and storing information. Most of the mechanised accounting systems have been superseded by the various digital computers now available and, particularly with the advance of micro computers, the electronic processing of information has completely transformed many of the book-keeping and accounting operations.

Working with a computer and the sophisticated 'accounting programs' readily available, the day-to-day business transactions can be competently and efficiently carried out, in a fraction of the time.

The 'grouping together' of similar types of operations has been the basis of many of the accounting programs, and some businesses have accounting programs designed and written to meet their own specific requirements.

A clear understanding of the double entry system and the fundamental principles of book-keeping and accounting will always be necessary if a full appreciation of the new technology is to be gained. The principles and procedures learned in the study and practice of the preceding modules will always remain the same; it is only the methods applied for recording, storing and retrieving the actual information that will change to meet the increasing demands of the modern world.

The accounts prepared and displayed throughout this book have all been shown with the page divided into two halves; the left-hand side of the page being the debit side, the right-hand side being the credit side; and the accounts have been totalled and balanced manually. These are known as 'traditional style ledger accounts'.

The development of mechanical and electronic equipment able to carry out calculations quickly and automatically has led to an alternative style of ledger account, which is known as the 'continuous balance account'. This style of account appears in three columns, the first column being the debit column, the second column the credit column and the third column the balance. The following is an illustration of a 'continuous balance account':

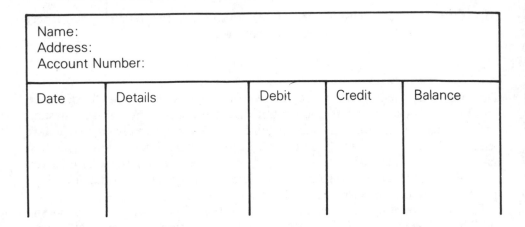

Name:				
Address:				
Account Number:				
Date	Details	Debit	Credit	Balance

When accounts are prepared using mechanised or computerised systems the balance on the account is recalculated automatically after each entry. It is important to note that in principle there is no difference between the 'traditional style account' and the 'continuous balance account'. However, it is a distinct advantage to the business to have the outstanding balance on an account continuously prepared, and when accounts are prepared manually the process involved to recalculate the new balance after each entry would take a considerable time.

The following is an example of a typical sales ledger account displayed in the 'traditional style':

B. Senior Account

19–8		£	19–8			£
Apr	3 Sales	235.00	Apr	10	Returns Inwards	46.00
	15 Sales	350.00		28	Bank	189.00
	25 Sales	145.00		30	Balance c/d	495.00
		730.00				730.00
May	1 Balance b/d	495.00				

The following is an illustration of the same account, in three column form with a continuous balance:

Name:	B. SENIOR			
Address:	34 Queensway, Leeds LS16.8 ER			
Account Number:	SL/18			

Date	Details	Debit £	Credit £	Balance £
Apr 3	Sales	235.00		235.00 DR
10	Returns Inwards		46.00	189.00 DR
15	Sales	350.00		539.00 DR
25	Sales	145.00		684.00 DR
28	Bank		189.00	495.00 DR

As this example is a customer's account in the sales ledger, the continuous balance will normally be a debit balance.

The principles of double entry are the same; it is only the function of recalculating the new balance after each entry, and the continuous form of presentation which has changed. At the end of the month, the balance remaining on the account is exactly the same using the traditional form and the three-column continuous balance.

The following is an example of a typical purchase ledger account displayed in the 'traditional style':

R. Reedman Account

19–8			£	19–8			£
Apr	12	Returns Outwards	25.00	Apr	7	Purchases	725.00
	29	Bank	700.00		17	Purchases	300.00
	30	Balance c/d	300.00				
			1,025.00				1,025.00
				May	1	Balance b/d	300.00

The following is an illustration of the same account, in three-column form with a continuous balance:

Name:	R. Reedman			
Address:	8 Crossfield, Bradford BD16. 2MN			
Account Number:	PL/8			

Date	Details	Debit £	Credit £	Balance £
Apr 7	Purchases		725.00	725.00 CR
12	Returns Outwards	25.00		700.00 CR
17	Purchases		300.00	1,000.00 CR
29	Bank	700.00		300.00 CR

As this example is a supplier's account in the purchase ledger, the continuous balance will normally be a credit balance.

The preparation of three-column ledger accounts with a running balance is a syllabus requirement for certain Examination Boards, and the student should now gain practice by working the following exercises:

POINTS TO REMEMBER   Examination questions relating to the construction of three-column style accounts appear rarely, and when they are required it is usually only the 'personal accounts' which are requested. The candidate will usually be given a list of 'balances', the amount of these 'balances' should first be entered in the appropriate accounts *before* beginning to record any further transactions.

The classified recording of information will inevitably change, but it is important to note that the fundamental principles of double entry remain the same whether the entries are made in the 'traditional style of account' or in the 'three-column form' with a continuous balance. It is only the method of presentation which appears differently.

Assignment Exercises

35.1
You are required to enter the following transactions in the *personal accounts only*, written in three-column form with a continuous balance. Do not write up the other accounts.

19–8
Jan 1 Bought goods on credit from D. Hall (£348); L. Walker (£576); B. Hagston (£850).
  4 Purchases on credit from L. Walker (£125); B. Dickson (£367).
  9 Returned goods to B. Hagston (£50); L. Walker (£55).
  16 Bought goods on credit from B. Dickson (£146); J. Dunn (£85).
  18 Returned goods to B. Dickson (£67).
  26 Paid D. Hall £348 by cheque.
  30 Paid B. Dickson £300 in cash.

35.2
Enter the following transactions in the *personal accounts only*, written in three-column form with a running balance. Do not write up the other accounts.

19–8
Feb 1 Sold goods on credit to M. Harding (£360); J. Johnstone (£98); E Briggs (£450); T. Myers (£212).
  3 Sales on credit to R. Godfrey (£330); P. Ellis (£421).
  6 Goods returned by J. Johnstone (£24); E. Briggs (£50).
  9 Sold goods on credit to T. Myers (£152); R. Godfrey (£135).
  12 Returns inwards from M. Harding (£60).
  15 Received £300 in cash from M. Harding.
  18 Sales on credit to E. Briggs (£220); T. Myers (£240).
  19 P. Ellis paid £421 by cheque.
  20 Goods returned by T. Myers (£52).
  25 Received a cheque of £400 from E. Briggs.
  27 Sales on credit to R. Kemp (£350); E. Briggs (£90).
  28 Received £74 in cash from J. Johnstone.

35.3
You are required to enter the following transactions in the *personal accounts only*, written in three-column form with a continuous balance.

19–8
Mar 1 Purchases on credit from J. Radcliffe (£525); P. Coates (£450); W. James (£695); P. Williams (£155).
  4 Sold goods on credit to J. Burns (£158); S. Daniel (£350); D. Hall (£212); P. Harper (£90).

6 Returned goods to P. Coates (£55); P. Williams (£25).
8 Purchases on credit from W. James (£152); P. Coates (£295); J. Allen (£355).
12 Credit sales to S. Daniel (£395); D. Hall (£422); J. Nixon (£125).
15 Paid J. Radcliffe £525 by cheque.
18 Goods returned to the firm by J. Nixon (£20); S. Daniel (£45).
21 Received £158 in cash from J. Burns.
25 Sold goods on credit to P. Harper (£155); J. Nixon (£120).
27 Purchased goods on credit from P. Williams (£240); J. Allen (£170).
29 Returned goods to J. Allen (£28).
30 Paid cheques to P. Coates (£395); P. Williams (£130).
31 Received £212 by cheque from D. Hall.

35.4

The accounts which appear on 1 June 19–2 in the ledger of R. Wilson, a stationery wholesaler, include the following:

	£
M. Porcher, a customer, balance	200 debit
S. Seaman, a customer, balance	75 debit
L. Tidmarsh, a supplier, balance	43 credit
A. Waters, a supplier, balance	75 credit
Stock of stationery in hand for own office use valued at	20

The following transactions took place during the first week of June 19–2:

19–2		£
June	1 Sold goods on credit to M. Porcher	270
	Bought goods on credit from L. Tidmarsh	75
	2 Returned goods to L. Tidmarsh	24
	Paid L. Tidmarsh amount due to date, by cheque	
	3 M. Porcher returned goods	48
	M. Porcher paid balance due on 1 June 19–2 by cheque less 3 per cent cash discount	
	4 Bought goods on credit from A. Waters	125
	7 Bought stationery for own office use from L. Tidmarsh	120
	Sold goods on credit to S. Seaman	150

You are required to write up the personal accounts and the stationery account as they would appear in R. Wilson's ledger. Sales, purchases and returns accounts are not needed.

To obtain full marks the personal accounts should be written up in three-column form: debit, credit, and balance.

(The Royal Society of Arts)

35.5

On 1 April 19–5 the following accounts appeared in the books of David Hunt, a sports goods wholesaler.

Sales Ledger		Purchase Ledger	
	£		£
W. Thomas	950	H. Roberts	600
R. Waters	1,100	F. Blake	160

Transactions during April 19–5 are summarised below:

Sales Day Book		Purchases Day Book	
	£		£
April 5 W. Thomas	1,400	April 9 H. Roberts	950
11 R. Waters	750	23 B. Mills	780
26 W. Thomas	1,840	26 F. Blake	84
	3,990		1,814

Returns Inwards Book		Returns Outwards Book	
	£		£
April 12 W. Thomas	190	April 30 B. Mills	200

Cash receipts and payments:

April   1 Cash at bank, £1,680.

4 W. Thomas paid the balance due on 1 April by cheque.

5 Purchased goods from F. Ripon for £430 and paid by cheque immediately.

10 Paid by cheque £600 on account to H. Roberts.

12 Accepted a cheque from W. Parker for £320 for goods sold that day.

15 R. Waters sent a cheque in settlement of the amount due on 1 April 19–5.

30 Paid by cheque Swift Motors garage bill for petrol supplied during April, £180.

30 Cash sales paid into bank, £950.

You are required to write up the ledger of David Hunt for the month of April 19–5 including his cash book (bank columns only).

To earn full marks the personal accounts should be submitted in three-column form with running balances.

In the general ledger the cash account only should be balanced.

(The Royal Society of Arts)

Specimen Examination Papers

THE ROYAL SOCIETY OF ARTS
EXAMINATIONS BOARD
SINGLE-SUBJECT EXAMINATIONS

S107 BOOK-KEEPING STAGE I (Elementary)
(JUNE, 1988)

(TWO HOURS ALLOWED)
*You have TEN minutes to read through this question paper before
the start of the examination.*

All questions are to be attempted.

You are advised to answer the questions in the order in which they are printed.

Marks will be lost for untidy work.

Answers should be written in pen or ball pen.

Calculators may be used.

*Marks will be awarded for method and you are therefore encouraged to show
your working for each question.*

SECTION A

1. W. Flower commenced business on 1st March 1988, paying £200 into a business bank account. During the next two months the following transactions took place. All payments are made by cheque.

			£
March	1st	Paid one month's rent	100
"	4th	Purchased goods for resale	500
"	18th	Paid vehicle insurance premium	50
"	24th	Banked shop takings for month	800
"	28th	Paid heating bill	40
"	30th	Cash drawn for self	100

April	1st	Paid one month's rent	100
"	4th	Purchased goods for resale	800
"	7th	Paid for repairs to motor vehicle	60
"	27th	Banked shop takings for month	950
"	28th	Paid heating bill	50
"	29th	Purchased new suit for self	100

You are required to:

(a) Write up the bank account, balancing at the end of each month.

(b) Write up all the other accounts. (Use one account only for all motor vehicle expenses) total and balance the accounts at the end of the two month period.

(c) Extract a trial balance as at 30th April 1988.

(26 marks)

2. K. Lynn runs a store which sells camping equipment and sports goods. Credit purchases for the month of May 1988 were:

4th May   Canvas Products Ltd   Invoice No CP1916
  4   2-person Ridge Tents   @£20 each
  4   4-person Frame Tents   @£110 each

9th May   Holiday Products Ltd   Invoice No IP1624
100   Beach Balls   @ £1 each
 20   Sleeping Bags   @ £11 each
  6   3-man Inflatable Dinghies @ £25 each

25th May   T. Wang   Invoice No TW1735
  6   Tennis Racquets   @ £10 each
  4   Badminton Racquets   @ £5 each
 20   boxes Shuttlecocks   @ £2 per box

30th May   Anglian Campers   Invoice No AN742
  5   Camping Stoves   @ £8 each

On the 14th May
  1 ridge tent was returned to Canvas Products Ltd.
  Advice Note AN27 damaged in transit.
All transactions are subject to VAT at 10%

All suppliers' prices are net and trade discount is not allowed.

You are required to:
Complete the day books below showing the amounts to be transferred to the nominal accounts at the end of the month.
N.B. The actual nominal accounts are not required.

(26 marks)

PURCHASES DAY BOOK

DATE	SUPPLIER	GOODS	INVOICE NO.	TOTAL	CAMPING	SPORTS	VAT

PURCHASES RETURNS DAY BOOK

DATE	SUPPLIER	GOODS	ADVICE NOTE NO.	TOTAL	CAMPING	SPORTS	VAT

338

3. The following are the net wages of four employees in your firm for the week ending 26th May 1988.

P. Hall	£142.70
A. Brewer	£152.76
D. Black	£137.92
R. Green	£158.14

You are required to:
Calculate the number of notes and coins of each denomination that you would need to collect from the bank in order to make up their pay packets. It is company policy to include a minimum of three £1 coins in each wage packet otherwise the minimum number of notes/coins must be used in each pay packet, e.g. one 20p coin would be used in preference to two 10p coins.

Your answer should take the form of a table under the headings below:

Amount	£20	£10	£5	£1	50p	20p	10p	5p	2p	1p

(*12 marks*)

4. J. Gordon is one of your suppliers. His account in your ledger is set out below.

J. Gordon

1987		£	1987		£
5 Dec	Bank	96	1 Dec	Balance b/d	98
5 Dec	Discount	2	9 Dec	Purchases	135
10 Dec	Returns	25	23 Dec	Purchases	56
28 Dec	Bank	105			
28 Dec	Discount	5			
31 Dec	Balance c/d	56			
		289			289
			1 Jan	Balance b/d	56

On 1 January 1988 you receive the following statement of account from J. Gordon.

		Dr. £	Cr. £	Bal £
1 Dec				98
6 Dec	Bank		96	2
6 Dec	Discount		2	–
11 Dec	Sales	135		135
14 Dec	Returns		25	110
24 Dec	Sales	56		166
29 Dec	Sales	80		246

You are required to:
(a) Prepare a statement reconciling the balance shown as due to J. Gordon with the amount shown as owing in your ledger.
(b) Explain why the entries debited in your ledger account appear as credit entries on the statement received from J. Gordon.
(c) Explain how the differences between the final balances can arise.

(*12 marks*)

SECTION C

5. The assets and liabilities of the Seashore Swimming Club at 1st June 1987 were: Balance at bank £580. Equipment £290. Sundry expenses owing £15. Stock of Refreshments £20. Rent prepaid £40. Accumulated Fund £915.

The following is a summary of the receipts and payments of the club for the year ended 31st May 1988.

Receipts	£	Payments	£
Opening Balance 1.6.87	580	Expenses of Dance	529
Annual Dance	917	Rent of Clubroom	540
Subscriptions	624	Purchase of Equipment	250
Locker Rents	248	Prizes for Competitions	95
Sale of Refreshments	268	Sundry Expenses	110
Competition Fees	142	Purchases of Refreshments	160
Sale of Swimming Permits	60	Licence Fees to Council	90

The following information is also available:
(a) Stock of Refreshments at 31st May 1988 was £10.
(b) Rent of Clubroom prepaid 31st May 1988 £50.
(c) Sundry Expenses owing 31st May 1988 £10.

You are required to:
(i) Calculate the club's bank balance @ 31st May 1988.
(ii) Prepare an income and expenditure account for the year ended 31st May 1988 showing clearly the profit/loss on the dance and the sale of refreshments and a balance sheet as at that date.

(*24 marks*)

340

PITMAN EXAMINATIONS INSTITUTE
150 BA

BOOK-KEEPING AND ACCOUNTS – ELEMENTARY
(Specimen Paper)

PART I (60 marks)

Read each question carefully. Choose the *one* answer you think is correct. Show your answer by selecting A, B, C or D.

Time allowed: 2 hours

PART I   requires your choice of answer only to be shown on the sheets provided. You are advised not to spend more than 1 hour 10 minutes on this part. *All questions should be attempted.*

PART II   Answer any *FOUR* questions.

1 Mr Jones, a butcher, buys a van on credit for use in his business. This transaction should be first entered in:

(A) the cash book.
(B) the Journal.
(C) the Ledger.
(D) the purchase day book.

2 Mr Jones records his purchase of the van by double entry by:

(A) debiting Bank account, crediting Motor Vehicles account.
(B) crediting Bank account, debiting Motor Vehicles account.
(C) debiting Supplier's account, crediting Motor Vehicles account.
(D) crediting Supplier's account, debiting Motor Vehicles account.

3 Invoices received for goods purchased would be first entered in:

(A) the sales day book.
(B) the purchase account.
(C) the purchase day book.
(D) the cash book.

4 A debit balance of £650 on P Carr Ltd account in the books of R Winn means that:

(A) P Carr Ltd owes R Winn £650.
(B) R Winn owes P Carr Ltd £650.
(C) P Carr Ltd has paid R Winn £650.
(D) R Winn has paid P Carr Ltd £650.

5 An invoice received for goods purchased showed:

20 tins paint @ £5 each   £100
less 20% Trade Discount   20
                                    £ 80

To record the discount of £20, it is necessary to:

(A) debit the supplier's account, credit discount account.
(B) debit purchase account, credit discount account.
(C) debit discount account, credit supplier's account.
(D) It is not necessary to enter trade discount in the ledger.

6 An invoice shows a total of £360 less $33\frac{1}{3}$ per cent trade discount and 5 per cent cash discount if paid by the 10th of the following month. If the account is paid by the 10th, then the cheque would be:

(A) £360.
(B) £228.
(C) £222.
(D) £240.

7 Which of the following is a personal account?

(A) Wages account.
(B) Sundries account.
(C) Discount received account.
(D) The Hexham Warehouse Limited account.

8 An error of commission is made if:

(A) a transaction has been overlooked.
(B) an entry is made in the wrong account within the correct class.
(C) a total has been cast wrongly.
(D) an entry has been made on the wrong side of the account.

9 A trial balance is a :

(A) record of the differences between the cash book and the bank statement.
(B) list of balances in the ledger.
(C) list of balances in the sales day book.
(D) statement showing the net profit.

10 A suspense account is opened when the:

(A) trial balance does not balance.
(B) balance sheet does not balance.
(C) profit and loss account does not balance.
(D) business is bankrupt.

11 In drawing up a trial balance, which one of the following should not be recorded on the debit side:

(A) Purchases.
(B) Sales.
(C) Drawings.
(D) Stock.

12 After the trial balance had failed to agree it was discovered that discounts allowed £25 had been posted to the wrong side of the discounts account. The correction to be made would be:

(A) Debit discounts allowed £25, Credit suspense account £25.
(B) Credit discounts allowed £25, Debit suspense account £25.
(C) Debit discounts allowed £50, Credit suspense account £50.
(D) Credit discounts allowed £50, Debit suspense account £50.

Questions 13 to 22 refer to the following Trading and Profit and Loss Account.

Trading Account

	£	£		£	£
Opening stock		700	Sales	24,770	
Purchases	18,615		less Returns	270	24,500
less Returns	280	18,335			
Carriage in		320			
		19,355			
Closing stock		980			
		18,375			
Gross profit carried down		6,125			
		£24,500			£24,500

Profit and Loss Account

	£	£		£
Wages		1,420	Gross profit B/d	6,125
Rent paid	360			
Rent accrued	90			
General expenses		220		
Carriage out		360		
Net profit		???		
		£6,125		£6,125

13 The missing net profit figure should be;

    (A) £1,675.
    (B) £2,675.
    (C) £3,675.
    (D) £4,675.

14 Total expenses were:

    (A) £210.
    (B) £2,450.
    (C) £810.
    (D) £2,575.

15 The cost of goods sold totalled:

    (A) £18,375.
    (B) £19,500.
    (C) £24,500.
    (D) £24,770.

16 The expense item of Rent totalled:

    (A) £360.
    (B) £270.
    (C) £90.
    (D) £450.

17 The turnover is:

    (A) £24,770.
    (B) £24,500.
    (C) £19,355.
    (D) £18,375.

18 The net cost of purchases is:

    (A) £18,615.
    (B) £18,335.
    (C) £18,655.
    (D) £18,375.

19 Purchases returned totalled:

(A) £360.
(B) £320.
(C) £280.
(D) £270.

20 Gross profit as a percentage on net sales is:

(A) 20%.
(B) 30%.
(C) 25%.
(D) $33\frac{1}{3}$%.

21 Net profit as a percentage on net sales is:

(A) 10%.
(B) 20%.
(C) 25%.
(D) 15%.

22 The value of unsold goods was:

(A) £980.
(B) £24,500.
(C) £6,125.
(D) £19,355.

23 If Stock at start is £760 and Stock at end is £830, and Purchases are £7,280 and Sales are £9,260, what is the cost of sales?

(A) £8,040.
(B) £8,870.
(C) £2,050.
(D) £7,210.

24 The balance sheet equation is:

(A) Capital = Assets + Liabilities
(B) Assets = Capital + Liabilities
(C) Liabilities = Assets + Capital
(D) Capital = Assets + Liabilities + Bank overdraft

25 Which of the following is an asset?

(A) Overdraft.
(B) Creditors.
(C) Capital.
(D) Premises.

26 On a balance sheet the fixed assets are included at:

(A) cost price.
(B) book price.
(C) selling price.
(D) replacement value.

27 If the capital of a business is £18,000 at the beginning of the year and £21,000 at the end, and the owner has withdrawn £5,000, the profit made during the year is:

(A) £5,000.
(B) £8,000.
(C) £23,000.
(D) £21,000.

28 A tax refund is:

(A) capital expenditure.
(B) a capital receipt.
(C) revenue expenditure.
(D) a revenue receipt.

29 If the cost of a machine is £8,000 and it is expected to last 10 years when its value is expected to be £1,000, what annual amount should be charge for depreciation using the straight line method?

(A) £800.
(B) £700.
(C) £900.
(D) £1,000.

30 Using the reducing balance method of depreciation, a motor car which cost £4,000 is depreciated by 20 per cent per annum. What is the value of the car at the end of its second year?

(A) £2,560.
(B) £3,200.
(C) £2,400.
(D) £3,420.

31 A fork-lift truck purchased by a business would be:

(A) capital expenditure appearing in the balance sheet.
(B) a revenue expense appearing in the trading account.
(C) a capital receipt appearing in the balance sheet.
(D) a revenue expenditure appearing in the profit and loss account.

32 Which of the following is not a capital expenditure?

(A) Breakdown van purchased by a garage.
(B) Cost of hiring refrigerating plant in a butcher's shop.
(C) Wages paid to own workman by a builder for the erection of an office to be used by his own business.
(D) Extension of a freehold factory building.

33 The distinction between capital and revenue is important because it:

(A) distinguishes between income and expenditure.
(B) separates assets and liabilities.
(C) allows the business to estimate bad debts.
(D) allows the business to determine what profits it has made.

34 A bad debt is a debt:

(A) incurred by the salesman.
(B) owed by one trader to another.
(C) unlikely to be paid.
(D) not shown on the trial balance.

35 A trial balance shows debtors as £3,250 and provision for bad debts as £250. After the trial balance had been extracted it was decided to write off £250 as bad debts and make the provision up to 10 per cent of the debtors. What would the new provision be?

(A) £325.
(B) £550.
(C) £300.
(D) £500.

36 Why do bank charges usually have to be taken into consideration when compiling a bank reconciliation statement?

(A) Bank charges are never entered in the cash book.
(B) The bank only makes charges when sending out statements.
(C) The bank does not usually inform its customers of the charges in any other way except on the bank statement.
(D) Bank charges need not be paid.

37 A request to a banker to make payments at regular intervals is known as a:

(A) bank giro.
(B) direct debit.
(C) standing order.
(D) credit transfer.

38 The cash book shows a balance of £850 but the bank statement shows a different figure. The difference is found to be a £10 credit transfer paid direct to the bank by a debtor. The bank statement showed:

(A) £840.
(B) £860.
(C) £850.
(D) £870.

39 Which of the following is not a liability?

(A) Expenses due.
(B) Rent received in advance.
(C) Subscriptions received in respect of the following year.
(D) Rates paid in advance.

40 The figures for the value of the stock are found by:

(A) physically counting the stock and valuing at cost price or market price, whichever is the lower.
(B) physically counting the stock and valuing at selling price.
(C) balancing the stock account.
(D) taking a percentage of sales.

PART II (40 marks)

Answer any *FOUR* questions. Each one is worth 10 marks. Ensure that your name is written clearly at the top of each of your answer sheets.

1 Prepare a balance sheet from the following information taken from the books of Bob King at the end of his first year of trading on 31 March 1981.

	£
Capital	6,000
Cash at bank	490
Stock	700
Freehold shop	5,000
Wages owing to staff	120
Drawing of cash for own use	1,270
Amount owed by business	3,200

Amount owed to business	3,900
Cash in hand	30
Shop fittings	1,200
Net profit made during year	3,270

2 Rule a petty cash book with four columns for Cleaning, Postages, Carriage and Office Expenses, and enter the items listed below. The book is kept on the imprest system.

1 June	Received £50 from the Cashier	
	Bought postage stamps	£6
2	Paid carriage on parcels	£4
3	Bought office stationery	£12
	Paid bus fares	£2
4	Bought postage stamps	£5
	Bought typewriter ribbons	£6
5	Paid for cleaning	£4
6	Paid carriage on parcels	£4
	Received cash from Cashier to make up the imprest amount	

Balance the book as on 6 June.

3 On 1 January the books of John Peel showed the following balances:

	£			£
Cash in hand	1,000	Debtors	D. Robinson	400
Cash at bank	5,000		H Jones	800
Stock	4,000	Creditors	H Taylor	700
Capital	10,000		B Towne	500

Open accounts in the Cash book and Ledger and then enter the following transactions:

2 January	Sold goods on credit to D Robinson	£ 400
3	Bought goods on credit from B Towne	£ 200
4	Cash sales	£ 100
5	Sold goods to H Jones	£1,000 less 10% trade discount
6	Paid H Taylor by cheque	£ 700
7	Paid by cash wages	£ 100
	D Robinson paid by cheque	£ 400 which was banked the same day

Balance accounts and extract trial balance as at 7 January.

4 Make out the Journal entries for the following provisions and adjustments. Date 31 March 1981.

1 Bad debt written off – D Brooks   £180
2 Depreciation of Fixtures and Fittings £200
3 Provisions for bad debts   £600
4 Money owing – wages   £150
5 Prepayment Rent   £370

5 The Town Society was formed on 1 July 1980 and at the end of the first year the Treasurer submitted the following statement to members:

Receipts and Payments Account for the Year Ended 30 June 1981

	£		£
Subscriptions	320	Cost of refreshments	20
Sale of dance tickets	80	Printing and Stationery	15
Proceeds of sale of		Rent	10
refreshments	30	Furniture	150
		Dance expenses	45
		Sundry expenses	15
		Balance	175
	430		430

You are required to prepare an Income and Expenditure Account for the year ended 30 June 1981, and a balance sheet as at that date. You are given the following information:

No subscriptions were paid in advance.
No depreciation on the furniture.
Stock of stationery £5.
Rent owing £10.

6 Mitchell's cash book showed a balance of £2,150 as at 31 December and his bank statement showed a balance of £2,195.

A comparison of the two records showed the following outstanding items:

non-presented cheques £250;
payment made by the bank out of his account under a standing order but not yet recorded in the cash book £40;
credit transfer from customer paid directly to bank account but not yet entered in cash book £175;

bank charges not in cash book £40;
takings deposited in night-safe on 31 December £300, but not recorded on bank statement.

Reconcile the two balances.

Index